THE RISE
RISHI SUNAK

Dr. Gopal Sharma

DIAMOND BOOKS

www.diamondbook.in

© Author

Publisher : **Diamond Pocket Books (P) Ltd.**
X-30, Okhla Industrial Area, Phase-II
New Delhi-110020
Phone : 011-40712100
E-mail : sales@dpb.in
Website : www.dpb.in
Edition : 2023

The Rise of Rishi Sunak
By - *Dr. Gopal Sharma*

PREFACE

If you have been following media-print as well as electronic - Rishi Sunak will not be an unfamiliar name for you. If you don't follow any of these, this name will still evoke so many cultural and religious feelings in you. That is why the preface for the book is unnecessary. "The rise of Rishi Sunak" is the real work which I have just completed and presented for your reading. Therefore, do not take me seriously in this preface because as I speak to you outside of what I have written, these marginal comments cannot have the value of the work itself.

I write these lines because I was asked to do so by the publisher who finds the manuscript incomplete without the preface. Now that the foreword-text-afterword triangle is complete, let me announce the completion of the project I named- The Rise of Rishi Sunak.

This is an account of the rise of Rishi Sunak as the fifty seventh British prime minister and the third Conservative prime minister this year who is trying to unite a governing party that is driven with divisions.

Mr. Sunak, 42, is of Indian descent and was born to parents who migrated to Britain from East Africa. The news was an ultimate Diwali gift for me and my countrymen. Just within seven years in politics he won the hearts of his people and made us proud of our ancient knowledge traditions. Many more books will be written on and about him but this is the first book of its kind that covers Sunak's ancestry and history starting from Gujranwala in Punjab in 1935 till October 2022 in 10 Downing Street (London). I find no one to thank and acknowledge but you who are the very reason for my writing. I write and leave...

Within you also there is a Rishi, read and explore!

–Gopal Sharma

CONTENTS

1

THE HISTORY AND THE ANCESTRY

Let me start from the middle. I wanted to start from the beginning but I can't because I don't know the beginning. I can't start Rishi Sunak's story from the end because the end of this story is beyond anyone's imagination. The extraordinary rise- slight tumbling- and again rise of Rishi Sunak, modern Britain's youngest, richest and first Hindu PM is not a fairy tale though he has been often called 'Dishy Rishi' and 'Britain's sexiest MP.' These are just some of the accolades that have been attributed to Rishi Sunak whose meteoric rise to Downing Street is just breathtakingly out of this world. He's the UK's third leader of 2022 but he's a man of many firsts.

The History

So what is his history? Seven years and few months… That's all it took for Sunak to rise to the top of politics. SUNAK'S IS A TRULY ASTONISHING POLITICAL STORY. His is in some ways the archetypal migrant success story. "Through a combination of lucky timing, the utter shambles of his Tory peers, and his undoubted competence, he has risen to the pinnacle of British politics seven years after he first entered it. He has done so despite not being obviously charismatic (though handsome and articulate, he has rather a reedy voice) or cut out for political greatness."[1]

Michael Anthony Ashcroft, Baron Ashcroft, KCMG, PC (born 4 March 1946) is a British-Belizean businessman, pollster and politician. He is a former deputy chairman of the Conservative Party. Ashcroft founded Michael A. Ashcroft Associates in 1972 and is the 132nd richest person in the UK, as ranked by the Sunday Times Rich List 2021, with an estimated fortune of £1.257 billion. He likes to write too. His life-mantra is: Let the others find you. In the course of my search and research, I found him and would like to say that we both like to write biographies. Ashcroft, like a soothsayer, wrote a biography -the tale of a super-bright and hardgrafting son of immigrant parents who marries an Indian heiress … the story of how he tore up the rulebook and went broke. He wrote a biography of Rishi Sunak-the first one. Therefore, I dedicate this book to him.

Ashcroft and I both realize in our own amusing ways that we are older than the Prime Minister. Ashcroft was born in 1946 and I in 1954. Ashcroft is a rich man, though perhaps not richer than Sunak family. I am a poor Brahmin from India who lives on God's mercy. The ultimate rise of Rishi Sunak took me beyond Ashcroft's narration and I began my work for you, my dear reader! As Tulsidas did more than five hundred years ago! Goswami Tulsidas read Valmiki's Ramayana and began his Ramcharitmanas. I didn't read Ashcroft but began.

> naana puraan nigam sammatan yad
>
> raamaayane nigaditan kvachidanyatopi.

svaantah sukhaay tulasi raghunaath gaatha,

bhaashaabandha matinjulamaatanoti.

For the gratification of his own self Tulsidas brings forth

This very elegant composition relating in common parlance

The story of the Lord of Raghus,

Which is in accord with the various Puranas,

Vedas and the agamas (tantras), and incorporates

What has been recorded in the Ramayana (of Valmiki)

And culled from some other sources (1-7)

I didn't read Ashcroft beyond Amazon's "look inside". I couldn't. I needn't. I had got myself Ready for Rishi and went straight to Lord William Hague of Richmond who had been aptly-quoted by Rishi Sunak when he wanted to self-introduce, "Rishi has proved to be a diligent constituency MP and it was no surprise to see him re-elected in 2017 and 2019. He is an exceptional individual and I believe he will continue to be a strong and effective advocate for our community."

Rishi's story in a nutshell is provided by Sunak himself as follows. This is just bare-minimum. If you are an impatient reader (and I am sure, you aren't) and have no time to delve deep along with me, this will give you a little bird's eye-view.

> I grew up watching my parents serve our local community with dedication. My dad was an NHS family GP and my mum ran her own local chemist shop. I wanted to make that same positive difference to people as their Member of Parliament and I was first elected to represent this wonderful constituency in 2015 and re-elected in 2017 and 2019. I live in Kirby Sigston, just outside Northallerton.

I have been fortunate to enjoy a successful business career. I co-founded a large investment firm, working with companies from Silicon Valley to Bangalore. Then I used that experience to help small and entrepreneurial British companies grow successfully. From working in my mum's tiny chemist shop to my experience building large businesses, I have seen first-hand how politicians should support free enterprise and innovation to ensure our future prosperity.

My parents sacrificed a great deal so I could attend good schools. I was lucky to study at Winchester College, Oxford University and Stanford University. That experience changed my life and as a result I am passionate about ensuring everybody has access to a great education. I have been a school governor, a board member of a large youth club, and have always volunteered my time to education programmes that spread opportunity.

I have been lucky to live, study and work internationally. I met my wife, Akshata, in California where we lived for a number of years before returning home. We have two daughters, Krishna and Anoushka, who keep us busy and entertained.

In my spare time I enjoy keeping fit, cricket, football and movies.

In July 2019 I was appointed Chief Secretary to the Treasury, having entered Government service as the Minister for Local Government in January 2018. In February 2020, I had the honor to be appointed Chancellor of the Exchequer, a position I held until July 2022.

On October 25, I was honored and privileged to be appointed UK Prime Minister.[2]

You can re-read the above information in a "Timeline" mode which is given below.

2015: Rishi Sunak was elected Conservative MP for Richmond, Yorkshire.

2016: Sunak is a lifelong Brexiter, and campaigned for Leave accordingly, a gamble at the time, but it paid off as it put him in good political standing within the Tory party for years to come.

2018: Under Theresa May, Sunak is given her first ministerial post as Number Three in the newly renamed Ministry for Housing, Communities and Local Government.

July 2019: Sunak endorses Boris Johnson for British Prime Minister and begins serving as Treasury Minister under then-Chancellor Sajid Javid.

February 2020: Sunak is promoted to the role of chancellor by Boris Johnson after Javid resigns over a power struggle between No. 10 and No. 11 Downing Street, making him the first Indian-origin to hold one of the highest positions in the British government

April 2020: After the UK went into full lockdown in March 2020 as the COVID pandemic took hold, Sunak received praise for a series of mini budgets for introducing measures such as the furlough scheme, which could save many jobs and businesses. runs to save her.

2021: Rishi Sunak has been tipped as a clear favorite to succeed Boris Johnson as Tory leader as Johnson's Partygate troubles begin, although the British Indian chancellor believes his focus is only on the cabinet A is on the post.

February 2022: UK Chancellor Sunak admits attending a party for his boss Johnson's birthday in the cabinet room of Downing Street, breaching lockdown rules in June 2020.

April 2022: In a tumultuous week, his wife Akshata Murthy's legal non-domicile tax status, meaning she does not pay UK taxes on her Infosys income, and that Sunak has her own US green card office in the media is garnering headlines.

July 2022: Rishi Sunak resigns as chancellor, shortly after taking over as health secretary from his former boss Sajid Javid at the Treasury.

July 8: Rishi Sunak begins efforts to replace Boris Johnson as the UK's PM.

20 July: Rishi Sunak edged past his party colleague by 137 votes to face off with Liz Truss in the final stage of the British PM contest.

August 5: Rishi Sunak wins over voters in a TV debate.

August 30: Rishi Sunak camp accuses Liz Truss of evading investigation.

September 1: Rishi Sunak ends campaign on personal note with parents, wife Akshata.

September 2: Voting closes in the race for Prime Minister of the UK between Rishi Sunak and Liz Truss.

September 5: Truss defeats Sunak in the race for the leadership of the Conservative Party to become the new British PM.

October 14: UK PM Liz Truss sacks Kwasi Kwarteng as chancellor amid economic turmoil.

20 October: Truss resigns as British PM after six weeks in the midst of open rebellion.

October 24: Rishi Sunak wins the Tory contest to make history as Britain's first Indian-origin PM.

This is all, in a nutshell…in brief…succinctly speaking. Let me elaborate it a bit. In fact, the entire book is a narration. Sing Heavenly Muse!

Rishi Sunak is a British politician of Indian origin, who has held office as the Prime Minister of the United Kingdom since 25 October 2022. He was elected leader of the Conservative Party on 24 October 2022. He was elected the MP for Richmond in Yorkshire in May 2015 (it is one of the country's safest seats, having been Tory since 1906) and was re-elected in 2019 with a majority of 27,210. Sunak served as Chancellor of the Exchequer from 2020 to 2022 and Chief Secretary to the Treasury from 2019 to 2020, and has been the Member of Parliament (MP) for Richmond (York) since 2015. He has inscribed his name in the history books of India and Britain. Before he gets a chance to show what kind of legacy he will leave behind, he has become a potential question to be asked in the competitive exams.

When people were asked what word or phrase first came to their mind when they think about the new PM, 'rich' was the most common choice. "Good', 'clever', 'honest', 'educated', 'self-made', trustworthy', 'nice' … were other adjectives used to describe him. It is commendable that Rishi Sunak himself did not add any of these nouns or adjectives to his name when he addressed the nation after taking oath as the Prime Minister, When he was about to enter 10 Downing Street as PM for the first time, he made no mention of being the first Indian-origin or person of 'color' to hold the top post. He did not give any such historical reason nor did he draw attention to anything which could have been discussed later.

While Sunak is the first prime minister of Britain with Asian ethnicity, several prime ministers have been noted to have different ancestries. Benjamin Disraeli came from a diverse European Jewish background, a community with historic roots in Asia. Boris Johnson's great-grandfather Ali Kemal Bey was Turkish. Lord Liverpool's great-grandmother Isabella Beizor was of partial Indian heritage.

Sanjaya Baru, former media advisor to former PM Manmohan Singh, writes on Rishi Sunak's achievement as follows. A Britain no longer great, a kingdom hardly united, has chosen a child of the empire to restore economic and political stability, even if not glory, in the 75th year of the jewel being plucked from its crown. Rishi Sunak, a person of Indian origin, is Britain's new prime minister. After all the usual skulduggery and backstabbing long associated with the very British political coups, Conservative Party members of parliament seem to have been reminded of Shakespeare's cautionary words (Richard II): "Forget, forgive, conclude and be agreed/ Our doctors say this is no time to bleed.[3]

Due to his Indian origin and being the son-in-law of one of India's leading technocrats, we-Indians- wish to know about him in detail. Here, one will find such a story that all the young men and women living in India and outside India will feel like their own story. You will get inspiration from this as well as guidance to move forward. I was the first one to narrate this undiluted and undefiled story of Rishi Sunak and Akshata Murthy (Namma Hudugi-Our Daughter) in Hindi before. I am the first Indian who is presenting a book-length study of the son of India. In a way, you are also the first one to hear and read it in this compact book-form. Both of us are fortunate because we are sons and daughters of India.

***

The Ancestry

"Sixty years after my Naniji boarded a plane in East Africa, on a warm sunny evening in October, her great-granddaughters, my kids, played in the street outside our home, painted Rangoli on the doorstep, lit sparklers and diyas; had fun like so many other families on Diwali. Except the street was Downing St. And the door was the door No 11." Recalling the journey of his family, Rishi Sunak said at a meeting of the Indian Global Forum in London.

UK Chancellor of the Exchequer Rishi Sunak opened up at length about his Indian heritage and growing up in Britain in a hard-working British Indian family at an awards ceremony celebrating Indian Diaspora achievements across different fields, "I'm incredibly proud of where I come from. It will always be an enormous part of who I am. And it brings me joy to live, and belong, in a country where, for all our faults, for all our challenges, someone like me can become Chancellor. Our task now is to make sure that's not the end of the British Indian story, but the beginning."

This is first hand information. There are many who claim they know about him. Let us read the following, to begin with. It is an extract published in The Siasat Daily (31 October, 2022) News Desk and was posted by Masrath Fatima when Rishi Sunak took over as the United Kingdom's first Indian-origin and Hindu Prime Minister.

> Rishi Sunak's appointment as the first Indian-origin Prime Minister of the UK has created echoes across the globe. His appointment is a flashpoint for his Indian roots and congratulatory messages poured in from the leaders of all major democracies, including India. However, soon after Rishi Sunak was announced as UK PM on the day of Diwali, his ancestral root was up for debate. Several

Pakistani nationals took to social media platforms to lay claim to Rishi Sunak's ancestry. A tug of war has begun between the people from India and Pakistan over his ancestral roots. The buzz around Sunak's origin erupted over the birthplace of his grandparents. Reportedly, Sunak's grandparents were born in Gujranwala, which is now situated in Pakistan. Known for its good food and culture of wrestling, Gujranwala is located around 1.5 hours away from Punjab province's provincial capital Lahore.[4]

"The story of a family that values commitment, determination, endeavor and the pursuit of education and opportunity goes back generations and covers three continents. It is the story of a family that was ready to take big risks in search of a better life." This is what an apt storyteller Lord Ashcroft mentions when he begins telling us about the rise of Rishi Sunak. Not much is known about Rishi Sunak's paternal and maternal grandparents, Rishi indicated in a tweet - When my grandparents emigrated here they emigrated to the United Kingdom. That's because it represented a set of values and ideas, and it's those values and ideas that are precious and that form the bond of the Union.(Jul 29, 2022)

The story lies in between and beyond. Let us unravel it.

The story of the Sunak family moving from India to Kenya in 1935 and settling in England in the 1960s is a story of Indian family solidarity and struggle on the one hand, with the fluidity and racism of the English public and mainly the elite, on the other. There is also an interesting narrative of his complicated relationship with the people around him. This saga has the magical realism of a Salman Rushdie novel and is as engrossing as Amrit Lal Nagar's stories. The personal family history of Sunak and Berry families, now revered by everyone as the 'Sunak dynasty', can be seen and read as the fulfillment of the

British dream. The idea that the UK is a land of opportunity is a valid one. People come from all over the world, and if they work hard, they can make their way to the top here. The key to success lies in 'hard work and determination'. Let me quote Rishi again, "As the child and grandchild of immigrants, I can testify to the openness, fairness, and, yes, warmth, with which British society welcomes talented individuals who seek to contribute to our society and become a part of our communities."

Rishi is married to Akshata Murthy, daughter of Infosys co-founder Narayana Murthy, and they have two daughters - Krishna and Anushka. Rishi's in-laws are definitely in India but they are neither going to tell me anything nor will I be able to ask them. I would like to meet Akshata's mother one day to speak to her and say, "Thank You!"

There is no such village or town in India where I can go to interview relatives or teachers associated with Rishi and tell you in what privations Rishi Sunak's childhood passed or with whom he was friends. Sunak lived and travelled in India when he got married with the daughter of India (namma hudugi).

Kamala Harris's mother was born in South India and studied in Delhi. Her relatives are still in Chennai and Delhi. Perhaps Rishi Sunak has no relatives on his father's side in India. His only relatives in the country are his in-laws and father-in-law, who are known for the well-known company Infosys. His father-in-law Narayana Murthy co-founded the company and is a well-known software giant. Mrs Sudha Murty is his mother-in-law and she is a household name for her simple living and grasping tales. Mr Murthy retired in 2011 and he and his wife lead a quiet comfortable life in a small flat in Bengaluru, South India.

***

The Twice Migrants

Neha Shah, an activist and researcher at the University of Oxford has found out that Indian migration to Britain took place in two significant waves. The first was in the late 1940s and 50s, when migrants were recruited directly from India by successive governments to fill the labor shortage that resulted from the Second World War. The second wave of Indian migrants to Britain were the so-called "twice migrants" who arrived from East Africa in the 1960s and 70s, having been expelled or encouraged to leave by the newly independent regimes in Uganda, Kenya and Tanzania. The Family of Rishi Sunak belongs to the second group.[5]

Indians share a long history with African traders in the Indian Ocean region. Their ties grew stronger in the 19th century when the British Empire, and especially the East African Protectorate (also known as British East Africa) was formed in 1885, and many Indians settled in the area that was then under British rule was under control. The Indian population grew rapidly in East Africa and prospered economically.

India was a colony even then. And the mindset of the ruler was also colonialist. Its sun never set and its empire was ever-expanding, which had a wide range of effects that still affect many communities today. Sunak's ancestors came from India via East Africa. Indian immigrants were invited by the British to act almost as a buffer between the natives and colonists on the African continent and as a source of cheap labor. They needed skilled labor even as far away as Africa and there was no shortage of them in India. Farmer laborers were going or being sent forcibly or willingly from UP and Bihar. Migration was also taking place from Punjab. There were young men who used to have golden dreams for their future, while some were struggling to earn their livelihood or do juun ki roti. On the political front, the tension between Hindus and Muslims was increasing and it was becoming difficult for Hindus to live in Muslim-dominated areas. Anti-colonial struggles grew and relatively prosperous Indians were seen as imperial allies. South Asians had long carved out an ambiguous niche for themselves in these societies. They were working as a link between the British rulers and the Africans. Asians often held government and bureaucratic positions, and some were also engaged in trade or business.

Indian migration to African countries took place in several phases. The initial migration was in the form of indentured laborers who were taken by the European imperialists to various colonies, mostly to cultivate sugarcane. Their first goal was to satisfy starvation and hunger. Indians stopped and settled at places like South Africa, Mauritius and Natal. Indians mostly from Gujarat and Punjab started settling in East African countries especially where the British rulers ruled. The first batch of migrants went there as railway workers. Later, professionals like lawyers, accountants, doctors, clerks and small businessmen also went to these countries and settled in many cities and towns. Most of them held British passports at the time.

Back home, India's colonial structure instigated the hostility between Hindus and Muslims. This was no doubt caused by Muslims being the minority in British-India, which drove this demographic to form a separate political identity away from British and Hindu influence. Hindus have experienced both historical and ongoing religious persecutions, systemic violence, in the form of forced conversions documented massacres, genocides, demolition and desecration of their temples as well as the destruction of educational institutions. For an educated upper-class Punjabi Hindu family the future was in the haze of turmoil as the tension between Hindus and Muslims was growing. They couldn't escape the happenings around them when the call for division of India was heard by them and Muslims around them became violent.

Rishi's grandfather and grandmother

Ram Dass Sunak and Suhag Rani Sunak, Rishi's grandfather and grandmother lived in undivided India. The year was around 1935 when both of them were leading a happy married life unmindful of what was in store for them. They lived in a town in the Punjab Province and used to look forward to a better future. Ram Dass Sunak and his wife Suhag Rani Sunak both were from educated families. Suhag Rani's father Mr Luthera was the postmaster of the Abottabad Post Office. So you can very well imagine that they were very much influenced by the British Raj and were in favor of the Raj and their appeal for education and modernity. That is why they were able to get many opportunities for themselves and their families. According to London-based historian Odhiambo Levin Opiyo, Sunak's grandfather Ram Dass married Suhag Rani in the 1930s and began making plans to migrate to Kenya at a time when the colonial government needed skilled workers in a country where most Africans lacked formal education to be hired.

At that juncture, they got the news that Britain wanted many skilled and unskilled hands in East Africa. For Ram Dass it was good news but he didn't want to leave his young wife behind in the area where violence was the rule of the day. As soon as he found the job of a clerical officer in Nairobi, Kenya, he made up his mind to try his luck and bought a one-way ticket aboard a ship and promised to send for his wife in time. "Dass" Opiyo writes, "bought a one way ticket to Kenya, boarded a ship which set sail for Mombasa. He then took a train to Nairobi, over 400 kms away, where he began working as a casual laborer while studying accounting."

Shri Ram Dass's departure to Africa led his wife Suhag Rani to go and live in Delhi with her parents-in-law. Ram Dass was an active and intelligent person. He didn't waste his spare time and went for further studies. He took courses to qualify as an accountant. Soon he got a job in the office of chief secretary in Nairobi as a clerk. He became a civil servant in Harambee House. (Harambee House is the office of the President of Kenya now.) Formerly an accountant, Ramdas became an administrative officer for the Kenyan colonial government. Over 50 years later, his grandson Rishi went on to work for Goldman Sachs and even starts his own hedge fund firm. It is wonderful to see how being good with numbers runs in the family.

Two years later, in 1937, as soon as he was comfortably settled, Dass invited his wife to join him in Nairobi.

Both of them left their ancestral village. The husband was in Kenya and the wife in Delhi. They met together after two years but their meeting place was neither Delhi nor Gujranwala. She went directly to join her husband in Nairobi in 1937. It was a final goodbye to their mother-land India; they didn't know this fact then. They were in a different city, country and culture. Whatever *sanskar* and teachings they received from their worthy parents were with them to guide them in time to come.

Once they settled in Kenya, they lived there comfortably and safely. India was in the vortex of turmoil and there was a movement under Gandhi going on to get total independence. They were aware of their homeland and didn't completely abandon the idea of going there again. In fact, they had six children-three sons and three daughters including Risihi's father Yashvir who was born in 1949. He was born in Nairobi, Kenya in 1949, to Ramdas and Suhag Rani Sunak. Like Tanganyika, Kenya was under British colonial control at this time.

When their children grew up and the question of their education arose, the parents thought that the daughters should go back to India to study and the sons should go to the West to study science and medicine.

Many Indian immigrants and their descendants still live in East Africa today, but many left in the late 20th century. In a way Sunak-family is the gift of Idi Amin to Britain. Indians would still be living in large numbers in East Africa if the Ugandan dictator had not initiated a series of expulsions from East Africa, first expelling Sunak's father and grandfather from their country in the 1970s.

Since the 1960s, the region had become a less hospitable place for Indians. The relative prosperity of Indian peoples on the African continent led to tensions and anti-Black attitudes reached a peak when Idi Amin seized power in Uganda and expelled Asians from the country in 1972. The Indian minority was expelled from Uganda under the orders of the then President Idi Amin. This was the time when a significant part of the Indian Diaspora left Kenya and Tanzania. Instead of returning to India, most of these Indians went to countries like America, Canada and UK etc.

At that time the environment for foreign immigrants in Britain was not the same as it is today. Satnaam Sanghera has this to say, "many immigrants of my parents' generation can still recall a time when white gangs roamed the streets of British towns and cities with iron bars and knives, looking for West Indians, Africans or Asians to assault, a judge at Birmingham crown court complaining in 1973 that "roughing up of coloreds is almost a hobby in some parts of the Black Country".[6]

The Rise of Rishi Sunak

In the context of Britain's rapidly changing demographics and socio-cultural realities, the then Labor Minister, Roy Jenkins, reflected on the philosophy of multiculturalism in 1967, "Integration is perhaps a loose term. I do not regard this as meaning the loss of their national characteristics and culture by immigrants. I don't think we need a 'melting pot' in this country that molds everyone into the same mold... So I don't see integration as a flat process of assimilation but as equal opportunity I define, in an environment of mutual tolerance, with cultural diversity.

In a nutshell, let me say that life in Pre-independent India was not a bed of roses for the family. When they went to live in Kenya it was just earning and living. When they reached the UK life changed a little bit but it went on as usual. "I didn't grow up in a wealthy family. My overriding memory of childhood is how hard my parents worked," Sunak recalled.

Maternal grandfather and grandmother

Raghubir Berry is the name of Rishi Sunak's maternal grandfather who, like his grandfather, was born in Punjab, India. Raghubir Berry's extended family is in Ludhiana where his relative Subhash Berry often narrates with great interest the stories of his visits to India. The Berry family earlier lived in the city's Karimpura locality and currently resides in Civil Lines. Rishi's maternal grandfather, Raghubir Sen, had five brothers: Ugra Sen, Bhim Sen, Vikramjit Sen, Gandharva Sen and Raghubir Sen. They were the natives of a village called Jassowal Sudan in Ludhiana district. At present in 2022, Raghubir Berry is 95 years of age and is recuperating and joining satsangs in London with his grandchildren.

He is also from Punjab and a typical Punjabi, but Raghubir Berry ji was married to a girl who was born in Tanzania. Saraksha was born in a rural area of Tanganyika (now Tanzania). This area was full of wild animals. It is said that she was brought up amidst the roar of lions. Saraksha had also learned Swahili language in her childhood but she remained bound and connected to India.

At the age of sixteen, Saraksha was married to Raghubir Berry, who was then working as a railway engineer in Tanzania. Rishi Sunak may not have any friends from the working class, but in Kenya, where his family settled down after they left Punjab, Indians worked hard to build the Kenya-Uganda railway line. His maternal grandfather and grandmother both were lucky, otherwise disease, decay and death by falling the prey of the wild lions was not rare there.

Raghubir and Saraksha had three children- Usha and two brothers Bharat and Ajay. Here also the aim of this family was not to return back to India. Let me repeat for clarity. Sunak and family and Berry and family are two families. The Sunak family was in Kenya and Berry family was in Tanzania. Both the families moved to Britain. Their lives got mingled together in a foreign land Britain.

In East Africa where they lived for so many decades was also changing. It was very difficult and dangerous to stay back. Many laborers later decided to stay, while some of them were forced to return. Interestingly, it is not the Indian or Asian group that migrated to Britain and America in large numbers in the 60s and 70s. There was an exodus of Asians in the 60s and 70s and it was humiliating to the point of expulsion, with most of the Indians evicted from East African countries like Kenya, Uganda, Malawi and Tanzania. The burden of the British yolk was too heavy to bear so the people revolted and the whites started leaving for good leaving the respective countries under and in the hands of those who had their own axes to grind. They declared an open war against those who were not Africans. Their position in the society had become such that when the freedom movement spread in these countries, Indians became easy targets of their wrath. When these countries started gaining independence one by one, Indians started to be driven out as per the policy of 'Africanisation'. Newly formed governments tried to ensure that power structures, business and other influential positions were filled by native Africans, and the colonialists and their Asian allies were gone.

Both the families in their respective East African abodes lived but desired to go back preferably to the land of opportunity. They wanted to go to Britain and settle down.

First let me tell you how Rishi's maternal grandfather and grandmother reached there. In a video, Sunak told a story about how her maternal grandmother had arrived in the UK "with the hope of a better life."

Let me tell you a story about a young woman who boarded a plane armed with the hope of a better life and the love of her family. This young woman came to Britain, where she managed to find a job. And it took her about a year to save enough money to take care of the children. One of those children was my mother, who was 15 years old. My mother studied hard and qualified to become a pharmacist. She had met my father in the National Health Service (NHS) and they both settled in Southampton. Her story did not end here. But my story started from there."

Let me retell you this tale in detail. This courageous woman, Saraksha, moved to Leicester in the 1960s on her own and somehow managed to reunite her family in 1969 within a year, working sometimes as a typist and sometimes in other small jobs. As I told you about her, she was bold and courageous-an extraordinary woman who grew up speaking Swahili in a remote hut in Tanzania. There was definitely a small Punjabi community there, but the company of foreigners was more. In 1966 she made the bold decision of selling her wedding jewelry to buy a one-way ticket to Britain. She traveled alone to Britain, leaving behind her husband and young children in Africa. She started living in the city of Leicester. After a year, she had accumulated enough cash to take care of the rest of the family. Her husband Raghubir Berry and their three children also came and joined the family.

Rishi's maternal grandparents moved from East Africa to the UK. Mr Berry also started working and got a prestigious job. Rishi Sunak's maternal grandfather worked there for decades in the Inland Revenue Tax Office as a tax collector. His work was recognized with an MBE (Member of the Order of the British Empire) in 1988 making him a Member of the Order of the British Empire.

An amusing anecdote is reported in the local papers. Raghubir Berry almost missed his appointment to collect his honor at Buckingham Palace due to the London traffic. But somehow he reached. In addition to his successful career, Rishi's maternal grandfather was an upstanding member of his local community. An article in the Leicester Daily Mercury reports, Raghubir Berry was president of the Hindu Religious and Cultural Society. Despite having moved from his Indian hometown to England, he clearly remained committed to his Hindu faith and Punjabi culture.

They benefited from the fact that they were close to the colonists and many of them were part of the administration and public service. They easily got adjusted to the new situation. Family connections in the UK helped him to get a job and settle there. The British government also helped them to settle so it was easier for them to get their privileges and stake claims.

***

The paternal grandparents also reached the UK in due course of time. In 1966, Yashvir's elder brother was lucky enough to get admission at Liverpool University to study electrical engineering. It was a golden opportunity. The family managed to get funds by collecting their entire savings. The same year Yashvir also joined his brother in Liverpool to complete his A-levels. Both of them led a modest life there but worked very hard to come up in studies. Ram Dass with his wife Suhag Rani in Kenya and some of their children getting education in India and the UK was a good arrangement though it was financially heavy. They were tied to their respective *dharma* and the future remained unpredictable.

As soon as it was possible, in 1966, Ram Dass and his wife Suhag Rani and the rest of the family also joined the two sons in Liverpool. Ramdass Sunak established a Hindu temple in Southampton in 1971 by forming a Vedic Society.

Now let us come directly and engage ourselves in the amazing tale of Rishi's parents. For the British media, the couple are said to be, "passionate British".

Raghubir Berry and Saraksha's daughter Usha was 15-16 years old when they settled there in the UK. She worked hard in school and secured admission in Aston University. Usha studied pharmacy. She graduated from Aston University in 1972 in Pharmacology. Mr. Yashvir reached Liverpool in 1966 to study medicine. He also did not settle down after A-level. He went ahead and studied further. He graduated in medicine from Liverpool University in 1974.

Usha met Yeshvir through family friends. And in July 1977, both of them got married. Rishi Sunak was their first child. Rishi's biographer has described Rishi's birth as follows.

Their first child, Rishi Sunak-he has no middle name- was born on 12 May 1980 at Southampton General Hospital.

The happy parents took him home to 54 Richmond Gardens, their sizable 1930s red brick house in the city's Postwood district, and a couple of miles from the surgery on Raymond road in Shirley where Yashvir now worked as a family doctor. Usha had been working as a manager at the local chemist, Weston Pharmacy, before she became pregnant for the first time, but she knew that with a young baby the role would be too much, and she left shortly before her son was born.[7]

Let me tell you, in India, we have no middle name. I am Gopal Sharma. Similarly, Rishi Sunak has no middle name. Ordinarily the first name is for the family-the parents and other close relatives and friends. Rishi's parents will never address him as "Sunak". He is Sunak for those who are 'others'. That is why, I am going to take liberty and address him as I like.

Yashvir was in the profession of medicine. He became a family doctor in the National Health Service and Usha Sunak started running a pharmacy. They moved to Southampton, and eventually had three children – Rishi, the eldest, Sanjay (born in 1982), a second son who is now a clinical psychologist and neuropsychologist, and Raakhi (born in 1985), the daughter who works at the United Nations.

This is a story - and it's a true story. This migration history is very different from those who moved to the UK directly from India or from Pakistan and Bangladesh. Your story and mine have also mingled and entangled in this story. I also spent not one or two but fifteen years in East Africa. I too taught my children abroad. But I have no story to tell you. The story of Rishi Sunak was made and told by many. It is Karma closely blended with dharma. Although Rishi's grandparents (maternal and paternal both) lived very different lives than the one that he does, there are some clear parallels. I am sure; you will try to

The Rise of Rishi Sunak

draw such parallels. If you have some time to spare, please read the following tweet by Aman Wahdud

> Rishi Sunak's grandparents migrated to Kenya from present-day Pakistan, in 1935 - still Rishi Sunak is of Indian-origin. Our great grandparents migrated a few hundred kilometers from present-day Bangladesh, much BEFORE 1935 - we are still accused of being of Bangladeshi origin!

Will you call it the South Asian-dilemma?

References

1 https://openthemagazine.com/cover-stories/a-desi-in-10-downing-street/

2 https://www.rishisunak.com/about-me

3 https://timesofindia.indiatimes.com/blogs/toi-edit-page/behind-10-browning-street-sunak-was-deemed-ok-by-english-upper-classes-who-control-londons-finainces

4 https://www.siasat.com/india-vs-pakistan-over-uk-pm-rishi-sunaks-ancestry-2446197/

5 https://www.theguardian.com/commentisfree/2020/feb/27/how-did-british-indians-become-so-prominent-in-the-conservative-party

6 https://www.thetimes.co.uk/article/rishi-sunak-britain-first-asian-indian-prime-minister-sathnam-sanghera-t33qqvwx9

7 https://books.google.co.in/ books?id=XFEFEAAAQBAJ&printsec=frontcover&dq=going+for+broke&hl=hi&newbks=1&newbks_redir=0&sa=X&redir_esc=y#v=o

□

2

CUTTING THE LONG STORY SHORT

It is my limitation that I cannot narrate the story of Sunak's grand- parents in detail who struggled throughout their lives. Their aim was fundamentally very ordinary and mundane. They wanted their children to prosper and knew fairly well that education and knowledge will be the only way to prosperity.

"Britain welcomed its first non-White Prime Minister, Rishi Sunak, a practicing Hindu, on the first day of the festival Diwali. You could be forgiven for thinking this is a ray of light for British race relations, and it has already been heralded as a 'historic moment' marking a change from when Sunak was born in 1980 when there were no Black or Asian members of Parliament." Kehinde Andrews, Professor of Black Studies at Birmingham City University and author of the book *"The New Age of Empire: How Racism and Colonialism Still Rule the World"* begins his article for CNN (published on October 26, 2022) with these words echoing our opinion also.

This son of the soil was born on May 12, 1980 at Southampton General Hospital. He seems to many of us a descendant of

Vishnugupt Chanakya, the pioneer of economics. He was born in the General Hospital. Southampton once again found a special karmic toehold in history, in 21st century, as the proud birthplace of the United Kingdom's first Hindu and first British Asian prime minister. He was born in Southampton, where he and his family still provide a meal once a year to local worshippers at the Hindu temple co-founded by Sunak's grandfather, Ramdas Sunak, in 1971 – shortly after he emigrated from India with his wife and their son, Sunak's father, Yashvir Sunak.

By the way, as Indians we hardly know about this place. But it will be interesting to read the following extract to know in detail about the place called Southampton. Vaihayasi Pande Daniel very beautifully and painstakingly collected this information. "The port of Southampton, and its 189-year-old majestic Royal Pier, has always been a place where history has been fashioned for Britain and the world. The *Mayflower* departed from this Hampshire town, in south England on an English Channel estuary, via Plymouth, in 1620, taking a sturdy bunch of 102 pilgrims across the choppy Atlantic, over ten rough weeks, to establish a 'New World' that became America and Canada. The ill-fated *RMS Titanic* sailed away to its doom from Southampton piers. During World War II, the port city was heavily bombed and in June 1944 platoons and platoons of British, French, Canadian and American soldiers -- some 3.5 million men -- left from its docks for the D-Day landing in Normandy to liberate France from the Nazis, which eventually won the war for the Allies 11 months later.[1]

Southampton once again found a special karmic toehold in history, in the 21st century, as the proud birthplace of the United Kingdom's first Hindu and first British Asian prime minister. The parents took him to 54 Richmond Gardens. This was his home which was built in the 1930s. It was a redbrick house in the Portswood district of the city. It was on Raymond Road in Shirley, a few miles from the hospital where his father Yashvir Sunak worked as a family doctor. His mother Usha worked as a manager in the local chemist's shop 'Weston Pharmacy'. She left that job shortly before Rishi was born. She later decided to work only where the working hours were short and there was no inconvenience in bringing up her children. Later, his brother Sanjay was born in 1982 and sister Raakhi in 1987.

This is what I quoted and indicated in the foregoing chapter. The marked quotation was from his biography which starts as follows, "How to make an ideal childhood? Some common themes are: loving parents, a stable home environment, opportunities to have fun, lack or absence of fear, time and space to play, a large house with a garden where children can run and run. The most expensive schooling that money can buy and lots of time together as a family, and most of the ingredients are definitely there." "The childhood of the future Prime Minister was remarkable in more ways than one. 'The small boy with jet black hair, a ready smile and lovely manners who used to wheel around on a bike with the other kids or kick a ball about with his little brother Sanjay' lived in peace with his friends."[2] He played and played and ate and ate. How could we say for sure?

***

Those who write biographies know that they can pass on anything as true and can claim that their side of tale is nothing but truth. It is difficult to separate what is fictitious, and what is true. There are two different "truths", which are "story truth" and "happening truth". "Happening truth" is the actual events that happen, and is the foundation or time-line on which the story is built on. "Story truth" is the molding or re-shaping of the "happening truth" that allows the story to be believable and enjoyable. Elizabeth Loftus discusses this idea in a way that's extremely compelling. The truth about Rishi Sunak is not hard to find but the findings are not always a click-away. What we get may be twice removed from reality. Therefore, '*Kursi ki peti khol lo*' Untie your seat-belts and relax. Believe me, I am an old man –

Neither father nor mother, nor any playmate;

Only an avenue, dark, nameless, without end

And tell me if I am not glad.

The poets and authors and those who narrate stories are often imaginative folk. That is why in my language-Hindi-a story is always told (ma kah eik kahani- mother, tell me a story). I tell you 'half-a-story' of a suitable boy that has more than half of his life ahead. One of Rishi Sunak's favourite authors is Vikram Seth.

When Rishi Sunak gave his first big interview to The Times, there was a statue of a Hindu deity on the PM's table in 10, Downing Street. From the back, it looked like either Lakshmi or Ganesh. A practicing Hindu!

***

The "East African Indian" community overturned misconceptions and perceptions about the Indian Diaspora in the UK. They went on to get success in business, education, government and finally politics in a logical sequence. It is no less than a miracle for the people of the deprived refugee class to develop in this way in a generation or two. Yashvir Sunak was a General Practitioner (GP) in the National Health Service

(NHS) and Usha Sunak was Pharmacist at Sunak Pharmacy in Southampton.

At present, his brother Sanjay is a psychologist and his sister Rakhi (Williams) is a specialist in emergency medicine in New York. Rakhi serves as the head of strategy and planning at the United Nations Global Fund. He himself is the Prime Minister. This is the present which has a long history.

"Dad was a National Health Service (NHS) General Practitioner (GP), and worked extra jobs, evenings, and weekends. Almost every night of my childhood, he worked until the early hours, writing up patient notes and referral letters. Mum owned a pharmacy – Sunak Pharmacy," he said.

Yashvir was busy with his GP duties and Usha in her pharmacy and kept on maintaining the family together. They had learned from their birth to pay attention to the education of their children. There was no negligence in this. Like many immigrant families, the Sunaks believed in the transformative power of education. With the success of the pharmacy run by Usha Sunak, as well as the income from Yashvir's General Practice, they were able to send their children to good local private schools.

When we are telling this story to you, we know that this is not a common story. This is the story of the Prime Minister of Britain. And when the story is big, then something or the other remains unfulfilled and untouched in it. At that time no one knew that Rishi would one day go so far. But now you and I know. This has also alerted the missing people of the story. Now many people have different stories to tell fond memoirs to concoct and retell. What would I have, no one would have such a device to know the truth. *'Honahar Birwan Ke Hot Chikne Paat'* (coming events cast their shadows before) but they are not so smooth that there is a fear of slipping. "Human memories are slippery.

Memory is slippery. It bends to our understanding of the world, twists to accommodate our prejudices. It is unreliable. Witnesses seldom remember the same things. They identify the wrong people. They give us the details of events that never happened. Memory is slippery, but my memories suddenly feel slipperier."

That's why without resorting to exaggeration, let's continue.

***

Sunak Pharmacy

The remarkable journey that took Rishi Sunak to Downing Street did not start at Southampton General Hospital, where he was born 42 years ago, but at a busy intersection on the A35, about half a mile away. Here, opposite Sainsbury's-Local, you will find a row of red-brick shops that today houses a baker, a barber's shop, a nail salon, a dental clinic, and a modest complex with a large sign on the door. There is a square clock and a blue insignia with flashing English letters NH to S. This little shop was called Sunak's Pharmacy for many decades. The King Edward VI School at the bottom end of Hill Lane bordering the lavish parks and gardens of Southampton Common was the city's most prestigious school. And at the top end, at the corner of the High Street, was Sunak's Pharmacy. Rishi's mother Usha used to run this pharmacy. Her service work continued uninterruptedly till her retirement. It was like their family venture. During his teenage years, Rishi used to deliver medicines to customers during weekends on his bicycle. Along with studying A-levels, he used to look after the accounts of the shop while studying economics. Rishi Sunak came this far through a combination of talent, hard work and good luck. Along with this, Sunak Pharmacy has an indirect contribution in ensuring that there was an excellent education for children.

Remember, among the ideals and inspirational characters Rishi Sunak has repeatedly cited is Margaret Thatcher, another shopkeeper's child (Europe's first woman prime minister. and Conservative PM). Rishi Sunak has compared former leader Margaret Thatcher's upbringing above her father's grocers to his childhood helping in his mother's pharmacy in Hampshire. Speaking to The Telegraph, the MP for Richmond said: '[Thatcher] talked about the person at home with their family budget. She talked about that really powerfully. That resonated with me, because that's how I was brought up. My mum was a small businesswoman, she was a chemist. I worked in my mum's small chemist in Southampton. I did my mum's books – that was part of my job. I also did payroll and accounts every week and every month.' "Our life was built around the business. Out of school, I'd serve customers or do deliveries; help dispense medicines; do the bookkeeping. And every Sunday we'd pile into the car to clean the shop, all of us together, the whole family. It was a family business – that's just what you do," he shared.[3]

His campaign launch video began with him saying: "Let me tell you a story about a young woman almost a lifetime ago who boarded a plane armed with hope for a better life and the love of her family. This young woman came to Britain where she managed to find a job but it took her nearly a year to save enough money for her husband and children to follow. One of those children was my mother; aged 15. My mum studied hard and got the qualifications to become a pharmacist. She met my dad, an NHS GP, and they settled in Southampton. Their story didn't end there but that is where my story began. Family is everything to me and my family gave me opportunities they could only dream of but it was Britain, our country that gave them and millions like them the chance of a better future."[4]

Rishi Sunak visited his family's old pharmacy in Southampton on 24 August, 2022. He spoke of the "strong family, community service" values he learned growing up that he wanted to bring to government. Though the business is no longer in the family's hands, the Sunak name can be seen on a parking sign at the back of the building. "[The pharmacy] shaped me to being the person I am today, these are my roots and it is those values that I want to bring to government," Mr Sunak said.

Oakmount School

Oakmount House, situated on the west side of Brookvale Road and south of Orchard's Way, was built in 1850 as a private residence before becoming a school in 1907. The school closed in 1989, but the house was modernized and retained when the surrounding area was developed.

The primary school Yashvir and Usha chose for their children was Oakmount School. This school had a great reputation. Only 150 children studied there and it was much better than the church school. Rishi was enrolled there at the age of four. The headmaster of this kindergarten in Oakmount, an old-time prep school, was Joe Savage. Sunak was so fast in studies that he went ahead of children of his age and started passing two classes in a year. His kindergarten teacher Mrs. Everest used to say that this boy would either become a brain surgeon or a heart surgeon. Rishi made such an impact even at the age of just four that one of his teachers predicted that he would be a brain or heart surgeon, can you believe this forecast? Little did they know that this kid would be winning hearts one day. In fact, the future prime minister was deemed so good academically that he could pass two classes in a year.

I don't have any specific anecdote when he was just in the school but my eyes sparkled when I read the following one somewhere.

During this year's visit to the temple, in July, the then chancellor was being introduced to a group of young children, aged four to nine, when one of them asked: "Are you the prime minister?" "We all burst out laughing," said Sanjay Chandarana, the president of the Vedic Society temple. "I don't remember what [Sunak] said particularly but obviously there was a smile on his face."

The Stroud School

Everything was going well at school, but suddenly during Easter of 1989 the news came that Oakmount School was going to be closed and this summer vacation would be their forever vacation. This news was worrying but true and then both brothers Rishi and Sanjay were admitted to another school – Stroud School.

Stroud School is an independent preparatory school in Romsey. A preparatory school is a fee-paying independent primary school that serves pupils up to the age of 13. Currently, this school charges per term fees of between £4,060 for Nursery to Year 2 students, and £6,515 for Year 7 to Year 8 pupils. His education at Stroud and from there King Edward VI Preparatory School in Southampton (now £17,000 a year) has given him the foundations to lead through challenging times with integrity and compassion.

This school functioned as a branch of another school and its children got priority admission in the other school. There was a lot of hustle-bustle in the school and there were also children of other Asian descent. Here too Rishi showed his strength and played a lot of games. He used to play all the three games of hockey, football and cricket and used to play a lot. An article from the Hampshire Chronicle mentions Rishi Sunak's time at Stroud: "Rishi Sunak went to Stroud School. He captained the Stroud cricket team and took part in hockey, football and athletics. He was head boy in his final year. There were discussions among the teachers. Judy Gregory writes on the Facebook page, "Yes, very proud to have known and taught him. He always stood out in the crowd as a genuine and caring boy. Very articulate and a great sense of humor!" Everyone used to tell his future was bright. Everyone used to congratulate his parents. His classmates still remember that the rituals of Rishi's parents made him so sharp. It is really surprising to know that teachers, fellow-students and parents of other students from his Hampshire prep school, Stroud, had seen sparks of greatness and genius in his eyes when he was just about 13 years of age. A student named Ollie Case was among her classmates at the school between 1989 and 1993, and the two continued on. Fellow Stroud pupil Ollie Case, who went on to be a teacher there, says in Lord Ashcroft's book: "He was someone that was talked about. The teachers would say, 'He's going to be a Prime Minister'." Oli became a teacher and he never tires of saying what the teachers then used to say about Sunak, "Rishi is going to become the prime minister one day." Schoolmates say he was destined for big things from the beginning. "Rishi was always expected to do something," former boarding school peer Tim Johnson once told Tatler. "He was always expected to be head boy as he was clever enough, reasonable enough and well behaved enough."

Rishi started participating in sports as well as cultural events. Young Rishi captained the Stroud Cricket team and took part in football, hockey and athletics. He was head boy in his final year. He was always ready to do small roles in plays and musicals. This gave him the skill to speak well in front of people. One of his teachers, Judy Gregory, once recalled of this teenager named Rishi, "Sunak always stood out in a crowd as a genuine and sensible boy. One more thing to remember is that he Apart from being eloquent, he also had a pleasant body, and you could call him cheerful."

Due to his personal qualities and popularity, Rishi got an opportunity to become the 'Head Boy' in his last year of school. It is said by all that the sage got only one mantra from his family and that was - *Vidya Dadati Vinayam* - he has to acquire knowledge and move forward with the help of that knowledge. This race to get ahead has led them to seek education in a better school than the one they can easily attend. So instead of going to Edward College, he decided to go to Winchester College. His classmates were going to Edwards, but his parents chose the more expensive college with higher fees. A few hundred yards away in Southampton was a good school in all respects, which did not require the daily run to Winchester, situated in the middle of the congested city. But the Sunak couple wanted to give the best education to their children.

Winchester College

"If ever there was a time for a Wykehamist, this is it. We've been drowning in spin and punch line politics for so long that we now universally hate politicians. Bravado is bust." Helen Kirwan-Taylor

"Boys from Winchester are different. The school's motto is "Manners Maketh Man", so they are known for their exquisite politeness and sheer brain power. It is boys from Winchester who run the civil service in effect the real holders of state power in Britain. The Winchester boys are those who become Archbishops, bankers and heads of professional associations. They leave the grubby populism of politics to Old Etonians like Boris Johnson." Denis MacShane adds.

The turning point in Sunak's life came at the end of primary school, when the hardworking boy from a working-class, middle-class immigrant family got a place at Winchester College. Speaking to LBC about Sunak, Matt Hancock said: "He's not of privileged background at all, absolutely standard background." and he's referred to himself as "professional middle class". Sunak's parents said that paying Rishi's Winchester fees was "quite a large financial commitment" because that amount was double the fees of his school in Southampton. Sunak was educated at Winchester College, a private boarding school, which admitted students then had to pay very high fees per year. Winchester College has a rowing club, a rifle club, an extensive art collection, they charge over £45,000 a year in fees.

Winchester is a boarding school for boys from 13 to 18-years-old, with girls admitted in the sixth form. It was a new world in which the Winchester boys even had a Victorian public-school language of their own, with bicycles being 'bogles' and cigarettes being 'trust'. All those boys were rich, very rich, and very few of them had to earn money by waiting tables during the summer months as waiters.

Intellectuals have presented this fact sometimes sarcastically and sometimes directly that education for all in general and that too quality education is such a medium through which they reach the ruling class. George Orwell wrote in 'The Lion and the Unicorn' in the first half of the 20th century, "England was ruled by an aristocracy, which was constantly recruited from parvenus (institutions of higher education)". given how much energy the -born men possessed, and given that they were buying a way into a class that had a tradition of public service in any way, one might expect that to produce capable rulers in some way In The Lion and the Unicorn, Orwell was not praising the new class of rulers, but was criticizing the old elite. He considered that both were disappointing: "One of the dominant facts in English life during the past three-quarters of a century has been the decay of capacity in the ruling class."

William of Wykeham was Bishop of Winchester and Lord Chancellor of England. He founded both the school and the university college, New College, Oxford, in 1382 to use the money from his positions. He founded Winchester College in 1394. Alumni of this college are known as 'Old Wykehamists' in memory of the founder of the school, William of Wykeham. It is a college which has had its own reign. This college is famous for its intellectuality. In fact, it has given only one Prime Minister – Henry Eddington – and that too two centuries ago. This institution last gave a candidate for the post of Prime Minister in 1801 but has given many ministers. Even more illustrious like Nawab Mansoor Ali Khan Pataudi, India's leading cricket player and today's hero Saif Ali Khan's father also studied in this college, General Sir Nick Carter (Chief of the Defense Staff), David J. Thules (Nobel Prize Winner in Physics) etc. and thousands more who were enriched in life by this college education.

You will be surprised to know that the shooting of some Harry Potter films was done in this college. 'As for famous OWs: it's quite the spectrum,' says the writer Nicholas Shakespeare. 'Apart from the author of Buffy the Vampire Slayer, the novelist Patrick Gale, and the former head of the army, Nick Carter, and before that Wavell and Anthony Trollope, it's hard to think of any colourful OW in political life since Oswald Mosley." Renowned novelist Jane Austen is perhaps one of Hampshire's most famous residents as she spent most of her short life here. After traveling to Winchester for treatment, Jane and her sister took up residence in College Street, next to the cathedral. Regrettably, he died two months later, and his body was buried in Winchester Cathedral. The English Romantic poet, John Keats also lived in Winchester. The poet resided here in the summer and autumn of 1819.

This college does not allow one to survive on the power of money but only on the power of intelligence along with money power. When Rishi Sunak entered this college at the age of thirteen, he entered the intellectual world where nothing happened without competition. 'The best part of Winchester is that it limits the amount of sociopaths coming in because of its focus on academics,' says Harry Knight, 23, an old Old Wykehamist (OW) currently finishing up masters in political history at UCL. 'Eton is all about the race to the top. Winchester is about the life of the mind.' Seeing the whole environment full of 'intellectually arrogant' teachers and genius students, Rishi felt that he would get both a challenge and a warning here. And he went ahead and accepted it.

The Sunak couple sent their two sons to study at Winchester College. The young Rishi never went downhill. He only traveled upwards. With the young Rishi and his younger brother Sanjay in the back of the car, Winchester made the daily 12-mile commute to college. Today, the whole world accepts that the people of India are engaged with their body, mind and wealth in the education of their children. The Sunak couple was rich but they were not wealthy enough, so they were worried about the expenses of their three children's education. Father was worried and that is why he encouraged Rishi to appear for the scholarship. The special thing about these examinations was that even if they did not provide much financial help, they used to get a lot of prestige. It was not easy to pass the exam. In Winchester these examinations were called 'elections'. These tests used to go on for several days. Rishi worked hard. Rishi, a 13-year-old teenager, could not get a scholarship to the famous public school Winchester, where fees are now £43,000 a year. This, according to him, was one of his first biggest failures.

Some money was also received from here and there. Father Yashvir, on the other hand, took up the part-time job of an occupational health advisor at John Lewis, which he continued to do for twenty years. This ensured the receipt of some more money. 'It was a big deal,' Rishi Sunak once told an interviewer when the incident was mentioned 'I missed it just a little bit and it was a big problem for my parents. I didn't realize until much later how much of a struggle it really was and what my parents had to do to make it less so. They saved a lot of money here and there, they sacrificed a lot, and everything for my parents was for their children to provide this great education.

The father, who was satisfied by spending everything in the education of the children, kept the Sunak family busy in sports and entertainment as well. There was no shortage of anything. Used to play tennis and also go out to eat. Due to the strong influence and support of the family and his hard work and sharp intellect, Rishi not only got success in the examination, he also became the shining star of his institution. Be it cricket, hockey or football, he has also shown in the field of play. While studying at Winchester College, Sunak did the strangest thing he ever did, sneaking a small portable television into his dorm room so he wouldn't miss any of the important Euro '96 games.

Senior journalist Saeed Naqvi, in one of his articles, while discussing the Indian family system and his great efforts for the education initiation of his children, narrates a parable to underline the contribution of his family to Rishi Sunak.

The planning by the Sunak family into the making of Rishi is exemplary. By way of illustration, let me first tell you a brief story of a planned future. A young man of modest means sought accommodation near a golf course so that his daughter could join the nearby school. He and his daughter would then join the golf club, at whatever cost, beg, borrow or steal. By the time she is past her higher secondary stage, ready for college, she will be an expert, if not a champion, golfer. This is high premium qualification for admission in the fanciest American colleges on his diligently drawn up list. The strategy worked.[5]

Such a senior journalist and commentator cannot be off the mark when he presents his conclusion as follows. "In Mr Sunak's case, the career was conceived and mapped with the best possible education as a stepping stone to networks, wealth and power. Stroud preparatory school, Southampton; Winchester College, where he was the head boy; Oxford, Stanford, and the campus secret societies on the way double distilling the elite network." [6]

It is a part of the tale that Rishi Sunak got his education in Private Schools and paid heavy fees. Those days he and his family didn't know that one day Rishi will be a political force and ultimately become the PM of the UK. Now that he is the PM and has a responsibility to protect the interests of his party, the opposition Labour leader Sir Keir Starmer has called on him to end the "scandal" of tax breaks for private schools. Mr Sunak's response has been according to his understanding, "Whenever he (Starmer) attacks me about where I went to school, he is attacking the hard-working aspiration of millions of people in this country; he's attacking people like my parents. This is a country that believes in opportunity not resentment. He doesn't understand that and that's why he's not fit to lead." Speaking about his time at Winchester in a documentary for the BBC in 2001, Rishi said: "At Winchester I was one of very few Asians, I mean the first generation into that level of society. It does put me in an elite of achievement definitely in society, but I'll always consider myself sort of, you know, professional middle class."[7]

In media profiles, Sunak's allies describe him as "immaculate", "calm" and "organized", qualities befitting of a former Winchester head of college. On the other hand, the attacks on him will never end. The British Press is brutal and vociferous. The wealth of his wife and his elite education will always remain with him and it will be very easy to accuse him of being out of touch with the mundane problems of the common men.

Kuti's Brasserie

Kuti Miah, a Bangladeshi emigrant, who came to Britain to work as a waiter in the mid-1970s, becoming a swanky restaurant owner less than two decades later, says enthusiastically that he has known Rishi since he was a few weeks old.

If you walk further through the port area to the Southampton Royal Pier building, 5.6 km from the hospital, you will come to a restaurant, classily done up in gold and blue, named *Kuti's Brasseri*. The eatery is situated on the waterfront in Southampton, Hampshire and the owner is a family friend of the Sunaks. His family had just become a Bangladeshi friend who came there in 1975 and became a restaurant owner from his industry. Miah got to know Rishi's parents in the 1980s. Dr Yashvir and Usha Sunak are both from Africa. When Miah began his brasserie, the Sunaks were frequent visitors marking family occasions with a dinner at Kuti's Brasserie, including every Christmas Eve.

Sunak worked as a waiter at Indian restaurant Kuti's Brasserie which is being owned by Kuti Miah. As a teenager, Sunak worked for one or two summers, in 1989-1999, at this British Bangladeshi-owned eatery, welcoming patrons and serving up its signature dishes. The experience gave him a huge appreciation of the business, of the importance of treating people fairly and the value of this most iconic of British Asian industry. Remembering Rishi's competence in work, Kuti Miah says, "He was very hard working. A very nice person. He can get on with everyone, the people with whom he was working. Everyone loved him -- the customers. He is a people person. He can very easily talk to people. You can see that now even. How he connects with the people -- very talkative person. He can explain things very nicely. He is very, very, clever with his mouth."

Kuti Miah was a Bangladeshi emigrant, who came to Britain to work as a waiter in the mid-1970s. He became a swanky restaurant owner in less than two decades. He has known Rishi since he was a few weeks old. He describes Rishi as "Wonderful! He was wonderful. People trust in him. He is a religious person. But he is very passionate about his work. He and his dad are very people-loving, human loving. They are very down to earth people." He adds, "I came to Southampton as a restaurant head waiter. Rishi's dad was my boss's GP. One lunch-time, Dr Sunak came for lunch. That's how I bumped into them. I open the door and I saw a pram with a baby (*Rishi*) and Dr Sunak and Mrs Sunak. I asked my boss who they are. He said: 'He is a GP'."[8]

Steady Study

Rishi joined at a young age and then threw himself into studies and all the activities for which the college was known. He made friends and won hearts with his kindness, humility, and gentleness. For A level, Rishi chose subjects - English Literature, Economics and Maths. He also took French and Biology for AS level. His parents were not particularly happy about his selection. What will the boy do after studying English or Economics? There was a concern in his mind that where does one get the meaning (wealth) by reading the scriptures? Rishi's mother was very worried about this for a long time. But this was Rishi's favorite subject. It became his favorite subject at the age of sixteen.

Sunak was different from the other sixth formers at Winchester: a lifelong nondrinker, he was not deterred by the charms of the pub. But there was something special about him, which set him apart from the general herd. He was an orthodox in every respect, and to his circle of friends he was one who, not only in his outlook and conduct but also in his religious outlook, was a Hindu who abstained from beef. "At Winchester I was one of very few Asians, I mean the first generation into that level of society," he once said. "It does put me in the elite of achievement definitely in society, but I'll always consider myself sort of professional middle class."

Winchester College preferred to treat the students as if they were young men, not milk babies. This was one aspect of the culture that Sunak particularly appreciated. His parents encouraged him to work hard from a very young age. He was a disciple who was slowly but steadily making progress. Now that he was in boarding school, he had to manage his own time, which he believes was one of the most valuable skills he acquired through hard work. Rishi was very much forthcoming in an interview when he explained.

> Winchester College loved to treat students as if they were actually teaching you to be able to understand your own life a little bit. "It was really teaching you to be able to just figure out your own life a bit...Homework was not 'here it is today, hand it in tomorrow'. It was much more 'here's all the stuff you need to do for next week'- you kind of organize your own time and figure out when you're going to do it...You can't get your parents to help you with everything, so it teaches you that independence and that self-motivation. That's probably the biggest kind of life lesson.

The Rise of Rishi Sunak

During school holidays, he helped his mother maintain the books of her pharmacy business. As a result, he began to take an interest in what the main political parties were saying about taxes and spending. He was also becoming aware of their parents' role and activities in the local community.

As the world was waking up in 1997, Sunak, as editor of the Winchester College newspaper, was writing articles expressing concern about the dangers of the European Union. At the age of 17, Sunak was concerned that Blair had "plans for the possible break-up of the United Kingdom and membership of an eventual European superstate". In May 1997, during the general election, he distributed leaflets for a few days for the local Conservative candidate. When Tony Blair won the election everyone was talking about it but not Rishi. His family story was closer to that of Margaret Thatcher than that of his bourgeois Laborite classmates. During the leadership election won by Ms Truss, Mr Sunak wrote in The Telegraph: "I am a Thatcher, I am involved as a Thatcher, and I am a Thatcher". I will rule."

Seeing the early results on election night 1997, Sunak sat down to write a thoughtful article for the school magazine, 'The Wykehamist', lamenting the news. His main complaint was with Europe. 'He relishes in the label of a patriot,' he complained of Tony Blair, 'but plans for a possible break-up of the United Kingdom and membership of an eventual European superstate.' The seeds of Brexit were already in his mind. Though he had been suspicious of the membership from the start, yet Sunak's political ambitions were not entirely clear.

Usha Sunak, his mother, used to be happy with the confidence of her sons. She used to feel that her sons had achieved something with great effort. She used to point out the differences between her and her sons, "They can stand up in front of the crowd and talk at any time. I can't do it like them. They come up with answers and arguments, and the only way I find to reason with them is by saying "I'm your mother."

You can see the success of it. You get an education, you get a good job, you have respect, you go up in your status, and things become easier," she told a BBC documentary in 2001.

What to tell about mother's love and care? Whoever she met, she used to brag about the progress of her children. Whoever used to come to her pharmacy would definitely hear and say something about Rishi. Without a comprehensive update on what the Sunak brothers had been up to in Winchester, Usha Sunak, who assembled the weekly prescription, would not allow them to leave the counter.

Incidentally, I may add here that according to a report in 'MailOnline', Sanjay Sunak studied at his brother Rishi Sunak's Stroud Private Primary School. Then he studied as an undergraduate at University College London in 1999 and as a postgraduate at Birkbeck, University of London. He then went on to study forensic mental health at King's College London, before pursuing a doctorate in clinical psychology from the University of Surrey. He also began working for the NHS during the period. Now he works as a consultant clinical psychologist working for a private clinic and Bupa, the private health insurer. Rakhi Sunak, after attending Oxford, founded the UNICEF Society there and married international aid specialist Peter Williams. She works in New York as chief of strategy and planning at the United Nations global fund for education in emergencies.

Expensive Education

Richard Beard, author of the book *'Sad Little Men: Private Schools and the Ruin of England'* (2021), elaborates on the expensive private education in Britain and the childhood studies of many politicians there. In 1975, as a child, Richard Beard was sent away from his home to sleep in a dormitory. So were David Cameron and Boris Johnson. Beard explains that the *"most convincing reason to go to a private school remains to have gone to a private school, with the prizes that are statistically likely to follow. Want to be a senior judge? Sixty-five per cent of them had the same education that helped form almost half the country's newspaper columnists and two out of the last three prime ministers. "* He sees elitism in education as an evil. Beard, whose book is partly based on his own experiences, believes that all-male boarding schools harden their students emotionally. He says that in order to survive the boys cannot show any vulnerability among their peers. In the words of Richard Beard, "The idea that, while attending Winchester College, he would never have thought that he would be at the helm of government seems to me very unlikely. Leadership qualities are one of the things they teach you." and you are bound to think of your future in those terms." So he must have thought that he would perform such functions, even though he had not explicitly thought of becoming Chancellor of the Exchequer." In the words of Laura Waddell, " Today's government frontbenchers, like Rishi Sunak, quite demonstrably have little insight into the plight of the common man. For those who grew up with an elite education, filing past statues of old boy British leaders into their lessons each day to remind them of their place in history, that exclusion was part of the deal for which their parents paid eye-watering fees."[9]

Until the age of 11, Sunak attended Oakmount Preparatory School and then Stroud Independent Prep School, which now charges up to £18,500 a year, he studied at King Edward VI's School in Southampton (now £17,000 a year) before going to Winchester College (now £43,335 a year). Five chancellors and a prime minister before Sunak attended one of the oldest public boarding schools in England. Another Eton's long-time rival had studied at Winchester. Boarding schools such as Winchester can prepare students well to move forward in politics, they form a worldview that goes far beyond the ordinary. Money is at the center of all this as everyone knows that studies cost a lot of money. Everyone knows the parents who study, teach and spend. But real money is intangible. The necessities of everyday life are taken care of for you. Then how can you really think of people who are struggling for five pounds and ten pounds?

(By the way, you will be glad to know that the all-girls private primary where Rishi's daughters attend - along with Harper Beckham, David and Victoria's youngest child - charges £22,350 a year. The boarding school Mr Sunak's eldest daughter attends charges an eye-watering £41,250 a year, taking their total education bill to £63,600. Attendees of the school have gone on to be MPs, broadcasters, top judges and members of the Queen's household. The Sunday Mirror revealed. You are an educated Indian and you will mentally calculate this amount and change it into INR. I wish to send my grand-children there.)

Sunak seems to have been adept at fitting in with predominantly white and upper-class establishments from an early age. These educational institutions historically prepared the country's richest men for powerful positions. Other Tory politicians of South Asian heritage had less privileged routes into politics – Sajid Javid and Priti Patel both skipped Oxbridge and were educated at comprehensive and grammar schools.

Hard work pays!

In August 1998, that summer – the heat of the France 98 World Cup and the Omagh bombing – Kuti Mia, the eponymous restaurant located behind the Curry House, overheard one of his waiters saying "You're going to be something special, Rishi!". Britain's future chancellor and future prime minister then reverently flashed his famous smile. Even today he says 'since then Rishi khub bolne wala tha, kya khub bolta tha.' Then 18-year-old Rishi Sunak was about to go to Oxford, but during vacation, he worked as a helper in Mia's restaurant, a close family friend, to earn some pocket money. 'I've seen him grow up, sir!' Miya, who came from Bangladesh, never tires of saying. Recalling Rishi's ability to work, he says, 'He was very hard working. A very nice person. He could work with everyone, the people he was working with. Everyone loved them - customers were happy with them. He is a popular person. He can talk to people very easily. You can still see it. How does he connect with people - Very talkative person… He can explain things very well. He's very, very clever at talking."

Miyan's son Armaan is now 25-26 years old and helps his father in the work. He was 7 or 8 years old when Sunak worked in his restaurant. Armaan also recalls Rishi's time when asked now, "I clearly remember both our families went on a trip to London, where we saw the movie 'The Lion King'. I remember Rishi as a very humble, well-spoken man who was destined to make it big."

Sports and Games

Rishi's parents were crazy about tennis. But Rishi loved football more than tennis. Father and son both were very fond of watching Football and loved to play Tennis. Father's love for the game was transferred to the son. Rishi's childhood hero was the team's star player Matt Le Tissler. Boy Sunak used to love him so much that he got a replica of his shirt and adorned himself with shirt no 7. His father Yashvir had a season ticket to watch the Saints and Sunak said that, for his 18th birthday, he was given a card signed by the whole squad, which then became "one of his most prized possessions". Jersey number 7, he used to flaunt many times by wearing it. "I'm a huge football fan, I'm from Southampton and if I've got to be able to run Southampton, I will." Rishi said once.

If the most diabolical thing Prime Minister Theresa May did as a child was to run barefoot in a wheat field. Sunak had left a small TV set in his hostel without permission to watch the Euro 96 match. His biography by Ashcroft claimed that "the naughtiest thing" he did while at Winchester College "was to smuggle a hand-held television into the school so that he did not miss any key games of Euro 96".The best gift he received on his 18th birthday was a card signed by the players of his favorite team. Rishi has this to say about it.

> We had this great song, "Football's Coming Home'... (A friend and I) had managed to smuggle into school some kind of old hand-held TV; this chunky thing with a big aerial that you could receive a TV signal from, but which obviously didn't work brilliantly...During the time when we were meant to be doing our homework in the evening, he and I nipped up to the top of the school, this attic, to go and watch TV ... There was an England game, someone had scored, and we were totally absorbed in the moment... and then obviously turned round and standing at the doorway was our teacher, who was nonplussed... He'd already busted us once a few days before, and told us to take this thing home, which we obviously didn't listen to. We were in full embrace, screaming and shouting "Three lions".

"Hats off to Qatar for hosting an incredible World Cup so far. The group stages will be remembered as one of the all-time greats". His love for the game continues.

Young Sunak not only loved the game of cricket, he supported England in every match and not India. Sunak was compared to former India cricketer Ashish Nehra on social media. People used pictures of Ashish Nehra while posting congratulatory messages for Rishi Sunak. Were Rishi and Ashish Nehra brothers who got separated at the Kumbh Mela?

Star Wars Fan

At a recent event in Exeter, he revealed the roles he would love to do in life if he didn't become a politician, saying he wanted to star in a Star Wars film or own his favorite Premier League club, Southampton. Sunak once said via Sport Bible, "It's been on my list of life ambitions, well, when I was a kid, I wanted to be in a Star Wars movie, so maybe it's a not a sensible thing."

A self-confessed 'Huge-star wars fan' with a sizable collection of lightsabers, he tweeted a photo of himself and his 'jedi master' Mr Javid at a screening of the rise of skywalker in 2019.

Sunak is, according to a report published in The Asian Age (7 Nov 2022), heavily influenced by the trade wars in Star Wars. Those who are unfamiliar with Star Wars should know that Star Wars is an American epic space opera multimedia franchise created by George Lucas, which began with the eponymous 1977 film and quickly became a worldwide pop-culture phenomenon. Satr Wars is a great place to find personal inspiration. It's a classic hero's journey, with a call to adventure for a reluctant young protagonist who is eventually thrust into greatness.

Sunak is said to be a fan of Star Trek but an even bigger one of Star Wars. Prof. David Kenny and Conor Casey write that Star Wars may not have the same importance as The Art of War or Machiavelli's The Prince as a political textbook. But it is full of interesting lessons and cautionary tales for those wishing to promote peace, order and good government in this galaxy or any other. They provide a few lessons for Sunak to keep in mind.

1. Incompetence leads to secession and strife- Sunak should remember that dysfunctional and incompetent governments create centrifugal forces that can break up even very old and established unions.

2. Trade keeps the peace but bores people- The other lesson here is that good trade keeps the peace, while trade disputes sow the seeds of much more serious conflicts.

3. Don't run from the background- You must be perceived as a political force, or a rebel alliance will come for you. Having just overthrown a prime minister lurking in the background, this is a lesson Sunak should know without having to learn from his favorite films.

4. Be careful when changing the deal- Sunak will have to make sure the UK delivers on its promises, or his potential partners could, like Lando, wonder what their deals are worth.[10]

Face to face with racism

It is not that in a community where white Englishmen are in abundance, no one will reprimand a black born there. No one will insult him. There are such people. Such incidents also happen. Film-maker Shekhar Kapoor recalled how he was subjected to racial discrimination by his own friends and was beaten up just because he went out with a white woman. Such incidents that happened in youth are remembered. Recalling one such incident, Sunak himself said in an interview.

> I was probably a mid-teenager. We were out at a fast food restaurant, and I was just looking after them. There

were people sitting nearby who- it was the first time I'd experienced it- were just saying some very unpleasant things. The 'p' word … And it stung. I still remember it: it's seared in my memory. You can be insulted in many different ways..but that stings in a way that's hard to explain really. Particularly because my little sister was quiet. Young, as was my brother. I just took them away, and just removed overselves from the situation.

Perhaps "Britain has outgrown its racism": "We must confront racism," says Rishi Sunak after Buckingham Palace incident when a black domestic abuse campaigner Ngozi Fulani was repeatedly asked where she 'really came from' by Prince William's godmother. Lady Susan Hussey resigned from her role in the royal household and apologized over the incident.

Lincoln College, Oxford

He was accepted as one of nine undergraduates to read Philosophy, Politics and Economics at Lincoln College, Oxford. Lincoln College is one of the smallest Oxbridge colleges, with only 70 graduates in each year group. His political career, too, has followed England's most traditional and comfortable path to power. Like five former Chancellors of the Exchequer, Sunak was schooled at the ancient and prestigious Winchester College; And like three of those same Wyckhamist chancellors, he was admitted, as expected, to study at Oxford.

More than any other course at any other university, more than any respectable or ordinary private school, and perhaps unmatched in any other democracy, Oxford PPE pervades British political life. Sunak also obtained a first class degree in Philosophy, Politics and Economics. Sunak studied at Oxford, which has given five of the last six prime ministers. Like so many of his classmates (Wyckhamists), Rishi chose Oxford for university education and like many ambitious young men who had gone before him, he chose subjects such as politics, philosophy and economics. Labor peer and thinker, Maurice Glassman, who studied modern history at Cambridge, comments on this: "PPE combines the status of a typical university degree – PPE with the stamp of a vocational course at school as good. It's the ultimate form of being.. It's perfect training for cabinet membership, and it gives you a distinctive view of life that is a very deeply cultural form." For some leaders, this degree is not a solution but a problem. Former government adviser Dominic Cummings wrote on his influential blog: "If you're young, smart and interested in politics, think very well before studying PPE ... it actually creates big problems because It encourages people like (David) Cameron and Ed Balls to spread bad ideas through a lot of make-believe and bluff." It is so funny that incidental former Prime Minister of Pakistan Mr. Imran Khan also opted the same subjects and studied. . Don't know how true this is!

Lincoln College (formally, The College of the Blessed Mary and All Saints, Lincoln) is one of the constituent colleges of the University of Oxford, situated on Turl Street in central Oxford. Lincoln was founded in 1427 by Richard Fleming, the then Bishop of Lincoln. Notable alumni include the physician John Radcliffe, the founder of Methodism John Wesley, antibiotics scientists Howard Florey, Edward Abraham, and Norman Heatley, writers Theodor Seuss Geisel (Dr. Seuss) and David John Moore Cornwell (John le Carré), the journalist Rachel Maddow, and the current British Prime Minister Rishi Sunak. Outside of Lincoln College, where he studied, Sunak had no special reputation or recognition. He was not like the young William Hague, who arrived at Oxford and became almost a Tory celebrity or young Boris Johnson who tore apart the Oxford Union. At Oxford, Sunak was as insignificant as Tony Blair.

No one took his ambition more seriously. Perhaps he took no interest in student politics and his political ambitions were taken with a pinch of salt. "His fellow students certainly said, slightly light-heartedly, that he wanted to become Conservative prime minister. But I don't think anyone took that too seriously—it was more of a joke," his former Oxford tutor, Michael Rosen, once said. He told in the BBC documentary – filmed in his final year at university – "it does put me in elite of achievement definitely in society, but I'll always consider myself professional middle class."

WhatsApp groups of his contemporaries buzzed about their new famous classmate, wondering how this great boy had been their classmate for years but was never noticed. "He certainly never came to the college bar," says one of the friends. "Not even once in three years. I'd be willing to bet if he ever set foot in it." I was somewhat known as a 'naughty teetotaler' who abstained from alcohol, and who sang everything from Karaoke to Ice Ice Baby at parties. 'Rishi was unknown to student politicians. That Mr Sunak went about his business and minded his own business, and that's all. Even the Oxford University Conservative Association is unable to claim to have recognized him as a past member. National Campaign Co-ordinator of the Labor Party Her rival Shabana Mahmood remembers Rishi as a "library geek" for her days at Oxford.

While at Oxford, Sunak's ambitions found other avenues besides running with the political herd. He joined Oxford University Investment Society which hosted talks by City high-flyers – and scored himself a graduate job at Goldman Sachs. It was a club that linked the students and the financial world. It was sponsored by investment banks etc. In his second year Sunak became president of the club. It was a good experience. As a president of the Society he gave eager young students some guidance. One of his tutors commented: "He was a really excellent student. He was really interested, he really wanted to understand, he cared about things, and he worked hard. He couldn't have been a better student really. He listened, he absorbed things, and he asked good questions."

He showed his natural talent for ballroom dancing, even being able to reach the semi-finals in one competition. In his biography of the Chancellor, Lord Ashcroft reveals that 'Dishy Rishi' has a talent for ball-room dancing. As an under-graduate at Oxford, Sunak made it to the semi-fial of a dance competition. 'He is something of a natural." Ashcroft writes.

Channel 4 recently revealed that just a year after graduating from Oxford, Sunak purchased a one-bedroom flat in the borough of Kensington and Chelsea for £210,000 after getting a considerable amount of financial help from his parents. Documents from the Land Registry showed that Rishi was able to purchase the property with an interest free loan of £105,000 from his parents - the loan was worth more than the average house price in Britain at the time. Sunak still owns the flat and it is now worth an estimated £750,000.[11]

Goldman Sachs

The Goldman Sachs Group, Inc. is a leading global investment banking, securities and investment management firm that provides a wide range of financial services to a substantial and diversified client base that includes corporations, financial institutions, governments and individuals. When Sunak graduated in 2001, he went straight to Goldman Sachs, as the ultra-ambitious did in those days. His first job was with Goldman Sachs. After Oxford, Rishi took a prestigious graduate job at Goldman Sachs and moved to London, buying a £210,000 flat in South Kensington with the help of his parents. Junior recruits at the investment bank learned to be very careful about everything they said and the impression they made, as Goldman uses a "360-degree process" in which employees are evaluated by both their boss and their peer group. is rated. "The result is you constantly have to manage your brand," any employee familiar with the system can tell you. "If you upset the people or let the team down... you're spewed out like toast." This kind of relentless constant evaluation made Sunak a useful training ground for politics.

During his Goldman Sachs days he started studying for a Chartered Finacial Analysit qualification. It is a three year course-CFA1, CFA2, CFA3. It is not easy to get through it. Sunak never rose to be much more than a junior member of financial firms he joined, that is why he constantly busy updating him professionally.

Today, it seems astonishing how far the world has come - the pinnacle of Blairism, financial arrogance, US imperialism and the Davos Consensus. Nevertheless, Sunak left this post in 2004 and took further steps. "Despite working for Goldman Sachs between 2001 and 2004, Sunak doesn't allude to his Goldman analyst years on his LinkedIn profile. Nor does he mention his subsequent career working for hedge fund TCI fund (The Children's Investment Fund) or for Theleme Partners, an equity investment firm which he apparently founded himself. All that matters in Rishi's history is his time in parliament and as Chancellor of the ExchequerEven if Sunak himself wants to play down his history in finance, it's unlikely to go unforgotten by the British electorate, for whom his former career in banking and his immense wealth by marriage are likely to be sources of growing contention in an era of fiscal restraint.."[12]

He left Goldman Sachs to do an MBA at Stanford in the US between 2004 and 2006.

Stanford, California

While Mark Zuckerberg was conceiving Facebook with his colleagues in Silicon Valley, Sunak, the future Prime Minister of Britain, was pursuing a two-year MBA course. He graduated in 2006, the year Twitter was founded. The course was not only valuable from the economic point of view, the most intelligent people of the world used to study in it. It is said that he picked up key aspects of his political philosophy during his time in California. He told the US venture capital journalist Harry Stebbings, of his time at Stanford: "Other than an appreciation of the weather, it's also a home of entrepreneurship, creativity, innovation, and those are probably the most important ways being out there in the US changed my life in terms of the trajectory that I was on."

Sunak got into Stanford through a Fulbright scholarship. You should know that this scholarship is very prestigious. Fulbright alumni include sixty Nobel Prize recipients, eighty-eight Pulitzer Prize winners and thirty-seven current or former heads of state or government. The Fulbright Program, the U.S. government's flagship international academic exchange, was created in the aftermath of World War II, with the goal of preventing future conflicts by providing opportunities for exchange and connection between U.S. citizens and people from other countries. Since its inception over 75 years ago, the Fulbright Program has provided over 400,000 U.S. students, scholars, teachers, artists and professionals — professionals — and foreign counterparts — the opportunity to study, teach and conduct research abroad. People from more than 160 countries have participated in the program. Sunak joins 40 other Fulbright participants who have gone on to serve as heads of state or government.

That's why it didn't cost him and his family that much. You should also understand that out of the recipients of this scholarship, 60 have been Nobel Prize winners and 90 have been Pulitzer Prize winners. Don't even ask the number of politicians and wealthy people who want to enter even after emptying the coffers. Was Sunak popular? It is useless to ask. Who is there who is not famous? (He reportedly got close to an Indian girl named Anuksha, but romance is not known.) According to Derrick Bolton, who was assistant dean of admissions at Stanford from 2001-2016 and remained friendly with Rishi-Akshata, "Mr. Sunak entered the program "very confidently". Among the classes Mr Sunak took was "The Paths to Power", intended to help students understand power and how to wield it effectively. He knew from a young age that he wanted to make an impact on as many people as possible."

This institution had a profound impact on his view of the world, fueling him with enthusiasm about entrepreneurship and giving him a global outlook. Sunak credits the time he spent receiving his Stanford MBA, which he received in 2006, with teaching him to "think big" about the world and for bringing a "start-up mindset" to governance like the US showed him the way, he is exemplary. That influence is reflected in his approach to blockchain and crypto. Stanford professor Paul Romer, who received the 2018 Nobel Prize, has been Sunak's idol and whose Charter Cities idea he quotes here and there. When Sunak lectured at a prestigious business school in London, he cited a lecture on innovation by one of his "inspiring" Stanford professors, Nobel Prize-winning economist Paul Romer, and described Romer's influence on him. Jeffrey Pfeiffer, who teaches a famous course called 'The Paths to Power', posted on LinkedIn that Sunak was among his students and that he hoped they would learn lessons about power "to reach positions where they are few in the world".

Ashcroft writes that Silicon Valley dazzled the young Sunak, and he once remarked how it was possible to drive 10 minutes from the Bay Area to pass hundreds of businesses that have changed people's lives. Sunak himself said once.

> Taking a ten-minute drive through the Bay area of San Francisco, it is possible to pass the headquarters of technology giants such as Apple and Google and hundreds of other businesses which have changed the way we live our lives today…I found working among all this young talent truly inspirational.

> At Stanford, you're in the heart of an ecosystem and a culture that is unlike anything else I've seen in the world,. Everyone is interested in changing the world, and they start with the biggest of dreams and the ecosystem around [Silicon Valley] is supportive of trying to help people realize those ambitions.[13]

He is fondly called 'a spiritual child of Silicon Valley' by some Americans. By his own account, his time there "changed [his] life", "living and breathing that entrepreneurial culture." When he was Chancellor of the Exchequer, he described his approach to being as a "start-up Treasury mentality". That is why some scholars have labeled him as the "first Californian Prime Minister." Sunak often says that his time at Stanford helped to convince him that the world was changing very fast and that the EU was failing to keep up and Britain needed to be more nimble.

Love Interest?

I am tempted to cite in full what Lord Ashcroft wrote about Rishi Sunak's mysterious love interest. I don't have any clue to find out the truth in the following lines. But "it is sometimes claimed, not entirely in jest, that Stanford MBA graduate students are not only shopping for a business qualification but also for a spouse."

> His love life is something of a mystery. At University, he became very close to a fellow student named Anoushka, but it does not seem that they were romantically involved; Any ex-girlfriends from his time at Goldman Sachs remain well below the radar. At Stanford, however, he would meet the person with whom he wished to spend the rest of his life: a young woman from an extraordinary Indian family whose parents were self-made billionaires.[14]

Through his finance career, Sunak either worked for or invested in major American companies – including some that would later shape his political fortunes. Rishi has seen a lot of America through his wife Akshata Murthy. According to 'The Guardian' magazine, through Akshata and her family's businesses, Sunak also has ties to companies like Wendy's in India and operates a joint venture with Amazon in India. This is also the implication of many Americans calling him the 'First Californian Prime Minister'. Perhaps this is also the meaning of calling them the 'spiritual children' of Silicon Valley.

Stephan Chambers, formerly head of the University of Oxford's MBA programme and presently director of the Marshall Institute at the London School of Economics underlines a significant quality of the present prime minister of his country as the first to hold an MBA degree which sets him apart from his peers. He indicates "those two years in brutally competitive Palo Alto changes more than how people dress." Chambers opines that "Sunak's Stanford education means he can run the numbers and pitich the vision. He can assess the net present value. He understands organizational behavior and market segmentation."

California

"In 1997 a business book predicted tech disruption, the alt-right and the rise of the super-rich. Now, in Rishi Sunak, its Silicon Valley world-view has taken over No 10." Quinn Slobodian.

Sunak returned to California in 2010 as co-founder of Thelem Partners, which invests in companies including News Corp. It owns Britain's largest-circulating newspapers The Sun and The Times, generally regarded as London's paper of record. Thelem invested more than $500 million in Moderna, and during the pandemic refused to disclose whether they were getting a cut of its Covid vaccine profits. He and his wife still own an apartment in Santa Monica and have put their green card on hold until October 2021, allowing them to enter the U.S. be allowed permanent residence in the UK. In his role as chancellor, he led the U.S. for 18 months. taxes paid. These American relations of Sunak were also severely criticized. People have quietly but surely said that they were not yet fully committed to staying in the UK.

Back to London

After completing a CV-topping MBA after two years in California, he returned to London and Mayfair in 2006, where a new kind of finance-economy was booming. It was a 'hedge fund'. He was hired by Sir Chris Hone at The Children's Investment Fund (TCI). It was a lucrative job at the London-based hedge fund, TCI Fund Management. A big role at the zenith of fame in an activist firm in Berkeley Square' was an odd job. He was trusted. And Sunak was accepted as a partner in the firm two years later. For a while, he and his new partner rode on the horses of success. Mr Sunak and his boss had studied the industry and CSX in depth for months and their mastery of the industry and CSX was astonishing.

Colleagues say about Rishi: "It is very difficult to dislike him. He is a very simple, humble kind of guy." The qualities that make up Rishi's personality become clear to you as you read his life story: clever and talented, extremely hardworking, ambitious, eager to learn, Disciplined, always well-dressed, he takes nothing for granted, absorbs every bit of information, approaches the less glamorous tasks of his responsibilities diligently and works in unison with his constituency. His only mischievous nickname among gossips in Westminster about Rishi after he became chancellor was "Baby Chino". It was first used in reference to his predecessor Sajid Javid. Javid found the nickname awkward 'Chino' which means "Chancellor in name only." In Sunak's case it could also be a jibe at his short stature as Rishi is only 5 feet 6 inches tall, and this is unlikely to affect him. Don't even get a chance to say anything.

Then came the economic crisis. In 2009, when the financial crisis deepened, top leaders at TCI left to start their own firm Theleme and they took Mr Sunak also with them For Sunak, watching hundreds of millions of pounds wiped off the value of investments was a bitter foreshadowing of the dire uncertainty he would face more than ten years later as chancellor when the UK economy plunged into recession.

The years in the US also informed his decision to back Brexit, he told the BBC in 2019. "The pace of change is just accelerating around the world - that was my experience being in California," he said. "My general broad view was given the pace of change... being independent and having the flexibility and nimbleness to react would be of enormous value to us."[13]

To Sum up, Rishi Sunak has about fifteen years' experience in financial services, in hedge fund management and venture capital companies, starting with an investment bank, Goldman

Sachs, and ending as director of his technocrat father-in-law's Catamaran Ventures. He knows what successful small and big companies look like and how to make money out of his own and other people's money. In his General Theory, John Maynard Keyes warned: "Practical men, who believe in themselves to be quite exempt from any intellectual influences, are usually the slaves of some defunct economist." Rishi Sunak became the PM after Liz Truss was forced out of office because she thought if she cut taxes growth would follow. Sunak, instead, had campaigned on a platform of sound finance for which it would be necessary to raise taxes so that the growth would follow. Handsome is as Handsome does.

Love and love marriage

Actually in the narration the protagonist very often takes precedence, and the narrator forgets even to tell the readers about his love-interests and marriage. The girls he met and the girl he met ultimately should be told in the proper sequence but I couldn't do it in my enthusiasm to tell you about Sunak's educational and professional growth. In Stanford, there, at the age of 24, he met a fellow student named Akshata Murthy. At Stanford, in keeping with the way she had been brought up, Akshata never flaunted her wealth, and many of her peers were unaware that she was very rich. I don't know whether Sunak knew about her wealth and all that, it is also not necessary now to beat about the bush. "It is easy to see why the pair were so drawn to each other: the parallels in their upbringings are remarkable. Both had grown up in households in which education and achievement were obsessions and hard work and decency were prized above all else. Both the family units were rock-solid, and Hinduism played a big part in their lives." This is what the fatherly biographer, figuratively speaking, has to say and we have no problem to accept this. Do we have?

It is said that he used to change and adjust his class schedule to 'be in a special class' with Akshata. Since Rishi is only 5 feet 6 tall (He can be said to be the shortest PM after Churchill.) So Akshata must have done some adjustments for them to take this relationship forward. They slowly came into the limelight by becoming a 'power-couple'. In a party, Rishi Sunak thanked Akshata and said, 'I thank you from the bottom of my heart that 18 years ago you decided to leave your high heels. Took it and decided to give a chance to the little boy walking with the backpack. Where else can you find a better example of the agility and sweetness of speech?

Sunak wanted to go back after his Stanford days but Akshata wanted to stay back in the USA as she wanted to do soemthing more. She enrolled on a postgraduate course in apparel manufacturing at the nearby Fashion Institute of Design & Merchandising. Sunak returned as he got a good job at The Children's Investment (TCI) Fund, a hedge fund run by the billionaire financier Chris Hohn. Though they were physically away from each other, they kept themselves in touch. For the next 2-3 years, they could meet in London, California and New York as when they got a chance to do so.

Back home. He must have told his parents and she hers. Getting to know his daughter's choice, Narayana Murthy once in a letter to Akshata said, "all that you had described him to be -- brilliant, handsome, and, most importantly, honest."

In January 2009, Sunak proposed to Akshata. He was explaining himself by staying far away for a long time. They tied the knot in August 2009. Some details of their marriage are available in Wedding Sutra magazine.

Key to Success: Study and Perseverance

A good education is more than an obsession for many British Indian families. It is widely seen as one of the easiest routes to success. A recent Institute for Fiscal Studies report stated that 'over 50 per cent of Indians… have tertiary [degree-level or equivalent] qualifications, compared with 26 per cent of the white majority'. In August 2022, Sunak tweeted: 'A good education is the closest thing we have to a silver bullet when it comes to making people's lives better.' The way Rishi viewed his education rather than his ethnic background; it seems that he saw the contribution of education as more important. "I am very lucky to have lived in these places; it has put me in an elite circle in the society. I've always considered myself professionally middle-class; I don't think being Asian is a defining characteristics," he said.

In a conversation with Nick Robinson, he said his family believes "education is everything". In a podcast recorded by two pupils at a school in Richmond, in his North Yorkshire constituency, he said when they began by asking him where he had been to school, and what type of school it was: "So I was very fortunate to go to this amazing school called Winchester College, and it's in Hampshire, and it's a very old boarding school but an absolutely marvellous place."

There are some videos on youtube in which Rishi is teaching some kids on zoom. Mr Sunak writes on a whiteboard in the background and teaches Mathematics to primary school children. After explaining proportion, proportion and fractions etc in Class 6 at St Paul's Primary School in Stanley, Kent, he takes some questions from the students. When one of them asked him what his favorite subject in school was, he replied that it was Mathematics. English Literature and Economics were his other favorite subjects. Samir Shah has very adroitly and succinctly summed up his (Sunak's) central ideas – based on his religious beliefs – are family values, hard work, and education. His lack of interest in identity politics will doubtless put him at loggerheads with the race lobby – but this is a Prime Minister who will see no tension between his faith, his race and his country.[15]

Shah's forecast is also worth noting in this regard when he says, "Sunak has already made some eye-catching remarks about education, from talking about a 'British Baccalaureate' to expanding the use of artificial intelligence in classrooms. Whether as a result of his religion or his cultural upbringing, it should come as no surprise if improving education becomes a central plank of a Sunak administration."[16]

Before you turn the page, let me cite an eye catching remark by Sunak about education. On 24 February 2022, Rishi Sunak gave the annual Mais lecture at Bayes Business School. During the course of his lecture, he said.

> Providing our people with a world class education is one of government's greatest responsibilities. This is a moral imperative. Education is the most powerful weapon we have in our fight to level up. And as new technology expands the skills our workers will need, our training system needs to match it. We need to move decisively from a belief that 'education' is a moment that exists at the start of your life, to one where it is a central experience throughout your whole life.

References

1 https://www.rediff.com/news/special/my-dear-friend-rishi-sunak/20221029.htm

2 https://books.google.co.in/books?id=XFEFEAAAQBAJ

3   https://www.thepharmacist.co.uk/news/pm-candidate-rishi-sunak-speaks-about-family-pharmacy/

4   https://www.dailyecho.co.uk/news/20578761.rishi-sunaks-southampton-childhood-education-career/

5   https://www.deccanchronicle.com/opinion/columnists/061122/saeed-naqvi-children-of-macaulay-go-global-with-sunaks-rise.html

6   https://www.deccanchronicle.com/opinion/columnists/061122/saeed-naqvi-children-of-macaulay-go-global-with-sunaks-rise.html

7   https://www.bbc.com/news/uk-politics-63806421

8   https://www.rediff.com/news/special/my-dear-friend-rishi-sunak/20221029.htm

9   https://www.scotsman.com/news/opinion/columnists/boris-johnson-what-top-tier-boarding-schools-can-do-to-britains-future-leaders-revealed-in-sad-little-men-by-richard-beard-laura-waddell-3671067

10 https://ustoday.news/rishi-sunak-big-star-wars-fan-looks-to-the-film-for-political-inspiration/

11 https://www.mirror.co.uk/news/politics/rishi-sunaks-privileged-childhood-no-27567616

12 https://www.efinancialcareers.com/news/2022/10/rishi-sunak-goldman-sachs

13-14 https://www.lordashcroft.com/2022/10/when-rishi-sunak-met-akshata-murty-the-birth-of-a-power-couple/

15 https://www.bbc.com/news/world-us-canada-63402491

16 https://www.spectator.co.uk/article/how-will-rishi-sunaks-hinduism-inform-his-premiership 17 https://www.spectator.co.uk/article/how-will-rishi-sunaks-hinduism-inform-his-premiership/ Sibling

❐

3

CHARACTER AND CHARACTERISTICS

From head boy, to hedge funder, to Chancellor of the Exchequer, to PM, Rishi Sunak traversed a long path with his own inimitable style and élan. Those who saw him grow up say that he has always been a 'brilliant talker'. His parents were also 'brilliant conversationalists' and 'very strong believers' who 'worked very, very hard', and inculcated those qualities in his son also. Though his parents and grandparents were from India via East Africa, yet over-time, they became 'passionately British' in work and deed. The virtues and characteristics of Sunak have been extolled many times over; "for his charming demeanor, his razor sharp brain and his acute financial sense". He has also been addressed as the 'Maharaja of the Dales' because of his Indian ancestry and Yorkshire home. Sunak's predecessor in his Richmond constituency, William Hague, praises him as "down to earth – a non-ideological Conservative". Writer Ben Judah, who has profiled Sunak, tells: "He has a spreadsheet mind." Former health secretary Matt Hancock says, "He's a true-born Englishman, but he brings many facets because of his heritage."

"Perfectly turned out in a suit and narrow tie, Sunak cuts a commanding presence compared to Johnson. Fitting the two men into Max Weber's equation, Sunak is "ethic of responsibility" made flesh while Johnson is his "ethic of irresponsibility." In a single word, we can say he is 'competent' for his job.[1]

Sunak is a completely conventional British prime minister, despite being a non-Christian. There are many who do not stop themselves and are free and frank in admitting that "Forcing an Indian cultural stereotype on Sunak feels inaccurate. To me, he feels like a very 21st-century product. The sort that went to Ivy League colleges, worked at Goldman Sachs or McKinsey, and flits between Silicon Valley, Canary Wharf and Dubai with consummate ease. The sort that could be found on a Peloton at a Fairmont Group Hotel early mornings and has premier mileage points on at least three airlines. The sort that could recommend the latest Peruvian-Japanese Michelin starred restaurant. The sort that is always jetlagged, always in a black limousine, always driving past at least 36 skyscrapers to a fancy short-term corporate apartment on the 33rd floor." [2]

Mark Harper, the former chief whip and an early Sunak backer, said: "The thing that tells me about his character, is that if you throw an emergency at him, or something unexpected or left-field – and frankly that happens to prime ministers a lot – he's got the capacity, both in terms of his intellect but also his character, to be able to grab it, understand it, and then make a well thought through decision at the right pace."[3]

A Tall Stature

In India, Lal Bahadur Shastri, is best remembered for his contribution at a difficult time. Nobody talks about his height. They always say something good about his great heights of character and perseverance. Similarly Rishi Sunak is best introduced as a person who thinks big and aims high. His height –physically speaking- is just below average when you compare it with the average Englishman's height, though it is not so far from the average as you might think. He is 170 cm or 5 feet 6 inches (*but the metric measurement equates to 5ft 6.9in, and so one can round that up.*), when the mean height of an Englishman is said to be 175.6 cm. He has the lanky frame of a taller man. He looks like a college-boy but he is not the shortest man to hold the job since Winston Churchill (5ft 5in). Sunak is like the president of Russia, Vladimir Putin, who is about the same height. On the other hand, Sunak is taller than the Former French president Nicolas Sarkozy (5ft 4in). There is a bizarre coincidence with some of Europe's leaders: Rishi Sunak, Emmanuel Macron, Olaf Scholz, Vladimir Putin, and Volodymyr Zelensky are all about 5'7". Bercow told the *Times* in 2014, "Whereas nobody these days would regard it as acceptable to criticize someone on grounds of race or creed or disability or sexual orientation, somehow it seems to be acceptable to comment on someone's height, or lack of it."

Rishi Sunak is an Asian and his height will never be a point of discussion in India. In his own country where there are many people who are so obsessed with height that one of the magazines published an article in which the height of many leaders, past and present, was given and discussed. "Mr Sunak's stature has attracted attention before, notably when, as chancellor in March 2021, he rather artfully positioned himself at the top of the stairs of No 11 brandishing that famous red box in time for the Budget, forcing his fellow Treasury ministers to line the steps below him, looking far smaller than their boss."

It is the greatness of Rishi Sunak that he doesn't refuse to own it. Height may be one of the markers of masculinity but he could win the heart of one of the wealthiest girls on this planet.

"I am incredibly grateful that 18 years ago you chose to give up your high heels and take a chance on the short kid with a backpack," he said to his wife Akshata Murty once.[4]

Virtuous life

Meaningful to the name Rishi, Rishi Sunak fasts on Mondays and this helps him in keeping his bodybuilding in shape. In interviews, Sunak claimed that he had never taken drugs or even a puff of a cigarette. He insists that he was never a 'rever' (going to parties or nightclubs), having worn 'shell suits' (brightly colored light-reflecting nylon pants and the same flamboyant jacket) as a child.

It is to be underlined that Rishi is a teetotaler, that is, he does not consume alcohol. It doesn't mean that he doesn't know the taste of it even though he was born and has been living in Britain. He was so nervous at the time of his wedding in 2009, the British media says (not me), that he promised his friends he would try a couple of shots before the wedding, and he reportedly did so.

According to parliament's website, "this custom (drinking) has its roots in the Speaker's function to communicate the Commons' opinions to the monarch." He was allowed to drink alcohol during his Budget speech due to tradition - but the Chancellor, being teetotal, has decided to ignore the historic ritual, opting for water."

> One Twitter user said: "Did you see Rishi Sunak talking about green growth whilst drinking from a single-use plastic cup?"
>
> Another one hit out: "Rishi Sunak using a plastic cup for his drink during the Budget statement?"
>
> "Seriously, can he not insist on a proper glass?"

In other words, you can say that he is a well-known abstainer from alcohol, making him possibly the first teetotal Prime Minister since David Lloyd George. Isn't it amazing that teetotal Chancellor gave alcohol duty the biggest shake up in 140 years in a historic budget speech when he cut the price of booze?

Fan and likes

It is said that Rishi has been very fond of sweets since childhood. He often starts the day with a double chocolate muffin. He wants two biscuits with tea in the afternoon as well. In a podcast, he can be heard saying that he had to get fillings on seven of his teeth because of excessive Coca-Cola drinking as a child.

Sunak "collects Coca-Cola stuff", as he once told two schoolmates, "I'm a Coke addict. I'm a Coke addict." So he said, "Coco-Cola-addict, just for the record." Rishi Sunak's biography published so far contain no evidence and no mention of the drug abuse that routinely abounds in autobiographies of senior Tories.

While addressing children in a library, Rishi had said that Roald Dahl is his favorite author of children's books and he has read many of his books to his two daughters. One of his favoruite books is "A Suitable Boy" by Vikram Seth.

The pictures show an ever-happy image of their geeky personality. He is an obsessive fan of Star Wars and the early Bond films. He once told some kids that he himself wanted to be a Jedi Knight when he was a child. It is possible that he may be looking to the films for inspiration, both personally and politically.

He seems to be crazy about electronic gadgets. A photo of him posing with a £180 self-heating coffee mug hit the headlines.

A video clip of Sunak holding his contactless debit card up to a barcode scanner - instead of tapping on a payment device - went viral, giving the impression that he rarely buys things in person. He later admitted that someone had to teach him how to use the card reader. In another resurfaced clip from a 2007 interview with the BBC, he admitted that he had no "working class friends".

Fashion and performance

Some people think that fashion is unimportant. They are wrong. Fashion is a question of life and death. If Prime Minister Narendra Modi is a fashion-icon in India, Rishi Sunak is in Britain. He could be the best-dressed prime minister the country have ever had, men and women included.

Here's the assessment of Dom Halas, executive director of the startup lobby group Codec, who has worked closely with him since he was chancellor: "innovation policy is an important part of his ideology. Sunak comes back to it again and again. Halas also notes the young Sunak's tech-love, saying: "People make fun of the fact that he wears a hoodie, but he's in his early 40s." Yes, he was born in the 1980s... I work with people who dress like that. He lives in that circle. He's not in that stuffy world where some of the politics People are."

Photos of Rishi are always seen in work mode. In these, the sleeves of Sunak's shirt are upwards. This is the Barack Obama model of power dressing. His personality has been analyzed so closely by the British press, even showing the red thread of worship around his right wrist. He is always photographed in work mode, with his shirt sleeves rolled up. This is the Barack Obama model of power dressing. His personality has been analyzed so closely by the British press that even the red thread of worship around his right wrist is regarded as a tribal rite, while other politicians around the world, who follow their religious beliefs (prayer rosary, cross) do not hesitate to show.

Hardly anyone mentions him, but Rishi's talk is different, he is a Hindu. Much has been written in the British press about Sunak's costumes and attire. Wearing 'anti-baggy suits' and expensive 'cashmere sweaters' is unusual even in British politics. That's why style-writers call him "Dishi Rishi". He has been described as both an "unlikely style icon" and "a kind of Austen heroine in a supreme hoodie". Some sarcasm, some envy and some praise with suppressed tongue. The Guardian magazine's Priya Elan once stunned people by comparing him to "a hired killer, planning a quick clean-up after his latest mission" after seeing his outfit. I can say without claiming anything that you have not even seen these clothes, shoes, and other material that he wears. Hearing the cost, you will start crying out of fear or with jealousy. Rishi's Henry Herbert suit cost £3,500. His £450 Prada loafers just show how 'out of touch' he is. Rishi spends money and you can immediately see that his clothing is worth it. They look even better. These new clothes communicate hope, longing and desire. Rest assured Rishi was an investment banker so he knows what to invest in, when and how much. 'In the margins of the COP, Sunak had his first meeting with Emmanuel Macron, President of France. The pictures from this event showed Sunak mirroring Macron in very regard; hair, clothes, frame, posture, beaming facial expressions. They even skipped towards each other like lovers on a beach; peas-in-a pod centrist technocrats.' depicts Patrick O'Flynn.

Sunak, in keeping with his clean, sharp lifestyle, regularly starts the day with a 6 a.m. Peloton workout and a breakfast of Greek yogurt and blueberries. He doesn't try to hide his habits. Sunak begins his days with Peloton workouts, but rehearses parliamentary affairs with a Twix bar and a can of Sprite. He wears plastic beaded kadas which may have been made by his young children (in other words, kuki ornaments) and also

'Kalava' which is indicative of Hinduism. There are skinny ties, Canada Goose puffers, and handmade project sneakers by Common. He also has an expensive £180 "smart mug" that keeps his drinks hot, indicating he may possibly be a 'gadget' lover. He once wore 'Prada loafers' while touring a building under construction, and in preparation for the Treasury's Budget Day, he wore a shocking pair of Palm Angels slides to 11 Downing Street.

Dishi Rishi

Sunak is Britain's first leader of color and the first Hindu to take the top job. At 42, he is also the youngest prime minister in more than 200 years, a political prodigy whose youthful looks, sharp suits, and smooth, confident manner saw him dubbed "Dishy Rishi" by the British media. As said, the dashing Rishi image was not created by Rishi Sunak. It got created on its own during the Covid-19 in the year 2020. When the whole world experienced the lockdown for the first time, Sunak came into everyone's limelight. "In a Cabinet weak on talent, Mr Sunak stood out, brimming with energy and thought. Not for nothing was he christened "Dishy Rishi". His popularity shimmered like a risen souffle at a time of crisis for the nation." the press commented. "He was seen by the party faithful, those who were voting, as too brainy, too quick and smart. He was a bountiful figure, considerate, caring and charming."

Sunak tweeted his work from home photo in a gray hoodie. In this photo his simplicity won the hearts of people. Sunak, who was seen in a hoodie instead of a suit, was busy with his work. "In the middle of a global health crisis, Rishi Sunak has risen from obscurity to become one of the most powerful figures in British politics. More importantly, posh white women adore him, making the rest of the world realise they can too!"[5]

In his article on him, Ruchira Sharma underlines the fact how the phenomenon – initially spawned by thirsty responses to a picture of him in a grey hoodie.

Some critics have called this image childish and 'manchild', "the recipient of puff pieces rather than asperities", as the 'Vice' magazine reported the trend with the following forewarning. "One inaccurate, oft-repeated claim by these lust-stricken columnists is that Sunak has come out of nowhere – a fiscally capable version of the "medic you had a crush on in the first term of your first year", as *Vogue* put it. But Sunak's past history as a banker and Tory MP should give anyone pause before uttering the words "Sexy Sunak".[6]

A lady wrote, "While Labour's Keir Starmer is at a first glance far more aesthetically pleasing, Rishi is the man we'd all self-isolate with. Rishi has only recently popped into our collective wank-bank. He's sexy because he represents hope that maybe the cabinet aren't all blundering, confused buffoons, that maybe we're going to be OK. Oh, Dishy!"[7]

#DishyRishi trend started on Twitter after this photo. This was not a new hashtag. Earlier this hashtag was for Rishi Sharma, who danced in a British TV show. The 'Daily Mail' newspaper apparently thought he was handsome, and a well-built young man. He is relatively young. He's certainly not Boris Johnson. 'The Sun' newspaper referred to him as a breath of fresh air. He looks more like a film hero than some middle-aged 40-year-old. "It's his edgy image that cuts off the disheveled Boris Johnson," says Borkowski. The star has glamor like George Clooney. His social media success is such that you could call him the country's first Instagram Chancellor. Made a plan to deliver food (hence dish-dish) and dish is a common term for good looking as in he is a dish or he is a dish looking man.

Rishi's rival party – the Labor Party – is also feared to find it difficult to defeat him in the upcoming election. There are many fans of his hero image. Not only have the media, young men and women also looked at this ideal family-man with envy. Journalist Helen Lewis, writing for 'The Atlantic', writes that people are more concerned with his wealth than his background. -- "Every time I see Rishi on TV, I have a burning desire to trick him and steal his lunch money." According to the political editor of 'Newsnight', Rishi Sunak is found by his colleagues and collaborators to be 'very fascinating'. Not only do they seem very personable, but they are such who understand their thoughts and say only what they can do. "He's seen as someone who's got a huge amount of competence and risen to the occasion of delivering a budget at short notice," says Novara contributing editor Ash Sarkar. "That's helped in part by the Greek chorus of posh white ladies saying they're thirsting over him."

Sunak once told the Radio Times he enjoys watching Netflix shows like Emily in Paris and Bridgerton and he is known for other nerdy hobbies: he's reportedly a big fan of Star Wars (he reportedly collects replica lightsabers) and the early Bond movies; he loves a gadget (remember that famous £180 self-heating coffee mug?); and has previously spoken about his "OCD approach" to stacking the dishwasher.

His favorite drink is a Mexican Coca-Cola made with cane sugar – once the subject of an unfortunate gaffe when he told school students that he was a "massive coke addict" before quickly clarifying he meant the soft drink. Sunak revealed that his cheat drink is the Mexican Coke - Coca-Cola produced in and imported from Mexico. "It's special Coke," Sunak explained on the podcast. "It's the only place in the world where Coke is made with cane sugar rather than high fructose corn syrup."

He's a fan of intermittent fasting; that he enjoys Greek yoghurt for breakfast on weekdays and pancakes at weekends; and that his favourite Peloton instructor is Cody Rigsby, who keeps him motivated with Britney anthems. "He is definitely my long-time favourite, which means you have to listen to a lot of Britney (Spears). But you know, no bad thing in trying to get you motivated, I guess. I am trying to diversify lately."

Food and Fitness

Apart from being a keen gamer whose favourite game is Mario Kart, per Mirror.uk, Sunak is also a fitness enthusiast. In 2021, when Sunak appeared on The Twenty Minute VC podcast with Harry Stebbings, he spoke about his diet and fitness regime."I wake up between 6 am and 7 am depending on what gym I'm doing," Sunak said. "In terms of breakfast, well, I do some intermittent fasting so most days, nothing. Otherwise, I'd probably have Greek yogurt and blueberries during the week," he added.

"On the weekend, we have a full-cooked breakfast on Saturdays; and on Sundays, we alternate between pancakes and waffles. So, we do American-style pancakes, we add crispy bacon, blueberries, strawberries, and pancakes. That's Sunday. And we interchange pancakes and waffles every week," he said. Sunak consumes sugary items in his mid-morning meal - a cinnamon bun or a pain au chocolat or a chocolate chip muffin. "And then I'd have a second breakfast mid-morning which is either a cinnamon bun or a pain au chocolat or a chocolate chip muffin. So I'd have a chocolatey, sugary pastry at some point." Sunak said on the podcast.

Sparkling Personality

Bright - sparkling smile that turns into a thoughtful gaze when more appropriate. Best Tailored Fit Suit. Well mannered speech. Honestly jarring characterization. An aura of confidence in the light of acumen. Rishi Sunak appears to be the "Disney Prince" version of a British politician Sunak is a stylish figure with a talent for managing the optics of his job. "Dr Rob Sutton comments. On social media, you can see memes of Rishi as James Bond ordering a Martini in Hindi. Bids are also being tightened on the similar faces of former Indian cricketers Ashish Nehra and Rishi Sunak. The brand and marketing expert Mark Borkowski said Sunak had Johnson and the rest of the cabinet worried. "It is his sharp image that is so striking against disheveled Boris that really cuts through," Borkowski said. "Sunak is always beautifully turned out, he has that George Clooney glamor. His social media is supremely successful, you could call him the nation's first Instagram chancellor."[8]

Rishi's personality has a distinct elegant charm of its own. 'Rishi the Cutie, with his lopsided smile and spaniel eyes, can disarm his worst critics' writes Shobhaa De. She is quick witted when she writes, "A smart-ish, short-ish, cute-ish, young-ish, brown-ish chap has moved house. Big deal! The whole world is going on and on about Rishi Sunak becoming the *gora log ka* PM like he has done the unthinkable, the unattainable, the impossible. Is it really such a feat? No, right? Had Rishi not been from a "certain background" (read non-white), he'd have been treated like any other bloke who has made it to No. 10 Downing Street, and accepted the worst job on earth right now."[9]

This quality is an admirable skill for a politician as most leaders lack it. Taking a fortune so quickly in life and marrying the daughter of a well-to-do Indian, securing a safe seat in the Parliament and pretending to be a Conservative MP without any special training and apprenticeship without any support, and then becoming the Finance Minister is not a feat. He did not show any special interest in politics in the university, yet then becoming the Prime Minister of the country within a short span of time is not surprising.

Honeyed tongue

It is claimed that no one ever heard any profanity from Rishi's mouth. He does not lose his balance even under stress. Those in the know say, "We never saw him quarrel or shout with anyone. If he felt angry, he kept quiet." He is reported to serve fine wine to guests at many of his homes, but he himself hardly touches alcohol. Needless to say, Rishi Sunak is the ideal young man. A schoolboy whom no one ever disliked, a hedge funder who gave no one a chance to repent, and a politician who does not drink and dine... Does not do anything, does not speak bad words, and makes friends, never an enemy. One who is a devotee of God, a believer, a devout Hindu, and does not hide his devotion, is not ashamed of his bhakti.

When he spoke the very first time, he was called "Sunak the Smooth: the sequel". Though he lacks the oratorical flair of the likes of Cameron, Hague or Portillo, his speech has always been workmanlike and clearly delivered. Its purpose is always served. He highlights his concerns well. He is also able to underscore that he is a "pragmatist" who finds "mindless ideology dangerous". When he was not the prime minister, he didn't speak much. His interventions used to be few and far between. Unlike Other senior ministers — Priti Patel, Dominic Raab, Michael Gove who used to be seldom out of the headlines, he kept his powder dry. That is why when he spoke, people listened with rapt attention.

There is plenty of evidence of Sunak's humility which has helped to deflect jealousy from colleagues. An example and illustration can be found in the statement given by MacGregor that underlines Rishi Sunak's courtesy and his expression of gratefulness for others and well-mannered and well-meaning behavior. Mark MacGregor was deputy director of policy exchange from 2013 to 2015. When the work for 'A portrait of Modern Britain' was over, Sunak, according to Mac, said thank you. "He said thank you, I tell you what, how often in politics do people say thank you? I've worked for MPs in elections where I've given up like three weeks of my holiday and brought tens of people with me to help them in their seats, and barely received a thank you, So often people don't thank you, and he is so polite, and I think that is an incredible strength for him."

Study the political life of Rishi Sunak and his growing influence. Both critics and well-wishers agree that he is a wiser politician than he appears to be. Underneath the outer shell is a shrewd strategist, clever at hitting the spot and making the right moves at the right time. He is a staunch Brexiter but he took a bitter sip of reality when Theresa May was prime minister. They have been quick to take personal loans for measures to mitigate the economic fallout of the pandemic. He had won over Tory MPs by giving them the impression that he was determined to share his disagreement over Covid restrictions without ever publicly debating the matter.

Brand Rishi

It isn't hard to see why politicians want to create their own brands. Branding not only gives them recognition for policies but also helps reach new audiences and of course potential voters. James Hardy is not off the mark when he says that good communications and branding are useful when the sun is shining – it becomes essential when the storm comes in. after all, says Marie Le Conte, a politician can be a product like any other; you just need to know how to market it.

Though Rishi Sunak was comfortable enough as a Tory MP, yet we can now say that he had his eyes fixed on a goal to reach the zenith of his career as a politician. That is why he marketed himself. Henry Hill, the news editor of Conservative Home said in 2020: Given that the prime minister seems fairly secure in post and we are three years away from a general election, why is he investing so much in building up his brand with the country at large? The only electorate he's likely to face any time soon is his Richmond (Yorkshire) constituency, who would return anyone with a blue rosette." How wrong was Henry Hill? Until Brand Rishi came in the limelight, Politicians used to rely on others to be in the news. They used to be there in talk-shows and *'aap ki adalat'* kind of programmes.

Sunak has tried very hard to build his image. The Clerkenwell Brothers co-founder Cass Horowitz has been credited with promoting Sunak through his organization. He and his brother Nicholas, the sons of novelist and Foyle's War creator Anthony Horowitz, run the digital marketing company The Clerkenwell Brothers, which describes itself as "the slingshot" in the David and Goliath story. Will Lloyd (unherd.com) wrote without mincing a word. "He has the calculator-gambler soul of an axe man, and ends up with a public image close to Marcus Rashford's. Scrooge is mistaken for Father Christmas. All the imagery — there is Rishi for the nerds, a Rishi for the boozers, a Rishi for the horny journalists, and a Rishi for the bumpkins — has been adroitly manipulated by his advisor and social media guru 'Cass' Horowitz."

Sunak is marketed by the agency in the same way as many other products, tequila, yoga mats and organics. Sunak increased his appeal by appearing in various outlets of 'Glamour' magazine and LADBable for his image building. While some of the social media campaigns were downright weird, the overall one ultimately built the brand Rishi. He also hired Mr Peston's co-host Allegra Stratton to run his communications team. It was Ms Stratton - who is married to Mr Sunak's former classmate, the political journalist James Forsyth - who is understood to have recommended Mr Peston for the job. He also started a YouTube conversation channel with celebrity chef Gordon Ramsay as its first guest.

Critics say a slick public marketing campaign has disguised a man with an ultra-privileged background, who is a committed Thatcherite ideologue. Jonathan Dean, an associate professor of politics at Leeds University, says this reflects broader political trends: "Forms of celebrity are increasingly prominent within politics, and that can either take the form of people who were conventional celebrities entering electoral politics, or it can also take the form of politicians trying to ape the publicity and performance traditionally associated with celebrity culture."[10]

Parveen Akhtar comments, "Choreographed snaps and videos more akin to a social media influencer than a politician have characterized his every move since becoming a cabinet minister in Boris Johnson's government in 2020." Giles Coren has also rightly pointed out that instead of a humorless wonk married to money I now see a kind of Guy Ritchie- directed backstreet hustler by way of Sexy beast with a splash of Ipcress-era Michael Caine who cannot fail to come back and win. This is because of "Brand Rishi".

Philip Sargent, author of *'The Art of Political Storytelling'*, says, "There is a certain blatant opportunism to it." "The particular approach he and his team are taking is probably a lot to do with the old advertising idea of positioning—finding a distinct personality within the market—hence the slick but homely image being pushed for him is different from the belligerent populist images that have dominated politics recently, and has the chance to stand out because of this." The journalist Isabel Hardman recently wrote: "It's not clear whether Rishi is announcing a package for the arts or launching his own aspirational menswear line." In July 2020, Sunak appeared on BBC Radio 4's flagship Today Programme where he was asked about 'Brand Rishi'. His response was to point out that his personal recognition was helping to get the message out.

When Sunak was asked about 'Brand Rishi' at an event, he burst out laughing. He argued that the most important thing was for people to get 'our message' and that in the process people mocked him, he was happy, not sad. Really 'Brand Rishi' has started working, that's why India's brand 'Amul' discussed it.

Rish the Dish

Some lust-ridden columnists and advocates of yellow-journalism have made a false but oft-repeated ridiculous claim. They never tire of saying that Sunak has come from somewhere outside. The way the magazine called 'Vogue' presented Rishi, he is completely different from that. Sunak's life as a banker and Tory MP has been kept an open book. If some freaks have the audacity to address Rishi as "sexy sunak" then it is their ignorance and stupidity. Rishi Sunak has also been dubbed 'a style hero', has now entered popular consciousness as 'dishy Rishi' (largely thanks to his tabloid nickname).

The talk show host Trevor Noah even described Rish the Dish as a "snack". He has joked that racists among the UK's white population might fear that the new PM would be tempted to sell Britain to India. In Noah's monologue, which was titled "Unpacking the backlash against new UK PM Rishi Sunak", he said: "Watching the story of Rishi Sunak becoming England's first Prime Minister of color, of Indian descent, of all these things and then seeing the backlash is one of the more telling things about how people view the role that they or their people have played in history."

"And what I mean by that is this, you hear a lot of the people saying 'Oh, they're taking over, now the Indians are going to take over Great Britain and what's next?' "And I always find myself going 'So what? What are you afraid of?'"

He continued: "You see people like Tucker Carlson [American Fox News host] all the time saying 'You know what they're trying to do? They won't stop until black people and women are in positions of power', so what?"

He added: "Why are you so afraid? And I think it's because the quiet part a lot of people don't realize they are saying is 'We don't want these people who were previously oppressed to get into power because then they may do to us what we did to them'."

Former chancellor and health secretary Javid disagreed: "Simply wrong. A narrative catered to his audience, at a cost of being completely detached from reality. Britain is the most successful multiracial democracy on earth and proud of this historic achievement." New Statesman writer Jeremy Cliffe also took issue with the comedian's claims and tweeted, "UK can't prevent US politicians and media (left & right) from crowbarring garbled accounts of British politics into their own culture wars - as Trevor Noah is doing here. But UK 'can' decide whether or not it wants to import US culture wars into its own politics."

Rishi Rich

Rishi Sunak had been nicknamed "the maharajah of the Dales". His privileged upper-class background and immense wealth works against him. It has earned him the sarcastic sobriquet ' Rishi Rich" which has been continuously giving him problems. "Rishi Sunak is almost certainly wise enough to know that in British politics, wealth is best kept in the background. If he has any doubts, the MP for Richmond, Yorkshire should ask the former MP for Richmond, Zac Goldsmith, son of a charismatic billionaire, whose failure to become Mayor of London was followed by the loss of his seat, twice in three elections. Like so many monied politicians, he has ended up in the Lords. If the new plutocracy is now to encroach on British politics, then better far that the billionaires know their place — what MPs refer to as "The Other Place."[11]

Diversity and inclusion are very important in politics and society, and in the words of Sir Keir Starmer, it sends the important message that "Britain is a place where people of all races and all faiths can fulfill their dreams."In response to press commentary about Sunak's upbringing and lifestyle, his team has stated: "Rishi is the product of a lot of hard work, kindness and sacrifice... He is dedicated to this country because of the opportunity it gave to him, his parents and his grandparents who moved here for a better life."

It's unclear how much Sunak earned till now, but his new job as Prime Minister comes with a sizable pay package: he'll now make more than $185,000 a year, nearly double his $95,000 wage as a member of parliament.

Symbol of the British Dream

If there's a concept called the "British Dream", Sunak embodies it. Liam Shrivastava of the Institute for Race Relations, a British think tank, who is also a local councilor for the opposition Labour Party, told once. "Rishi Sunak is a multi-millionaire but this allows him to tell a compelling, aspirational story, and it can be framed as progress." He says, "One of the key things that we see the Black and Brown candidates doing is mobilizing their own identity in order to tell a seemingly progressive story of

British meritocracy and hard work, whilst concealing their own class position and economic power."[12]

The people of England are very proud and it seems like they have achieved something called the "British Dream". People are familiar with the 'American Dream', but the British also have dreams and believe that if you work hard, you can achieve anything. Rishi Sunak is a 'self-made man' in his view. He married into a family with a wealth of wealth, but has built up a lot of wealth himself and he truly embodies this British aspirational ideal. Britain's High Commissioner to India Alex Ellis on the stage of India Today Conclave said that Rishi Sunak is a man of Punjabi mood, he is Hindu but his heart and mind is completely British. Rishi has taken over the reins of Britain at a time when there is turmoil in the whole world. His history is undoubtedly related to India, but he is the Prime Minister of Britain.

Sibling Shine

According to a report in the MailOnline, Rishi Sunak's siblings Sanjay, 40 and Raakhi, 37, have also 'strived to match Sunak's youthful successes. His younger brother Sanjay is remembered by friends as less chatty but, although two years younger, followed a similar trajectory in his early years of education. His parents paid for Sanjay to go to the same private primary as Rishi, Stroud School.

Sanjay followed in his parents' footsteps to work in medicine, specialising in psychology, he enrolled as an undergraduate at University College London in 1999 before moving on to postgraduate studies at Birkbeck, University of London, specializing in criminology. At King's College London he studied forensic mental health before doctorate studies at the University of Surrey in clinical psychology. While studying and teaching there he also began working for the NHS. Now 40, he is likely to earn a six-figure salary as a consultant clinical psychologist working for a private clinic and Bupa, the private health insurer.

Rishi's sister Raakhi, works in New York as chief of strategy and planning at the United Nations global fund for education in emergencies. As an undergraduate, she founded Oxford's Unicef society, growing its membership to around 400. Now known as Raakhi Williams after marrying international aid specialist Peter Williams, she helped to organize last year's COP26 climate change conference in Glasgow for the Government before moving to America to work for the UN.

The ultimate family man

"I learnt early on that family matters. Families nurture our children and teach them good conduct; support us, unconditionally; pass on culture, religion, and identity. No government could even begin to replicate the profound bond family forms," Rishi said once.

The strong family spirit remains at the heart of Sunak's leadership bid, from being the frontrunner among his party colleagues through to the final stages of voting by Tory members. He is a doting son, a dear father and a sincere husband. Let me give you some of the instances when he spoke his heart out and revealed to us his innermost feelings. At the final hustings in Wembley, London, he said, "That is something that is really hard for me because I love my kids to bits, I love my wife to bits and unfortunately, I have not been able to be as present in their lives at all in the past few years as I would have liked to have been." He was in tears when he thanked his parents for all their support and inspiration and said, "It was their example of service and what they did for people that inspired me to enter politics."

Like Obama, Rishi also has two daughters. But unlike Obama's wife, Mrs. Sunak is no Michelle. In fact, no one knows what their point of view is. I also don't know why people talk more about his/her wealth and less about his/her knowledge and wisdom?

In an interview, Sunak spoke about his experience with parenting. He said that he was "very lucky" because when his children were born, he was running his own business with partners and was in control of his time. Sunak added that he was "very much around" for his children after they were born.[13]

This story is neither of Akshata nor of other characters. They are the witnesses and co-operators of our sage's life, character and activities. With Akshata, he is enjoying the happiness of married life as a couple. Being the father of two cute girls, he follows the religion of his ancestors. Carolyn Iggulden, in an article written for 'The Sun' magazine, considered him the ideal Indian to follow the Grihastha Ashram carefully. She writes, 'Rishi Sunak is a teetotal, Peloton riding family man who learned the value of hard work at his mom's pharmacy.'

Akshata remains totally Indian, as Rishi is completely British. When her non-domicile status became controversial, she wrote on social media: "He's never asked me to abandon my Indian citizenship, ties to India or my business affairs, despite the ways in which such a move would have simplified things for him politically." Rishi revealed in a recent interview that one of the secrets behind their happy marriage was that they were very different people. While he described himself as "incredibly tidy", he said his wife was "very messy" but also the more spontaneous one.

> Just as Liz Truss was quitting as PM that day, after a tumultuous six weeks in power, he was treating Krishna and Anoushka to lunch at TGI Fridays. He was gearing

up for a game of ten pin bowling when he got the call saying there would be another leadership battle. The former Chancellor was also looking forward to his first family holiday away in three-and-a-half years. Fast forward just a matter of days — and he entered Downing Street to face one of the toughest in-trays in history.

Within Westminster, Rishi is well-known as a man who likes to start work early and finish late. His glamorous wife Akshata Murty, the billionaire daughter of India's 6th richest man, is reportedly devoted to her husband of 13 years and doesn't mind when he works until midnight. The highly-disciplined new PM likes to start everyday with an early morning workout, either on the treadmill or on his beloved Peloton bike. He once admitted his favorite Peloton class is one inspired by Britney Spears.[14]

On providing strong role models to his daughters, he said, "After having our first girl I was pushing for a second girl and having two sisters in the house is really special. Look, that's one thing we try to do." They are very strong role models for them. They also take very seriously the task of choosing the books they need for their daughters. Books by Elena Favilli and Francesca Cavallo, Cleopatra, Frida Kahlo, Marie Curie They give their daughters books to read about the lives and achievements of women such as Maya Angelou, Ruth Bader and Michelle Obama. They respect their daughters' views. A BBC TV show on climate change presenting his argument in the debate, Rishi had said, "I also take the advice of my two daughters on this subject. They are experts in my house in these matters."

According to a BBC report, Sunak told that when her daughter Krishna was 11 years old, she wanted to walk to her primary school in London. As a result, before Sunak resigned as chancellor in July, the family moved out of their flat at 11 Downing Street to live near their daughter's school. Sunak recently tweeted how her daughter Anushka performed the Kuchipudi dance with her classmates for the Queen's Platinum Jubilee celebrations at Westminster Abbey in June. Sunak cited some recent attacks on women and girls in the UK to make it clear that this is a priority issue for her.

"I want to make sure my kids and other people can move around safely, which is what every parent wants for their kids," Sunak said. Making it safe is something that is very important to them personally.

Fair-weather friends only?

Once when Rishi was a student, he was asked by a documentary filmmaker about his friends, to which he replied, "My friends are aristocratic, upper class, and working class, then correct themselves." Said - No, not working class. Needless to say that Rishi probably has no special knowledge of the poor, poverty and middle-class.

Let me tell you about this in detail. The year was 2001. Rishi was just a young man of 21 years of age. He was being interviewed by BBC about "Middle Classes- Their Rise & Sprawl". When he was asked about his social circle, he gave an innocent reply, "I have friends who are aristocrats, I have friends who are upper class, I have friends who are working class."

But he quickly corrected himself.

"Well, not working class," he added and his father who was there just looked at his son.

"I mix and match, then I go to these kids in inner-city state schools and tell them to apply to Oxford, and talk to them about people like me."

"And then I shock them at the end of chatting to them for half an hour and thell them I was at Winchester and my best friend is from Eaton or whatever, and then they're like, 'oh, OK."

The documentary was OK. It didn't elicit much response. But in 2022, it became viral.

Sometimes, parents go out of the way to provide for their children and never tell them their difficulties and sacrifices. Till date, no journalist went to his parents to ask their story. But every Amitabh has a Bachchan behind him. Sunak knows that his parents sacrificed a great deal but he never reveals.

When the boy of 21 years turned into 42 years of age and a candidate for the coveted post of the PM, he was asked again about the same interview.

"You talked a lot about your supposedly ordinary origins, your background. Why, when you were young, did you say you had no working class friends?"

Sunak replied: "Andrew, we all say silly things when we are students. I've talked about my background. My family were welcomed here as migrants."

I grew up working in my mum's pharmacy. You don't grow up doing that unless you encounter lots of people.

"We served our community and my parents worked hard to provide opportunities for me, that is ultimately why I want to be prime minister, because this country allowed my family the opportunity.

"As prime minister, I want to do the same for everybody."[15]

A friend in need

In Britain it is said that every sensible prime minister has an "honest friend". Winston Churchill had Norman Brooke, who claimed to have prevented at least some of his worst decisions. Harold Macmillan had John Wyndham, Harold Wilson had Lady Falkender, Tony Blair had Alastair Campbell and Peter Mandelson. Boris Johnson had Dominic Cummings.

"I have friends who are aristocrats, I have friends who are upper-class, I have friends who are, you know, working-class. Well...not working-class." Long ago Rishi Sunak said and people still remind him of his childlike innocence. The old BBC video of Rishi Sunak doing the rounds on social media is from 2001. "I mix and match and then I go to see kids from an inner-city state school and tell them to apply to Oxford and talk to them about people like me. And then I shock them at the end of chatting to them for half an hour and tell them I was at Winchester and one of my best friends is from Eton or whatever. And then they're like: 'Oh OK'," Rishi Sunak said in the documentary. That is why Labour's deputy leader Angela Rayner said, "Rishi Sunak has no mandate and no idea what working people need."

Forsyth's best friend is Rishi Sunak. They are godparents to each other's children. They were best men at each other's weddings. Presently, James Forsyth is political editor of The Spectator and one of Sunak's closest friends. Can we say that the kind of friend we are discussing about is Frosyth for Rishi?

A day after Rishi was sworn in as the PM; "Independent" had a caption: Sunak is keeping his friends close, and his enemies closer. Andrew Grice wrote that Sunak's mantra is to "keep your friends close and your enemies closer". It's fitting that Michael Corleone said it in The Godfather. Sunak is no Mafia boss but he does have many enemies. Anita Pratap of "The Week" concludes: Sunak treads in a treacherous environment of prowling enemies and harsh economic conditions. But silver linings glimmer. Most people see the foolish hollowness of Johnson's "cakeism"—you can have your cake and eat it, too, and then Truss's "fantasy economics". People now want governance to be less theater and more carpentry—doing the nuts and bolts of economic repair. Many conservatives understand that they have one remaining chance of reversing their own and the country's fading fortunes. It is the last brown hope. Sunak's biggest asset is his awareness that his coronation comes with a crown of thorns.[16]

The rise of Rishi Sunak has been so swift and fast that he got no leisure time to stand and stare and make enemies on the go.

References

1 https://www.dailymail.co.uk/news/article-11042927/ Golden-boy-Rishi-Sunaks-high-flying-siblings-strived-match-youthful-success.html

2 https://www.theguardian.com/culture/2022/nov/17/our-rishi-sunak-comic-anuvab-pal-pm

3 https://www.theguardian.com/politics/2022/aug/06/rishi-sunak-tory-leadership-private-school-prime-minister

4 https://www.bloomberg.com/opinion/articles/2022-10-24/who-is-rishi-sunak-uk-s-first-hindu-prime-minister

5 https://www.independent.co.uk/news/uk/politics/rishi-sunak-height-how-tall-b2212471.html

6 https://www.vice.com/en/article/k7ed3e/rishi-sunak-chancellor-dishy-rishi

7 https://www.gq-magazine.co.uk/lifestyle/article/rishi-sunak-hot

8 https://www.theguardian.com/politics/2021/feb/27/rishi-sunak-instagram-chancellor-and-prime-minister-in-waiting

9 https://www.deccanchronicle.com/opinion/columnists/ 281022/shobhaa-de-we-want-banana-leaves-pappadums-at-downing-st.html

10 https://www.opendemocracy.net/en/rishi-sunak-could-become-pm-heres-what-he-doesnt-want-you-to-know/

11 https://www.thearticle.com/rishi-sunak-and-the-irresistible-rise-of-the-new-plutocrats

12 https://time.com/6224407/rishi-sunak-prime-minister-world-reactions/

13 https://www.shethepeople.tv/news/rishi-sunak-on-akshata-murty-marriage/

14 Rishi Sunak is teetotal, Peloton riding family man who learned value of hard work in mum's pharmacy | The Sun

15 https://www.huffingtonpost.co.uk/entry/rishi-sunak-no-working-class-friends_uk_62e41f0de4b0d0ea9b76cee3

16 https://www.theweek.in/theweek/more/2022/10/28/ britain-pm-rishi-sunak-economic-and-political-challenges.html

4

THE BIRTH OF A POWER COUPLE

It is being said and being discussed that even Lord Derby, who was loaded, was not richer than Queen Victoria. Rishi Sunak is such a leader of Britain, who has to face sarcasm and criticism many times for being the son-in-law of a rich Indian technocrat. Rishi Sunak's wife, fashion designer Akshata Murty, is even richer. She has less than one percent of the shares in her father's company, but it is also a lot. According to the information of media reports, Akshata Murty is the owner of total assets of $ 1.3 billion i.e. 10.6 thousand crore rupees, in which the largest share is of Infosys' share. She is also a director of three corporate venture capital and private equity firm Catamaran Ventures, fashion stores Newell & Ling Wood and gym chain Dime Fitness. "The British media likes to see Akshata and Rishi as a gilded power couple with sprawling properties in London and California, sharing a love for luxury labels and throwing champagne and caviar garden parties. But they are more a power partnership, firmly committed to each other and to the middle-class values of "humility and integrity", two qualities with which Sunak said he would govern."[1]

Akshata Murty, wife of Rishi Sunak, a very well-known personality all over the world including Britain, is the daughter of India's famous industrialist Narayan Murthy and philanthropist-literateur Sudha Murthy. Akshata Murty is still an Indian citizen. Akshata's life is in more ways than one the reflection of her mother's wonderful life. Rishi and Akshata are made for each other and they are very often called 'The power couple".

Parents : Sudha Murty-Narayana Murthy

Nagvar Rama Rao Narayana Murthy (born: 20 August 1946) is the founder of Infosys Technologies, a well-known Indian software company and a well-known industrialist. Infosys is one of the largest tech companies in India. It is currently present in around 50 countries including the UK. Its headquarters is in Bengaluru. The company recorded revenue of $11.8 billion in 2019, $12.8 billion in 2020 and $13.5 billion in 2021. Narayana Murthy stepped down as Infosys chairman in 2011, but still holds 0.39 per cent of the company's shares.

It will not be out of place to mention Infosys and its founder as more people around the world had heard of Infosys than Rishi Sunak till Sunak became the PM. Sanjaya Baru has very aptly put it, "It is not a coincidence that in the Western media Britain's new Prime Minister Rishi Sunak is often referred to as the son-in-law of the man who created Infosys. Rather than Mr Sunak brand Infosys, Infosys brands Mr Sunak." That is why the story of Mr Murthy and Mrs Murty along with their daughter Akshata should be told in right earnest.

Turning Point

As a young Marxist, Narayana Murthy, the humble son of an 'anti-American and pro-USSR' teacher in Mysore, was arrested in 1974 by Bulgarian guards on the Yugoslavian border for looking at actual existing socialism. He was kept for five days without food and water in Bulgaria for the crime of asking questions about the life of the people there and was ordered to leave the country via Istanbul. 'I lost faith in communism,' he still remembers. The illusion of the idol was dispelled. Murthy returned to India 'cured' of his delusions, with dreams of applying his engineering skills to start a company. In 1981, a year after Akshata was born, software engineer NR Narayana Murthy along with six partners founded Infosys, an IT company, using $250 borrowed from his wife. The company was so modest that for two years they did not have a computer and the firm's office was Narayana Murthy's own room. Nearly 40 years later, the company has now grown into a company synonymous with transformation into an IT powerhouse of India. Today, more than 300,000 employees work for Infosys in approximately 50 countries. It has bagged lucrative contracts for providing IT services to companies and governments around the world, including the UK.

Sudha Murty, his wife belongs to a middle class family, not a rich family. Her father was a professor and doctor, and she married into another teaching family. Her father-in-law was a school teacher and her brother is a professor; her sister is a professor. The only exceptional person in the family is her husband who went into business.

> "I'm a very independent person. In my day people used to say, 'Oh my God, what a girl!' Not so today. My husband Narayana Murthy is -T-H-Y, right? I am Murthy - T-Y. From here I think my freedom is visible.... A verse I was taught as a child... My grandfather was a great scholar of Sanskrit and I asked him why Krishna is respected so much in India. He said, 'na rukmini vallabha na aniruddha pitah na devaki nandahara krishna swayam

krishna' - Krishna is respected not because That he is Devakinandan, the son of Devaki, not because he was the husband of Rukmini, not because he was the father of Aniruddha, but because he was Krishna in his life. I am the same."[2]

A prolific writer, engineer, professor and philanthropist, Sudha Murty is a force of nature. Smashing glass ceilings at a time when there were very few women leading the way—she was the first female engineer to be hired by TELCO, India's largest auto manufacturer—her story is an exemplary account of a formidable trailblazer, who braved the road less travelled.[3] This independence is also visible in her daughter Akshata. She is still known by her surname 'Murty' after marriage and not by the surname 'Sunak'.

The Murthy couple is now role-models for the middle class in India. Both are seen as nationalist geniuses. The life of these two has become a synonym and example of simple living and high thinking. The Murthy couple never became part of the aristocracy. Someone has rightly called Shri Narayana Murthy the 'Mahatma Gandhi of Corporate India'.

Rishi Sunak's father-in-law, NR Narayana Murthy, lives with his wife Sudha in the same Bengaluru flat they started living in decades ago. He still drives the same small car, washes the dishes, and cleans his own toilet. There is no glitz in their life, no fashion, no lavish vacations or private jets, no luxurious houses, no luxury brands. Everything about them is simple and no-nonsense. Murthy is an introverted person who probably likes to contemplate more than studies. Sudha Murty in her book 'Three Thousand Stitches' mentions how her husband cleans his own toilet, a task that many Indians usually leave to others. Apart from reading and writing, charity and social service is another passion of theirs. "The real power of money is in giving it," is one of their famous sayings.

Sudha Murty worked as an engineer in the 1980s, but took up teaching at a college to spend more time with her children. Today, of course, Akshata is the owner of immense wealth, but her childhood was like that of common Indian girls. She was very gentle by nature, though her brother was the naughty one. The Murthy couple was not wealthy and it is said that in school, Akshata was once denied participation in a play being performed during her school's cultural program because her parents could not buy a costume for her. It is also said that her idealistic father had given strict instructions to follow many rules in the house like Gandhiji and wanted to inculcate high Indian values in his children.

I am a witness to this myself as I was working in Tata Institute in Bangalore from 1980 to 1985 and this couple was looked upon with respect. Don't know how many times I must have seen him at the crossroads of Malleshwaram and Jayanagar then. How could I have known that their son in law was going to be a man of history!

Born to Narayana and Sudha Murty, Akshata and her younger brother Rohan were raised by their grandparents while their mother and father pursued careers in engineering and science. They brought Akshata two months after her birth in Hubli (city near Goa) to Mumbai, but quickly discovered that it was a difficult task to nurture a child and manage their careers along with that. So, they decided that Akshata would spend the initial years of her life with her grandparents in Hubli. (see the letter given at the end of the chapter to know the predicament of a father)

Narayana Murthy built the $4 billion IT Company Infosys on the strength of his perseverance, and Sudha Murty became

India's first woman engineer at the most famous car manufacturer, Tata Engineering and Locomotive Company (TELCO). Then on the strength of her self-study and social-work, she got the title of well-known writer and social worker. It would not be an exaggeration to say that Sudha Murty's writings remind one of RK Narayan in Indian English.

As said earlier, Sudha Murty did not allow her children to grow up in an environment of luxury and show off. According to reports, there was not even a television in their house during her childhood. Not only this, Sudha ensured that her children went to school in auto-rickshaws instead of luxurious cars. Mr Murthy was too busy to devote real time with his children and family and it was Mrs Murty who took care of them. It is said that she wasn't a strict mother to her son and daughter in any way but was the one to take care of their homework. "All of their credentials, accomplishments are all thanks to her." Mr Murthy tells others.

In her early days, Akshata went to Baldwin Girls' High School, Bangalore. However, she went abroad for higher studies. Akshata went abroad to study economics and French at Claremont McKenna College in California, before completing a degree in 'Design and Merchandising of Fashion' in Los Angeles.

A love story born at business school

Little is known about the beginnings of Murty and Sunak's relationship, but he reportedly switched his class schedule "to be in a particular class" with her, and he has since joked about how she didn't let his height (just 5ft 6in, making him the shortest PM since Winston Churchill) put her off. "I am incredibly grateful that 18 years ago you chose to give up your high heels and take a chance on the short kid with a backpack,"

She joined Stanford University for MBA where she met Rishi and their love story began. Akshata had studied at Claremont McKenna College, in Claremont, California. Her uncle Shrinivas Kulkarni (Sudha's brother) is a renowned physicist at Caltech, in Pasadena, California, separated by a mere half-hour drive. Sunak then came after graduating from the prestigious Oxford University after earning a first-class degree and gaining admission there as a Fulbright Scholar. Akshata worked at Deloitte and Unilever before going to Stanford. Murty was described by Tatler as "an artistic and fashion-loving student with a deep passion for India's traditional craftsmanship." In 2005, she did her MBA from Stanford University, where she met her future husband, Rishi Sunak. They fell in love with each other and decided to tie the knot. Sunak has put his love into words many times.

During his campaign against Liz Truss, he had said that he was grateful to Akshata for giving the 'short-kid with the backpack' a chance in his/her life. Rishi knows and understands that financially Akshata and he are not equals. In a nod to their common background, Sunak once candidly admitted, "You know what you mean to me, and I'm incredibly grateful that you kicked off your heels 18 years ago to give a chance to the guy with the short backpack." It is true that Rishi Sunak's height is just five feet six inches and if Akshata continued to wear high heels, she would have appeared taller than her husband.

Marriage Bells

Recognizing their daughter's choice, the enlightened Murthy couple pondered and found that their daughter desired a 'brilliant, handsome, and honest' boy. Murthy's early impressions of his son-in-law come to the fore in a warm letter he wrote to his daughter for a 2013 book (Legacy: Letters from Eminent

Parents to Their Daughters - Sudha Menon). He wrote, "... when I met Rishi and found he was everything you described him as - brilliant, handsome, and most importantly, honest - I understood why you let him steal your heart."

Seeing the humble nature of Rishi Sunak and forecasting his future as an experienced man of the world, he resolved to marry them both. Narayana admits that he initially felt "sad and jealous" of his daughter's relationship, but all of that changed when he met the future chancellor. "I ... found him to be all that you had described him to be – brilliant, handsome and, most importantly, honest. l understood why you let your heart be stolen." I repeat.

The couple married four years later in 2009 in a grand ceremony in the city of Bengaluru, India. They married on 30 August 2009 in a simple yet elegant ceremony at Chamaraj Kalyana Mandap, Jayanagar, and the reception was held at The Ballroom, Leela Palace Hotel, Old Airport Road, Bengaluru. The wedding banquet was organized by 'Adiga Caterers' who are famous for Kannada cuisine. This sattvic (no onion and garlic) meal was a traditional Mysore Brahmin meal (Narayana Murthy is from Mysore) with a Dharwad touch (Sudha Murthy's home town). The highlight of the menu was Mandige, a sweet dish from Hubli. The food was served in plain biodegradable banana leaves. Azim Premji, Kiran Mazumdar-Shaw, Anil Kumble, Nandan M. Nilekani, Captain G.R. Gopinath, Prakash Padukone, Syed Kirmani and Girish Karnad were among the dignitaries present. Mr. TV Mohandas Pai, one of the founders of Infosys, who met Sunak at their wedding, now recalls that he found Sunak to be a "complete, honest, energetic, much focused" young man. And who was already the "apple of the Murthy family". "He was very polite, very well behaved and very mature," he still says today.

When Rishi and Akshata married in August 2009, the wedding was attended by James Forsyth as best man, his best friend from their time at Winchester and future political editor of Spectator magazine. Michael Ashcroft writes in his 2020 book 'Going for Broke: The Rise of Rishi Sunak' that the usually self-confident Sunak was left a bit troubled and self-conscious by the sight of his wedding extravaganzas.

On the other hand, some reporters called it 'no tamasha'. It was a low-key affair. The following is what a wedding-sutra commented.

Akshata's wedding reflected the mindset, values and lifestyle of her parents. Though everyone has heard about the Murthys simple lifestyle, they had presumed the most awaited event in their life would be a grand celebration. And the simple, traditional wedding surprised all; while many were touched by the low key festivities where guests were paid personal attention to, others were amazed as to how one of India's richest families could host such a no-fuss traditional affair.[4]

After a brief stay in India (some say it was about four years), he moved to the UK, and Rishi became the MP for Richmond, Yorkshire in 2015. The couple has two daughters, Krishna and Anushka, but little is known about them, as their parents have kept their identities private. The elder one is believed to have attended Glendower Prep in South Kensington, London, the same school where David and Victoria Beckham's daughter Harper attended. It is also known that their first daughter was born in 2011.

Akshata Designs

In 2007, Akshata established her own fashion design business, named 'Akshata Designs'. Akshata has been featured by 'Vogue India' and she is the owner of Akshata Designs. "I am all about protecting the story behind a particular garment, its authenticity, craftsmanship and a rich heritage," she says. Akshata was also quoted as saying: "I believe we live in a materialistic society, and globalization over the past few decades has made it easier to sell products to customers around the world." It was the culmination of her life-long love of fashion, which astounded her "no-nonsense engineer" mother, Ms Murthy told Vogue India in 2011. The company's website said it aimed to provide a "sustainable source of income" for women artists and craftsmen in rural India.

> Ever since I was a little girl I have always loved clothes. My mother, a no-nonsense engineer, was always baffled why I would spend so much time creating different outfits from my wardrobe...I'm about the story behind a particular garment, it's authenticity, craftsmanship and protecting a rich heritage. I care about doing something in India, for India because it's part of our family's DNA. You also once said that you hope your label is viewed as a passport to different cultures...I believe we live in a materialistic society; and over the last few decades, it has become easier to sell products to a wide audience, given the advent of globalization. People are becoming more conscious about the world they live in. Doing good is fashionable...[5]

Richness unfathomable

The U.K.'s new prime minister and his wife, the daughter of an Indian tech billionaire, have a collective net worth higher than the personal fortune of King Charles III. The cofounder and retired chairman of Indian tech giant Infosys N.R. Narayana Murthy's net worth is estimated by Forbes at $4.5 billion.

She has an estimated wealth of Rs 5,956 crores (USD 721 million) which was more than the late Queen Elizabeth II's approximate wealth. She is also the director of at least three companies – Catamaran Ventures, Digme Fitness and the New & Lingwood.

Akshata Murthy is a citizen of India, the country of her birth and home of her parents. India does not allow its citizens to hold citizenship of another country simultaneously. So they are bound to follow the rules and regulations of India.

According to a media report published in April 2022 based on information shared with the stock exchanges, Akshata Murthy's wealth was more than that of the Queen of Britain. Rishi Sunak's father-in-law Narayana Murthy's Infosys is one of the largest tech companies in India. Nowadays it has a business network in about 50 countries including the UK. The company's revenue was $ 11.8 billion in 2019, $ 12.8 billion in 2020 and $ 13.5 billion in 2021. Akshata Murthy received a dividend of Rs 126.61 crore in 2022 for her stake in India's second largest information technology company Infosys. Akshata had faced controversies over her tax status on her income outside the UK. Akshata, daughter of Infosys co-founder Narayana Murthy, held 3.89 crore or 0.93 per cent shares in Infosys at the end of September, according to information made available to stock exchanges. She is a "non-dom" in the UK i.e. she still holds an Indian passport. She is living as a foreign national who paid a £30,000 flat fee in lieu of millions of pounds in income tax on income outside the UK. This revelation almost doomed her husband's political career.

A day after Rishi resigned as chancellor in July, Akshata offered tea and biscuits to waiting journalists outside her London home. But ignoring his/her hospitality, some egoists on

Twitter discussed the price of designer mugs. One wrote: "The price of that mug can feed a family for 2 days." What should I say to you, what Goswami ji has said - it is a feeling. How would the English people know the Indian spirit of hospitality? Do you know? In English, what to talk about the guest, the guest is called 'host', which sounds like 'ghost' and seems to be of the family of 'hostile' (distracted). If they knew the importance of 'Atithi Devo Bhava', they would have taken Akshata's hospitality on their heads. Remember, if the media and the so-called journalists go on spreading all these witticisms and don't stop, rather because of some arrogance, they play the game of sending curses to the goddess of 'wealth', they are defaming Indian values and those academics, those best lives. Discrediting the values, discrediting the Gandhian methods that the Murthy family has kept as their guide and inspiration throughout their lives and with great passion, faith and pride have handed over their daughter to them.

Akshata is still Indian, even though her husband is British. When her non-domicile status became controversial, she wrote on social media: "He has never asked me to give up my Indian citizenship, ties to India or my business affairs, despite the fact that such a move would harm his Things would have been easier politically." Rishi Sunak felt "very upsetting" that his wife has faced criticism over shares she owns in a tech company operating in Russia. He compared his feelings to those of film star Will Smith, whose wife was mocked at the Oscars. Sunak joked: "Both Will Smith and me having our wives attacked - at least I didn't get up and slap anybody." He told the BBC's Newscast podcast: "I think it's totally fine for people to take shots at me. It's fair game. I'm the one sitting here and that's what I signed up for, "But it's very upsetting and, I think, wrong for people to try and come at my wife."

Rishi revealed in an interview that one of the secrets behind their happy marriage was that they were very different people. While she described herself as "incredibly clean", she said that his wife was "very disheveled" (Very Messi), but also more comfortable. As one writer quoted an MP in 'Tatler' as saying: "As one writer huffed in the Tatler, quoting an MP: "He's got an extremely devoted wife. She's got no problem with him staying out until midnight doing what has to be done. If I did that, my wife would have my head for dinner." Clearly, he hasn't had any dealings with Indian women." In the similar vein William Hague says. "She is a brilliant woman in her own right. Sometimes with people's partners, in politics, you find they say, 'I'm not doing this, I'm not doing that.' But she was very, very supportive of his choice of career. I've never detected the slightest doubt or reservation in Akshata with what he's doing, even though it's meant quite an upheaval."

One of the many things between Akshata and Rishi Sunak in which they have a lot of similarity is that the parents of both of them have given true meaning and character to the word couple. They have literally followed the promises given to each other at the time of marriage. Both remained working and educated their families to the best of their ability. They were also very fortunate in the fact that they saw their children flourish and see them climb heights.

Let me conclude with an anecdote provided by Gaitri Issar Kumar, a retired IFS officer and former Indian high commissioner to the UK. "Both he and his wife, the charmingly unassuming Akshata Murty (She surprised us by arriving without any fuss or protocol at the Indian High Commission and then preferred public transport while leaving), are proud of their Indian heritage. India, too, is proud of PM Rishi Sunak. We wish him success." This is called to be "in pursuit of a meaningful life."

***

Ask Mr Murthy and Mrs Murty anything about their son in law, the answer will be short and to the point. "I look after my own country's things, he looks after his." Sudha ji replied. He is their son-in-law. Period.

"We are proud of him and wish him success," Infosys co-founder Narayana Murthy said in his first comments on the elevation of his son-in-law Rishi Sunak as Britain's prime minister.

For Murthy, Sunak is the ideal son-in-law. Murthy made him the director of his new company Catamaran Investments. In this way Murthy gave a new height to his son-in-law. As a result, Sunak made up his mind to take part in politics seriously. Narayana Murthy spent his days in the run-up to the 2015 general election, hardly anyone noticing who he was, putting pamphlets and campaign material for his son-in-law in a letterbox in North Yorkshire. There have been discussions of the humility and kindness of both of them.

Sunak told "The Sun" newspaper, "If I can achieve even a tenth of what my father-in-law has achieved in his life, I will be a happy man. I am really proud of what he has achieved." Rishi Sunak, Sunak said about his father-in-law in a TV interview after he became MP, that being Murthy's son-in-law was "a huge advantage", but "at the same time Sunak then revealed that she had received some priceless advice from her father-in-law." He always tells me to live honestly and do the right thing. Rishi Sunak is also proud of his father-in-law. During an interview he said, "My father-in-law started from zero and had just a few rupees, which my mother-in-law saved and gave him, and now he is one of the biggest and most respected industrialists in the world. They have successful companies that employ thousands of people across the United Kingdom. In the TV debate, Rishi said, "It's an incredible story and it's actually a story that I'm really proud of and as Prime Minister I want to make sure that we here at home (in the UK) can make more stories like him.

Rishi Sunak has spoken many times about his enormous pride and admiration for everything his father-in-law has achieved. Speaking with reference to the attacks on his wife and her family over the continued presence of Infosys in Moscow amid the ongoing Russia-Ukraine conflict, he said, "I think it's totally fine for people to take shots at me. It's fair game. I'm the one sitting here and that's what I signed up for." It's very upsetting and, I think, wrong for people to try and come at my wife, and you know, beyond that actually, with regard to my father-in-law, for whom I have nothing but enormous pride and admiration for everything that he's achieved. And no amount of attempted smearing is going to make me change that because he's wonderful and has achieved a huge amount, as I said, I'm enormously proud of him."[6]

***

Letter from a Father to His Daughter

It is universally acknowledged that a father-daughter relationship is very special. They say a daughter may outgrow your lap, but she will never outgrow your heart. The birth of a daughter is a life-changing event for a father. When a father writes for his daughter he pours his heart out for her. 'Letters from a Father to His Daughter' is a collection of letters written by Jawaharlal Nehru to his daughter Indira Nehru, originally published in 1929 by Allahabad Law Journal Press at Nehru's request and consisting of only the 30 letters sent in the summer of 1928 when Indira was 10-year-old.

In the letter, published in Sudha Menon's book 'Legacy: Letters from eminent parents to their daughters,' Murthy articulates how Akshata's birth changed his life. Murthy's letter to his daughter Akshata became so viral that some part of it was published in the newspaper in many Indian Languages. It is well said that only a truly global leader like Narayana Murthy can tell his daughter to become a citizen of the world in every sense while simultaneously asking her to be a proud Indian, wherever in the world she lives. Now that she has religiously adopted her father's wishes, the value of this letter becomes really manifold.

Here's the full text of the letter-

Dear Akshata,

A regular April evening in Mumbai, in 1980, suddenly became special for me—I received the much-awaited news of your birth.

In those days we could not afford a telephone at home, and my then colleague, Arvind Kher, came all the way from our office in Nariman Point to our house in Bandra to tell me that your mother had delivered you, back in Hubli, her hometown.

'So, how does it feel to be a father?' asked Arvind. I replied that, for the first time in my life, I felt the compelling need to become a better person.

For now there was someone in whose eyes I could do no wrong. Someone, for whom I'd always be a hero. Someone, whose life would be shaped by my actions. I told him I felt a sense of awesome responsibility. I suppose, Arvind could see that becoming a father had completely overwhelmed me.

Akshata, becoming a father transformed me in ways that I could never have thought possible. I could never go back to being the person I used to be before. Your arrival in my life brought unimaginable joy and a larger responsibility. I was no more just a husband, a son, or a promising employee of a fast-growing company. I was a father, who had to measure up to the expectations his daughter would have of him at every stage of her life.

Your birth raised the benchmark of my life, in every aspect.

My interactions at the workplace became more thoughtful and measured; the quality of my transactions with the outside world more considerate, dignified, and mature.

I felt a need to deal with every human being more sensitively and courteously. After all, someday you would grow up and understand the world around you, and I didn't want you to ever think that I had done anything even remotely wrong.

My mind often goes back to the initial days after your birth. Your mother and I were young then and struggling to find our feet in our careers. Two months after your birth in Hubli, we brought you to Mumbai, but discovered, quickly enough, that it was a difficult task to nurture a child and manage careers side by side. So, we decided that you would spend the initial years of your life with your grandparents in Hubli. Naturally, it was a hard decision to make, one which took me quite a bit of time to come to terms with.

Every weekend, I would take the plane to Belgaum and then hire a car to Hubli. It was very expensive, but I couldn't do without seeing you.

What never ceased to amaze me was how you created your own little happy world at Hubli, surrounded by your grandparents and a set of adoring aunts and relatives, oblivious of our absence from your life.

I still remember the joy I felt when I walked through the door of your grandparents' house on weekends to pick you up and hold you close. As soon as you saw me, you would switch your allegiance, and we would become one inseparable unit.

Neither your grandparents nor tachi (her aunt Sunanda) were allowed into our inner circle as long as I was there! Everyone used to be amazed by this and we would all have a good laugh. Of course, I would secretly swell with pride at your loyalty. Most of all, I felt so grateful to you for your belief in me that continues even today.

I am often asked about the qualities that I have imparted to my children. I tell them that it is your mother who shouldered this great responsibility and I am ever so grateful to her for bringing you up to be the fine individuals you are.

She communicated values more by action than by talking about them. She taught Rohan and you the importance of simplicity and austerity. There was this one instance, in Bangalore, when you were selected for a school drama for which you were required to wear a special dress. It was in the mid-eighties, Infosys had just begun its operations, and we did not have any money to spend on non-basic goods.

Your mother explained to you that we would not be able to buy the dress and that you would have to drop out of the performance. Much later, you told me that you had not been able to understand or appreciate that incident.

We realize it must have been a bit drastic for a child to forgo an important event in school, but, we know you learnt something important from that—the importance of austerity.

Life has changed for us since then and there is enough money. But, you know, our lifestyle continues to be simple. I remember discussing with your mother the issue of sending you kids to school by car once we were a little comfortable with money, but your mother insisted that Rohan and you go to school with your classmates in the regular autorickshaw.

You made great friends with the 'rickshaw uncle' and had fun with the other kids in the auto. The simplest things in life are often the happiest and they are for free.

You would often ask me why there was no television at our home when the rest of your friends discussed stuff they watched on TV. Your mother decided early on that there would be no TV in our home so that there would be time for things like studying, reading, discussions, and meeting friends. She insisted that it was important to create an environment conducive to learning at home. Therefore, every night we dedicated the time between 8 pm and 10 pm to pursuits that brought the family together in a productive environment. While Rohan and you did your schoolwork, your mother and I read books on History, Literature, Physics, Mathematics, and Engineering, or did any office work.

It is quite a well-known fact that when a daughter gets married, a father has mixed feelings about it. He hates the fact that there is somebody else in his daughter's life with whom she shares her affections—a smart, confident, younger man who gets the attention that was earlier his alone. I, too, was a little sad and jealous when you told us you had found your life partner. But when I met Rishi and found him to be all that you had described him to be—brilliant, handsome, and, most importantly, honest—I understood why you let your heart be stolen. It was then that I reconciled to sharing your affections with him.

A few months ago, you made me a proud grandparent. If holding you in my arms for the first time gave me indescribable joy, seeing Krishnaa, your lovely daughter, for the first time at your home in Santa Monica, was a different experience altogether. I wondered, whether from now on, I would have to behave like a wise, grand old man! But, then I realized the bonus to growing older and becoming a grandparent. I would have the joy of pampering a child silly!

Besides, you know what they say about grandparents and grandchildren having a common enemy—the parent! I am convinced Krishnaa and I will eventually exchange notes and crib about you and be completely on the same page when it comes to criticizing you!

Jokes apart, Akshata, having Krishnaa will bring home to you the magnitude of the job at hand. In some ways, you already know it. Remember that day when you wrote to me saying how, for the first time in your life, you knew that I was not completely crazy for calling you up almost every day when you were studying abroad, checking on your well-being, checking up on whether you were eating well and resting, and making sure you were comfortable in every possible way? I was amused when you told me you were doing the same with your infant daughter, checking on her every few minutes, worrying if she was fed well, and sleeping enough, even though you know that she sleeps most of the day and night! That is what being a parent means, my dear.

As you begin the next phase of your life Akshata, I would like you to look back at the time you and Rohan were growing up. Your mother, when she realized that her job as an engineer with a corporation kept her away from you both for long hours, quit the job and decided to become a college professor instead. She wanted to be at home when you both returned from school.

Do you remember coming home and regaling your mother with stories about your day at school, having a hot snack, and later in the evening going over your homework with her? I know career aspirations receive much attention in this competitive world. However, what was important in your mother's time will remain the same even today, despite the much-changed world in which you live.

Having a child is an eternal responsibility, Akshata, and having to simultaneously deliver a hundred percent at work is like walking a tightrope. You are lucky to be in a position where you can take a break from your career for a short period and focus on your baby. Hundreds and thousands of women around this country do not have this option. At Infosys, I have talked to young mothers who leave their little children at home and have to perform consistently well at the workplace. I am reminded of how you are balancing your act and that makes me understanding and considerate to them. The world admires a woman who brings a sense of balance to all the three responsibilities—being a loving wife, a caring mother and a competent career woman. I have no doubt at all that you will strike a healthy balance in these responsibilities like you have in everything else.

Tell Krishnaa lots of stories and instill good values in her through them. Tell her, like I told you, stories of the accomplishments, courage, compassion, sacrifice and adventure, of your aunts, uncles and grandparents. Through them she will know her ancestors intimately and be inspired by their lives. It is also how she will develop love and respect for your elders and make a bond with the past and the present.

There is a joke in our family that the only person I am scared of, who can rein me in, is my daughter. Throughout my career—at the Indian Institute of Management, Ahmedabad, while working in Paris at Patni Computer Systems and finally at Infosys, I really did not have a boss.

In the first three places, since I worked hard to deliver whatever I agreed on time, within budget, and with the requisite quality, my bosses left me alone. Since I founded Infosys, I had no boss! So, the only boss I have known is you! Who else can order me around about my eating habits, my sleep patterns, my incessant traveling, and my refusal to go for regular medical check-ups? Rohan is my buddy, but you are the one who instills discipline in my life.[7]

Take care, my child!

Lovingly,

Appa

References

1 https://openthemagazine.com/cover-stories/rishi-sunak-and-akshata-murty-a-grounded-partnership/

2 Telegraphindia.com/entertainment/murty-not-murthy-my-husband-spells-his-name-wrong-says-sudha-murty-as-she-talks-books-marriage-and-infosys-at-an-authors-afternoon-only-t2-was-there/cid/1563069

3 https://www.readersdigest.in/features/story-the-simple-life-in-conversation-with-author-philanthropist-sudha-murthy-127154

4 https://www.weddingsutra.com/celebrity-weddings/celeb-weddings/akshata-murthy-and-rishi-sunak/

5 https://www.vogue.in/content/meet-designer-akshata-murty

6 https://www.business-standard.com/article/current-affairs/uk-chancellor-rishi-sunak-speaks-of-pride-in-father-in-law-narayana-murthy-122040101342_1.html

7 https://www.shethepeople.tv/news/fathers-day-special-letter-to-his-daughter-narayana-murthy-to-akshata/

❐

5

A SON RISES

"I'm incredibly proud of where I come from. It will always be an enormous part of who I am. And it brings me joy to live, and belong, in a country where, for all our faults, for all our challenges, someone like me can become Chancellor. Our task now is to make sure that's not the end of the British Indian story, but the beginning."

—Rishi Sunak

On 24 October 2022 my eldest son Ankur Sharma stood outside the Tory Party Headquarters in London with his wife Akshitara Singh and their infant son Aryav. They took us along with them to witness an event of a life-time. We were on-lookers and could watch the event from a considerable distance. The security *bandobast* was at place and the common men were not allowed to reach there where the Tories could assemble. My elder son Ankur looked at me with furtive eyes and said, "I see history being made here today… Daddy! Write this in your new book. If one day your grandson also becomes the prime minister of the Netherlands, then his story will have you as one of the characters."

We had gone there to catch a glimpse of Rishi Sunak, the son of India, and be a part of the historic moment. The 'Enthusiasm of an Expatriate' was written around as my daughter-in-law akshitara spoke, "This sounds very exciting. I am very happy to be here and experience it."

"Rishi Sunak started campaigning for the post of British Prime Minister on Tuesday, 12 July. Just a month before this, in June 2022, Rishi's father Yashvir Sunak and mother Usha Sunak had wished their son success by going for a *darshan* in the Darbar of Mata Vaishno Devi in Katra (J&K), India.

Anshul, my younger son, added, "Jai Mata di!"

My happiness knew no bounds. My wife too gave all the credit for their success to Lord Shiva. In India, Akshata and Rishi are either the incarnations of Sita-Ram or Shiv-Parvati. Common-folk are bhakatas and this is the way they show their reverence and express their goodwill. My wife, Shashi, was sure it was a Monday and a Monday is an auspicious day for Rishi. We were far away in the crowd keenly watching something beyond our imagination. "It is an emotional, heart-warming and symbolic moment for a grandchild of the British Empire to take up the highest office of the land," she said.

Our British host was also happy and called it a defining moment in the history of their country. She was apprehensive and worried about his tenure too. "He is too open and loud about his Hindu religion and culture. The British public will look at every step taken by him with the harshest scrutiny."

As soon as Rishi got out of the car, cheers broke out and although the reactions were divided between cheering and clapping, it was in stark contrast to the bitter division and chaos which had for weeks engulfed the Conservatives. They greeted the former chancellor with hugs, kiss and pats on the back as they welcomed him to the party's campaign headquarters before his victory speech. The new prime minister climbed the packed stairs and made some very important non-verbal statements of his intention. His expressions were clear and varied. He greeted each person using a different greeting style. Greeted someone the way Indians greet with folded hands, someone with an Islamic way and someone else in some other way and did it continuously. He also patted the children and also looked fervently towards the young men and women gathered in a good number. He shook hands with a few. This was not a formal handshake. Rishi was very successful in giving the impression that he was interacting with each and every individual in a very personal and individual way. Once he arrived in front of the party headquarters, the victorious Prime Minister gathered to enjoy and celebrate his massive victory.

He shared a few moments with us. His gesture to the wider audience at the top of the stairs was one of restrained triumph. Rishi used a fresh smile, hinting at a broad seriousness of his vocation. "General election now!" was shouted by a handful of protesters as Mr Sunak's car drove by. He was greeted with cheers and applause, but went inside without making any public comments. We're still waiting for him to say anything in public despite now being the prime minister in waiting.

***

He didn't say anything in public. We were told that he delivered a short speech inside. It would have been good to have heard him. But after a while, we could only read this tweet.

> The United Kingdom is a great country but we face a profound economic crisis. That's why I am standing to be Leader of the Conservative Party and your next Prime Minister. I want to fix our economy, unite our Party and deliver for our country.
>
> pic.twitter.com/BppG9CytAK
> — Rishi Sunak (@RishiSunak) October 23, 2022

This was a day old tweet and interviews were being shared and circulated. The time was running at a speed we ordinary folk can't fathom. I must cite for you an extract of the interview just to familiarize you the gravity of the political, economic and overall situation of the British people.

> The BBC's Nick Robinson has delivered a zinger to Rishi Sunak over the "emergencies" battering the UK that the ex-chancellor says he wants to fix. As the interview wrapped up, Robinson said to Sunak: "In just half an hour, you and I have gone through a whole series of emergencies – there's a whole lot more I'm sure you wanted to say more on. "An emergency in the economy, an emergency over energy bills, an emergency in the NHS, an emergency with our borders, and our standards in public life. "When you discover who's been running the country for the past 12 years, you're going to be really cross, aren't you?" Sunak paused briefly before replying: "Well, no actually, there was lots that I was very proud of to have participated in government. "We talked about the pandemic response, protecting over ten million jobs, saving business, ensuring that our economy remained resilient through the worst shock it had faced in 300 years. "I'm proud of what I achieved in government, I'm not going to run away from that and, actually, that's why people should now look at me as the person who can be the person who can be the person to lead us forward.[1]

The conservatives needed a leader who could unite Britain, lead all parts of the United Kingdom through the huge economic challenge they were facing and win the next election. It was their choice based on their requirement and need.

***

Cameron did a Nostradamus!

David Cameron, the flashy Etonian car salesman, 15 years younger than his former Gordon Brown and seemingly full of youth and energy compared to Brown, was a worthy prime minister. Polly Toynbee and David Walker, in the book "*Cameron's Coup*" (Guardian Books), managed to encapsulate their argument about the worth of Cameron in the two opening sentences of the book - "Asked why he wanted to be Prime Minister, David Cameron said, 'Because I thought I'd be good at it'. He wasn't." We are not here to discuss David Cameron and his times. But it looks like the appointment of the first British-Indian premier was predicted by former UK PM David Cameron years ago.

David Cameron congratulated Rishi Sunak – and himself too. He pointed out that 10 years ago he said he thought the Conservatives would be the first party in the UK to have an Indian –heritage PM. As party leader Cameron put in a lot of effort into getting his party to select more female and minority ethnic candidates, and that had been linked to Liz Truss appointing a cabinet last month in which none of the top four jobs was held by a white man.

> "Huge congratulations to @RishiSunak on becoming PM to lead us through challenging times. I predicted a decade ago that @Conservatives would select our first Brit Indian PM & proud today that comes to be. I wish Rishi the v best, he has my wholehearted support."

Rishi Sunak's entry into Number 10 Downing Street is an unprecedented historical event. His election as the fifty-seventh Prime Minister of Britain is being watched with pride, love, joy and elation across India. Not one but many stories are being narrated as proof of Rishi being of Indian origin. Everyone of consequence and even those who are of no-consequence are prompted to add their expert opinion. The Political Pundits and Sooth-Sayers both have a hey-day.

The Conservatives under David Cameron came to power in 2010 as the largest party in a coalition with the Liberal Democrats. It won the general elections in 2015, 2017 and 2019, the last with the party's biggest majority since the 1980s. David Cameron quit as the leader of the Conservative party and prime minister of Britain when 'Remain' lost the Brexit referendum and 'Leave' won. Cameron had said yes to the referendum on British membership of the EU in the hope that he would be able to persuade the majority of British people to vote for 'Remain'. After leaving office, Mr Cameron got a job as an adviser from his own former adviser, Mr Greensill.

The credit of the rise of Rishi Sunak is being taken by the party as a whole and by individual leaders. David Cameron once called him "the future of our party." Former UK Prime Minister David Cameron, who rarely comments on politics since his resignation in 2016, also came forward with a tweet. Through this tweet, he indicated that he had predicted and foresaw a decade ago about it. He also attached a solid proof with this tweet. He added a link to the news of the event that He attended in April 2012. He was then leading a coalition government with the Liberal Democrats. Then at the launch of the Conservative Friends of India, Cameron said, "We were the first party to have a woman prime minister (Margaret Thatcher), we were the first party to declare a Jewish prime minister in the form of Benjamin Disraeli and when I look at the talent behind us and I think we are going to be the first party to crown a British Indian as Prime Minister…" Cameron reiterated his prediction to a packed Wembley Stadium during the visit of Prime Minister Narendra Modi in November 2015 to a large number of expatriate Indians:

"It won't be long before a British Indian Prime Minister arrives at 10, Downing Street." Be long before there is a British Indian Prime Minister in 10 Downing Street).

Though David Cameron, who, at the reception in Wembley for Narendra Modi in 2015, wooed the Indian prime minister by speaking a few words in Gujarati, while his wife, Samantha, wore a sari, yet no one took this statement of Cameron seriously then. But sometimes common people also predict like soothsayers. Goddess Saraswati resides on their tongue as well. After seven years of this coincidence, today Rishi Sunak is the Prime Minister of the United Kingdom. He is the foremost beneficiary of the 'Cameron Doctrine' that was put in place when he became one of the Conservative leaders in 2005.

Conservative MPs rejoiced in Rishi Sunak as a proof of the country and their party's commitment to diversity. They remarked, "Labour talks a lot about diversity but the Conservatives act." Compared to the Labour Party, the Conservative Party has been ahead in appointing women as well as minorities to Shadow and Government high office. They are also proud of it. Some gave a balanced overview, "Rishi Sunak is more competent than most of his Cabinet colleagues, but it's a very low bar. He oozes charm, but has a colossal ego, no understanding of life on a low income and pays only lip service to net zero: the fate of the planet doesn't bother him. He should be judged by what he does, not by what he has."

'Indian son rises over the empire': PM Rishi Sunak makes history and headlines. NDTV headlined its main story on Rishi Sunak: "India's son rises over the empire. History comes full circle in Britain." "The empire on which the Sun never sets is ruled by an Indian!" Arab Times gave the caption.

***

We all were very happy there. People back home were celebrating the festival of lights. They were doubly happy. This Diwali was very special for India's magnificent cricket victory defeating arch-rival Pakistan and Rishi Sunak, a person of Indian origin, a practicing Hindu and our own Narayana Murthy's son-in-law, becoming prime minister of UK. What a day it is for India, that too on our 75th year of independence from Britain!

Aha! This festival brought such happiness! See! Celebrate! A youngman of Indian origin has taken over as the PM of Britain on the auspicious festival of Diwali, which means that the Hindu Gods and Goddesses have blessed him. Lakshmi's able son Rishi Sunak had already pleased Goddess Lakshmi and due to this he was also the cause of envy and jealousy for many. On this day Lord Rama's coronation ultimately became a certainty in Treta Yuga. In India this news was a reason for all round celebrations here and there. Not only Narendra Modi, there are other sons of India in the world who have become the flag bearers of the eternal culture and civilization of this country. Once upon a time this country-the Great Britain- used to rule over us, today after 75 years of independence, we have turned the table. MA Ibrahimi, a former chief secretary of Bihar, tweeted in a reference to India's colonial past: revenge of history as well, Destiny. From Diwali gifts to 'Azadi Ka Amrit Mahotsav', Indian politicians have given many flavors to the ascension of Rishi Sunak to the post of the Prime Minister of Britain. BJP's Member of Parliament Bandi Sanjay Kumar tweeted a picture of Sunak and his wife praying in a Hindu temple. "True essence of #AmritKaal, as Indian Origin Rishi Sunak becomes the Prime Minister of former colonizer United .Kingdom. #AzaadiKaAmritMahotsav celebrations continue. More power to India," tweeted the MP from Karminagar, Telangana.

Sunak became Conservative leader in the most auspicious times for the Indian Hindus, though for the British people it was the most inauspicious time. The British folk are reminded of the words of their own novelist Charles Dickens who wrote in "A Tale of Two Cities": It was the best of times, it was the worst of times, it was the age of wisdom, it was the age of foolishness, it was the epoch of belief, it was the epoch of incredulity, it was the season of light, it was the season of darkness, it was the spring of hope, it was the winter of despair. The festival of life is celebrated on the night of amaavsya- the dark night. What a kismet!

This festival- this Deepotsav festival of Hindus, is celebrated every year in memory of Lord Rama's return to Ayodhya after fourteen years of exile. A world record is being created in Ayodhya by lighting lakhs of earthen lamps simultaneously. Processions are being taken out. Crackers are being burst in spite of pollution across the country. There is no limit to enthusiasm. India has once again defeated Pakistan in the game of cricket. That's why fireworks are unbridled even during the day. It has been going on since yesterday itself because the news of Rishi's victory reached India on the day of Dhanteras. BBC's Radio (4) Service - Service in Bengali broadcast this talk on the day the Tories elected a new leader, Akhandadhidas, a Vaishnava Hindu teacher and theologian, compared the expected victory of the sage Sunak to Lord Rama's exile "Today, many Hindus and Sikhs around the world are celebrating Diwali, the annual festival of lights. I think for many people in the UK this past weekend the story of Rama's homecoming has become a part of our association to the current political landscape may seem unusual. The possible return of an exiled ruler, or the incarnation of a sage, would be difficult not to relate the sage to Sanskrit terminology and tradition. For a Hindu Rishi Sunak to become

The Rise of Rishi Sunak

the leader of the British nation... The story of Diwali The parallels here are very clear and political, like the residents of Ayodhya, the kingdom of Rama, all those years ago, we too were facing a time of deep anxiety and desperation... It is said that life for the citizens of Ayodhya had reached a standstill. In such circumstances, hoping for a savior- Naturally, someone should fix everything."

While we Hindus not only in India but all over the world are praying to Goddess Lakshmi for prosperity and success, one of our Hindu sons named Rishi Sunak has become the Prime Minister of Britain at the beginning of Diwali festival. This news has filled the hearts of not only the Hindus of India but also the Muslims of Pakistan, because Rishi's grandfather had gone abroad from undivided India before independence. Ram Dass Sunak and his wife must be happy in heaven. Mr Yashvir Sunak and his wife are celebrating in the UK. Rishi's father-in-law and mother-in-law are feeling proud in Bengaluru. Why shouldn't they be filled with pride, what can be a greater moment of happiness than this?

On 24 October Billionaire businessman Anand Mahindra shared a Twitter post. Mahindra also mentioned a quote by Winston Churchill in his post. Anand Mahindra said that Winston Churchill joked on the occasion of India's independence in 1947, labeling all Indian leaders as low-level and powerless. But on the occasion of the completion of 75 years of the country's independence, a person of Indian origin has given a befitting reply to them by taking over the reins of Britain." Today, during our 75th year of independence, we are set to see a man of Indian origin being anointed as the Prime Minister of the UK. Life is beautiful! Churchill said many other such arrogant things for India, Indians and Gandhi. He had a deep hatred for Indians. However, he himself preferred India as long as it remained a

British possession. According to his colleague Leo Amery, he portrayed Indians as "beastly people with a beastly religion". Now that a sincere devoted Hindu Rishi Sunak is sitting at the same place where he once used to sit, it is not difficult to guess how much his soul must be reeling in pain.

Rishi Sunak has become the Prime Minister of Britain. Some people will find it strange for Indians to be happy. Nevertheless, the truth is that he is not only an Indian by heritage and culture, but also the respected son-in-law of a well-respected family of India. It is well known to you and us that Rishi Sunak is not the representative of Indians, but of his own party - the Conservative Party. But still, his reaching this position is a matter of pride and pleasure for all of us. It is also a moment of hope and faith for them, whose sons and daughters have settled in Europe and America in the last so many decades.

There are as many people in India who have so much to say about this while celebrating his victory. Everyone claims to know a lot. We come across many unknown facts about the Prime Minister of the UK, which have no evidence, no rhyme or reason. There is just faith and there is a lot of pride - mixed pride. Some don't know anything but create the illusion of knowing a lot. It is said that at the age of four, Rishi Sunak's teacher predicted that this child would do great things in life. And others say that marrying the billionaire daughter of a multi-billionaire was Rishi's "great deed" by which he proved his guru's prediction to be true. Some are telling his success as the fruit of his devotion to the mother-cow; while some are getting fascinated by the mantra by pointing to the Raksha Sutra tied around his wrist.

Ham eise hee hain -We are like this only. The book I am writing and you are reading after buying it is also in one way the fruit of this amazing fascination for Rishi who is of the same age as my own son Ankur is. There is a relation of this nameless bond and relationship behind it too. Our shastras call it 'Badrayan sambandh'.

The residence of the Prime Minister of Britain is called 10 Downing Street. It is natural to be pleasantly surprised to know that a Hindu will have a residence in it. It is a matter of great pleasure, and that too on Diwali day. The devout Hindu former Finance Minister and now Prime Minister of Britain, who took the oath of allegiance by placing his hand on the Bhagavad Gita when he was elected as an MP in the House of Commons, took time even during this long campaign on his Hindu-faith and occasionally visited the temple. That's why many people of the country and abroad kept on praising him from the bottom of their hearts. Don't know how many people were praying for his success. How many prayers for victory have been answered? Sunak has got the victory, which was forcibly taken away from him some time ago. I am overwhelmed with raw emotion and if I ignore those who are votaries of Standard English and start writing in my own Indian English, ignore my shortcomings.

Three things are true of Rishi Sunak. One – he is the new Prime Minister of the United Kingdom. Two – he is South Asian, specifically of Punjabi descent. Three – his appointment makes history, marking the first time a non-white person has held the title of Prime Minister of Great Britain. The rest? Well, that's up for debate. For instance, Isabella Silvers argues that Rishi Sunak becoming our first Asian PM is no reason for other people to celebrate. She is of the view that a brown Prime Minister may be historic, but we can't separate politics from the person. As a British-Asian woman, she doesn't see his position as anything to celebrate. It's hard to see his appointment as a sign of progress for people of color when he was not elected by the public, instead losing the initial leadership contest to another white PM.

Post-Liz Truss,Sunak only nabbed the role after all of his other opponents dropped out of the race.[2]

Even labour peer Paul Boateng is elated to find Rishi Sunak as the PM and celebrates, 'Britain has shown the world that you can have truly multi-racial democracy and it's something I've fought for all my life."

Obama Moment

This is, allegedly, a historic moment being compared to former US President Barack Obama's win - although Sunak won via the mandate of the people, not via a select few. Only few OECD countries have achieved such a feat. Joe Biden, a pretty caustic critic of Britain for an American president, called it a "global milestone." In other words, the UK underwent its own 'Barack Obama' moment. By voting for Barack Obama, the American people had created history in 2008. With Rishi Sunak, the British people created a similar history in 2022. Though Obama was a liberal and Sunak is a conservative, yet in democracies when a leader hails from a minority community, it goes to the glory of democratic credentials of that country and mirrors social maturity of the people.

"It's like for the UK, it's the Barack Obama moment, where a non-white person becomes Prime Minister for the first time, also a person from Indian origin and Hindu which is another dimension and everyone is very proud," said the president of the temple, set up by Ram Dass Sunak, Rishi Sunak's grandfather in 1971. It's a proud moment, the temple is buzzing right now, a lot of people are showing their own pictures with him, when he was here before he took pictures with every single person who was in the temple." Sanjay Chandarana, president of the temple, told the news agency: "Rishi comes regularly to the temple, even now." He continues, "He is an intellectual guy, he looks at things practically, he is humble at the same time, he understands what is required, he will lead the country through the economic challenge and I believe he will be a good Prime Minister without a shadow of a doubt."

Faustine Ngila writes, "New UK Prime Minister Rishi Sunak is African. Not by birth but through his roots which historians trace to East Africa. Sunak's parents are part of thousands of Indian Diaspora who moved to the UK from East Africa in the 1960s after the region began 'Africanizing' its economy." "It's another Obama moment for us. We pride ourselves in seeing him steering the UK's rocky boat back to stability," commented Julia Onyango, a fishmonger based in Kisumu, a city located 58 kms from former US president Barack Obama's K'Ogalo village where his father was born. The Taifa Leo newspaper called Mr Sunak's rise another "Barack Obama moment". "Sunak's case is nearly similar to that of former US President Barack Obama, who is an American citizen but has Kenyan roots as his father was born in Homa Bay County," Citizen Digital website said. Popular newspaper commentator Macharia Gaitho said "Kenya has conquered the British Empire".[3]

Sandip Roy of "The Hindu" doesn't subscribe to this idea and asks us not to be carried away by such labels. He says, "Party-poopers have pointed out that the arrival of the "UK's first Indian-origin Prime Minister" will not mean the Kohinoor is coming back or a Jallianwalla Bagh apology is in the offing. The rise of Sunak in the land of that old racist Winston Churchill is historic but those calling this an "Obama moment" for British Hindus forget Barack Obama was actually elected by the voters."[4]

It is also noteworthy that Barack Obama visited Kenya six years after he became the President. A billboard outside Nairobi airport reads: "Welcome Home, Mr. President." The year he won the US elections, the Kenyan government had declared a national holiday in celebration. Obama began his speech, "Habari Zenu. Wakenya mpo... I am proud to be the first American President to come to Kenya and, of course, I'm the first Kenyan-American to be President of the United States." Something of that sort, we Indians can expect from Rishi Sunak.

Similarly Arun Sinha writes an opinion piece in "Telangana Today" suggesting us not to get carried away by emotion. "We need to be temperate in tomtomming triumph. Today in our country, emotion is battering reason monstrously to drive it out of the national psyche. It is doing the same thing in the Rishi Sunak case. We need to save reason from emotion's assault in this case." I am in agreement with him. Maybe you also don't want to be emotional. But do you like to be called "they"? Sinha continues, "They want to wear him as a jewel in their Hindu crown...They in fact would not give an inch to any of the Semitic religions —Islam, Christianity or Judaism — in India. They want their followers to 'conform to Hinduism' to prove their 'Indianness'. They make a Catch-22 offer to them: "You are free to worship your God but you must follow the Hindu culture." Now, the culture of a community is no different from its religion. Asking non-Hindus to follow Hindu culture amounts to asking them to follow Hindu religious culture."[5]

The difference of opinion between the two set of people is palpable. The common folk are elated and imaginative; the intelligence of those who write is based on their thinking. Without reacting or refuting these scholar journalists, I would cite a stanza from one of Atal Bihari Vajpayee's poems.

And so a new milestone's been crossed.

How many more remain, no one knows,

And no one knows when the final

Destination will arrive.

References

1 https://www.huffingtonpost.co.uk/entry/nick-robinson-rishi-sunak- conservatives_uk_62f3ed25e4b0acf9d0042a6d

2 https://www.cosmopolitan.com/uk/reports/a41767583/rishi-sunak-first-asian-prime-minister/

3 https://qz.com/east-africa-is-having-another-obama-moment-1849714121

4 https://www.thehindu.com/society/rishi-sunaks-elevation-turns-the-spotlight-on-indias-famous-sons-in-law/article66056281.ece

5 https://telanganatoday.com/opinion-proud-hindu-and-proud-pluralist

◻

6

THE SUN SETS

I don't know for sure but one of my friends told me quoting a holy book that from the rising of the sun to the place where it sets, the name of the Lord is to be praised. I pray to the Lord and I am also bewildered to notice how the sun sets but the son rises. It happens at the same time, figuratively speaking.

Once upon a time, the British Empire spanned the globe. This led to the saying that the sun never set on it, since it was always daytime somewhere in the empire. The phrase "the empire on which the sun never sets" (Spanish: el imperio donde nunca se pone el sol) was used to describe certain global empires that were so extensive that it seemed as though it was always daytime in at least one part of its territory. George Macartney wrote in 1773, in the wake of the territorial expansion that followed Britain's victory in the Seven Years' War, of "this vast empire on which the sun never sets, and whose bounds nature has not yet ascertained." A rejoinder variously attributed to an unnamed Indian nationalist runs in one variant, "The sun never set on the British Empire, because even God couldn't trust the English in the dark".[1]

"Indian son rises over the empire. History comes full circle in Britain," an NDTV headline underlined the irony with all its might. Echoing similar sentiment, 'The Mail' headline read, "A new dawn for Britain" with the sub-head: "Rishi Sunak becomes our youngest modern PM - and first with an Asian heritage". "From Age of Empire to Rishi Raj as Sunak moves into No 10," roared The Times of India. "India was [once] under the governance of Britain. Now, an Indian-origin man has become the Prime Minister of England," a Zee News anchor spoke tongue in cheek. "Another Diwali gift to the country. Indian-origin Rishi to rule the whites," said Dainik Bhaskar. Karnataka Chief Minister Basavaraj Bommai said that Indian-origin Rishi Sunak becoming the UK prime minister meant that the "wheel has turned full circle". 'The Week' asked in return, "A full-circle moment for the British?" "The Brits ruled over us for 200 years. They'd not have dreamt that one day an Indian would become their PM. The wheel has turned full circle," Bommai replied.

In this time of victory festival, everyone in India too - from common men to film stars, industrialists such as Amitabh Bachchan and Anand Mahendra, everyone is writing and tweeting. Taking to Instagram, Amitabh Bachchan shared a picture and wrote, "Jai Bharat.. Britain finally has a new Viceroy from her motherland as its Prime Minister." Former Indian diplomat Kanwal Sibal tweeted about the "poetic justice" of an Indian leading a country that had once colonized and ruled India. An op-ed in the 'Deccan Herald' enthusiastically discusses the "contrary cultural colonization of the UK" to be ensured by Indians. Novelist Chetan Bhagat wrote, " 1608: East India Company arrives in India at a port near Surat …414 years later…on Diwali day. 2022: Rishi Sunak becomes PM of UK. Time changes everything. Happy Diwali all!

Less than a century earlier, the clubs run by the British in India and Africa were out of bounds for anyone except the whites. Apartheid policy prevailed. Today, their prime minister is a man of a race, creed and caste that most British people of the time despised and treated inhumanely. The Times of India declared in its Delhi edition, "History comes full circle as 1980-born Rishi Sunak becomes the first person of Indian origin ... to become prime minister of a once-colonial power from which India gained independence 75 years ago."

Since the mid-1800s, the British controlled almost the entire subcontinent; however, after a conflict, that they called the Sepoy Rebellion and we called it the War of Independence, the British monarchy assumed control of the major part of the Undivided India leading to a period of rule known as the "British Raj." Columnist Devika Rao sums it up as follows.

> India was a place of interest for much of European history, including prompting the voyage of Christopher Columbus in 1492. The British were no exception and engaged heavily in trade with the country through the British East India Company. The company had a monopoly in Indian commerce by the 1700s and started creating its own army in the area, even recruiting some Indian citizens in the process, called sepoys. In the mid-1800s, they controlled almost the entire subcontinent; however, after a conflict, called the Sepoy Rebellion, the British monarchy assumed control of what is now India, Pakistan, and Bangladesh, leading to a period of rule known as the "British Raj."[2]

The Empire Strike Back! Commentators say that Rishi Sunak is the revenge of the Empire on its English colonizers and masters who ran a deeply racist imperial wealth gathering operation not in the distant past. Indians have not forgotten the chaos that followed the country's independence in 1947 and the bloody partition that followed, during which 500,000 to 2 million people were killed and an estimated 15 million were uprooted. The significance of Sunak's appointment is that this underlines the success of the Indian Diaspora in the UK, where around 7% of the population is of South Asian descent. The Evening Standard lamented on 27 October, 2022. "The single photo that shot around the world of King Charles III, the grandson of the last colonial Emperor of India, shaking the hands of his new prime minister, Rishi Sunak, the grandson of colonial subjects of that same Raj, who would not have been allowed to use the same toilets as whites in the great imperial bases, let alone set foot in the white-only clubs of that era, is an image of enormous power."[3]

Hip Hip Hurray!

There is a wave of excitement throughout India and its diaspora over the appointment of Rishi Sunak as Prime Minister of Britain, and that too at the age of 42. Eminent litterateur EM Forster (1879-1970) in his inimitable style had recommended democracy to be given only two cheers (cheers) instead of three, about a hundred years ago. He wrote in one of his articles "So two cheers for democracy: one because it accepts diversity and the other because it allows criticism. Two cheers are enough: there's no occasion to give three." But when we see this important historical act of Rishi Sunak, we feel like doing not three but thirty cheers. Rishi is not among the drinkers, then instead of talking about cheers, discusses another litterateur.

Shafi Rahman in London writes for India 'Today' about the Rishi Raj and begins his eloquent feature. "The lights had long dimmed on the Empire when the sun never set and on Diwali day this year, Westminster was drowned in a festive light of diversity, as the Empire struck back in style." The amusing anecdote he provides is hilarious and hitherto unknown. Read it just for fun. "In 1869, telegraph pioneer John Pender set up the British Indian Submarine Telegraph Company to lay undersea cables from Britain to India. When English author John Ruskin was told about this venture, he asked, half in jest "I wonder what the message will be." A century and a half later, a man of Indian descent, well-tailored and whip-smart, has become a powerful message unto himself, to a country that has itself become a joke as it grapples with an economic crisis and political instability.[4]

Churchill Forewarning!

"In 1947 on the cusp of Indian Independence, Winston Churchill supposedly said "...all Indian leaders will be of low caliber & men of straw." Today, during the 75th year of our Independence, we're poised to see a man of Indian origin anointed as PM of the UK. Life is beautiful," Mahindra wrote on Twitter. In his tweet, there is a painful history and a joyful actuality of the day.

"One of the best things about being Chancellor is working in some of Britain's most historic buildings. This week I went to the balcony where Churchill made his victory speech 75 years ago today. It reminded me that when Britain comes together we can overcome anything. #VEDaySunak" This is another tweet of one who has been an avid admirer of Churchill. He has been a British citizen by birth and as such has described himself as a Churchill admirer since childhood.

Former UK PM Sir Winston Churchill is famous in British history for a number of reasons, including leading his country out of crisis during World War II. Winston Churchill was the first Prime Minister of Queen Elizabeth II. He held office from 1940 to 1945 and from 1951 to 1955. Churchill also received the Nobel Prize in Literature for his history of World War II and for his speeches that resonated around the world. He is also remembered for his eccentricities and the public comments he made are not taken well by Indian scholars. His thoughts were not appropriate about Indians, their struggle for freedom and Gandhiji. He was like Rudyard Kipling, who wrote famously of the 'White Man's Burden,' regarding colonialism as a means of civilizing the natives, a "divine burden to reign God's empire on Earth."

Churchill had an animal kind of loathing for Indians — though he quite liked India itself as long as it remained British property. He had stated that he did not become prime minister to liberate India. India had no right to aspire for freedom. Indians won't be able to rule the nation, even if they gain independence, how the pages of time have turned!

According to his colleague Leo Amery, he referred to Indians as a "beastly people with a beastly religion." As recorded in the diaries of Churchill's Downing Street secretary, John Colville, on returning from Yalta in February 1945, "the PM said the Hindus were a foul race, 'protected by their mere pullulation from the doom that is their due'. And he wished Bert Harris [head of the RAF Bomber Command] could send some of his surplus bombers to destroy them". Churchill reportedly said in the British Parliament, " "If Independence is granted to India, power will go to the hands of rascals, rogues, freebooters; all Indian leaders will be of low calibre and men of straw. They will have sweet tongues and silly hearts. They will fight amongst themselves for power and India will be lost in political squabbles. A day would come when even air and water would be taxed in India."

Churchill's soul must be groaning in his grave that the Indian race which was considered by him as worthless, where their 'father of the nation' was called by him a 'half-naked fakir', how did a person of the same Indian race become the Prime Minister of Britain? How silly and narrow-minded was he!

75 years ago, a half-naked fakir returned to India from South Africa and forced the British to leave India. About 50 years ago, a group of families turned to Britain from East Africa and made their mark. Mihir Bose says, "Those Asians faced well documented racism and hardship, but still, with pluck and with much entrepreneurship, made their mark on British society and the British economy. It is the children of these East African Asians, who have done well, and particularly the Hindus: around two thirds of Hindu men are in managerial and professional jobs, but only around a third of Muslim men."[5] Jai Ho!

"The single photo that shot around the world of King Charles III, the grandson of the last colonial Emperor of India, shaking the hands of his new prime minister, Rishi Sunak, the grandson of colonial subjects of that same Raj, who would not have been allowed to use the same toilets as whites in the great imperial bases, let alone set foot in the white-only clubs of that era, is an image of enormous power. Britain can only rise above its worsening reputation by showing it is not the caricature in Putin's speeches or The New York Times, but what it really is: one of the most successful multicultural societies in the world. More so than the US," says Ben Judah, British journalist and author of' "This is London" and "Fragile Empire".[6]

Living Bridges

On October 24, 2022, Narendra Modi congratulated Rishi Sunak. In his message, he called PM Sunak an example of 'living bridge', that the UK Indians are. He wrote, "Warmest congratulations Rishi Sunak! As you become UK PM, I look forward to working closely together on global issues and implementing Roadmap 2030. Special Diwali wishes to the 'living bridge' of UK Indians as we transform our historic ties into a modern partnership." "For hundreds of years, Indians have traveled to various parts of the world and have created thriving communities in several countries. Sunak's parents were born in Kenya and Tanzania respectively. By mentioning 'living bridges', PM Modi meant that the descendants of Indians are the living, breathing, and flourishing representatives of India's timeless culture and energy."[7]

In the words of Dominic Asquith, former British High Commissioner (2016-2020), "The phrase 'Living Bridges' was coined by Prime Minister Narendra Modi to describe the unique phenomenon of what the India-UK partnership is all about. It is the people-to-people connections, the myriad institutional linkages, free flowing exchange of culture and ideas that sits separate from our government-to-government relations."Referring to the "living bridge of Indians" cultural diplomacy, India's former ambassador to the US Harsh Vardhan Shringla had previously described Indian Americans as "an organic bridge between the world's two largest democracies". Thus for India, Rishi Sunak's appointment as UK Prime Minister provides an opportunity to strengthen the narrative of 'living bridges' and boost its cultural diplomacy. It was during his first visit to the UK as Indian Prime Minister back in November 2015 that Narendra Modi coined the phrase "Living Bridge" during his historic address to a gathering of Global Indians at Wembley Stadium in London. The phrase has since become etched in the bilateral vocabulary as a symbol of the vibrancy of the UK-India relationship. However, what had remained unquantified so far was an estimate of the kind of monetary value that can be attached to the many successful diaspora-owned businesses in the UK.[8]

The Rise of Rishi Sunak

"We know the UK-India relationship is important. We represent the living bridge between our two countries," said Sunak, in response to a question about the UK-India relationship coordinated by Conservative Friends of India (CFIN). "It's a privilege to be here because *aap sab mere parivar ho* (you all are my family)," he said in Hindi.[9]

Let us close the discussion with the opinion of Upala Sen who poses a relevant question, "PM Modi referred to the new British PM as the living bridge of UK Indians. But is there really any kinship?" The answer may be in Upala's opinion"Well, hundred or more years ago, some people jumped the mother ship and for valid reasons, mostly reasons of unbelonging. In that leap of faith was born a new people."

piṇḍe piṇḍe matirbhinnā kuṇḍe kuṇḍe navaṃ payaḥ |

jātau jātau navācārāḥ navā vāṇī mukhe mukhe ||

- subhāṣitaratnabhāṇḍāgāra

Varied is the intellect in different people; varied is the (taste in) water from different sources; varied are the customs for different descents; varied are the speech from different visages. Each person is different and each has a different perspective. It is these varied perspectives that make the world different and beautiful!

References

1   https://time.com/3969097/shashi-tharoor-oxford-union-debate-reparations-india-britain/

2   https://theweek.com/feature/briefing/1017872/rishi-sunak-and-the-complicated-history-between-britain-and-india

3   https://www.standard.co.uk/comment/rishi-sunak-empire-britain-india-king-charles-colonial-past-reputation-b1035674.html

4 https://www.indiatoday.in/magazine/cover-story/story/20221107-the-rishi-raj-challenges-and-pitfalls-2290451-2022-10-28

5 https://www.theguardian.com/commentisfree/2022/oct/26/rishi-sunak-tory-hindu-labour-conservative

6 https://www.standard.co.uk/comment/rishi-sunak-empire-britain-india-king-charles-colonial-past-reputation-b1035674.html

7 https://www.opindia.com/2022/10/pm-modi-congratulatory-message-to-rishi-sunak-living-bridge-meghalaya/

8 https://www.indiaglobalbusiness.com/igb-archive/the-living-bridge-effect-on-uk-india-ties

9 https://www.iglobalnews.com/newsviews/we-are-the-living-bridge-between-uk-and-india-rishi-sunak

❐

7

BRITISH RAJ TO RISHI RAJ

Barbad ihna azadian ton hoye tusi vi ho,
hoye tusi vi ho, hoye assee vi haan/
Akhan di laali paying dasdi hai, roye assee vi haan

Late Ustad Daman, the poet of the gardens in Lahore, had written the above rhyme. It can be roughly translated into English as follows:

> We have been ruined by this Independence and so have been you
>
> The redness of the eyes shows that we have wept and so have you!

"The UK once the super power that produced the colony that grew into the USA is now America's mad little pet. The absurd Boris Johnson is just a B-Movie, Z-list version of the supreme absurdity –the reality TV stars Donald Trump." David Sinclair's book "Superheroes and Presidents: How Absurd Stories Have Poisoned" (2021) ends with this sentence. Can we add something to it to make it worthwhile? Versifiers in India try to play with words and say.

do sou saal gulami jheli, jhelen julmon sitam

aaj achanak, badali kismet, raja hue hain ham

Two hundred years, suffered slavery, suffered oppression,

Today, luck suddenly changed, we have become kings.

The Road to Somewhere

Asian migration in Britain is a complex story. They didn't come at a time in a ship. There were two distinct migration streams. The first stream of migrants can be called the "direct-flight" migrants. They arrived soon after Britain left the subcontinent, and were mainly rural migrants from Punjab and Gujarat, with a large number of Muslims from Mirpur in Pakistan-occupied Kashmir. Rishi Sunak's parents and grandparents were not among them. His ancestors had been encouraged by the British to migrate to East Africa, to act as middlemen between the British and the Africans. They lived there, settled there but later were forced to run away to save their lives and property. These Asian migrants who migrated from East Africa have historically had more reason to be grateful to the British. They had two roads to go back. They could have gone back to India or they could have tried their luck in Britain.

Two roads diverged in a yellow wood,

And sorry I could not travel both

Two roads diverged in a wood, and I—

I took the one less traveled by,

And that has made all the difference.

They took a calculated risk and reached there where they made a mark. They were allowed to stay but they had faced racism and violence. These hardworking families made their mark and prospered in due course of time. Sunak's parents are among those who worked day and night and tried to educate their children. Rishi and his brother and sister did remarkably well. The rest is history.

"In his book, The *Road to Somewhere* (2017), David Goodhart detected two types of public figures: the 'somewhere' man, rooted in national particularities, and the 'anywhere' man, the Davos man. Rarely in the political world is there a demand for the latter. Britain of 2022 is the aberration."These are the words of India's leading analyst Swapan Das Gupta. You may or may not agree with him, but this is what Swapna Das Gupta emphasizes. He understands that Rishi Sunak is a staunchly successful politician, a man whose presence enriched the Conservative Party and made immeasurable contributions to government. Yet, being a unique personality is different from being a party leader, someone whose face is presented to the entire electorate, not just a constituency. He says, "As a politician of Indian ethnicity, Sunak was always a baby step short of being entirely an insider in the charmed circles of the Conservative Party. He may be the MP for Richmond in Yorkshire, a rural constituency that doesn't boast any significant numbers of Asian voters. Indeed, his constituency has spared him of the need to dabble in identity politics, although he remains a proud Hindu, a vegetarian and a teetotaller."[1]

In the early 1960s, politicians such as MP Cyril Osborne argued strongly against immigration from the former colonies. In an interview, Osborne declared that England was "a white man's country and I want it to remain so." Conservative candidate Peter Griffiths used openly racist language in his 1964 election campaign: "If you want a nigger neighbour, vote Liberal or Labour."A decade and a half ago, the Conservative Party had just two MPs (out of 198) from racial minority backgrounds. The party was out of power at the time, and knew it had to improve its image in order to be successful long term in modern Britain. So, in 2006, newly-elected party leader David Cameron made a conscious effort to ensure that the party more accurately reflected the nation he wanted to lead. David Cameron, who became its prime minister four years later, included racial minorities and prioritized women. Sajid Javed was Minister of Culture, Sports and Media in the Cameroonian cabinet; He is of Pakistani origin. His father was a bus driver. Sajid later worked as an employee of Deutsche Bank on the strength of his hard work.

Former Prime Minister David Cameron is credited with changing his party's approach and developing a personality like Sunak. He predicted in 2012 that very soon his party would have its first British-Indian prime minister. And his words came true within 10 years. Not only in Britain but also elsewhere, such as in Italy and Germany, have right-wing parties taken the lead in promoting women and other social groups.

Inspiration

Sunak started seriously thinking about returning to the UK and getting into politics in 2013. Rishi's father-in-law Shri Narayana Murthy had also given him similar advice that he should think of stepping into politics instead of business as public service can also be done through it. "When it came to doing these jobs – it was actually my father-in-law," Sunak told people attending a private hustings at the UK home of former partner in Blackstone Franks Subhash Thakrar in August 2022, during his first leadership contest.

> "I was always struck that a man who was so successful and created one of the world's most successful companies, that employs hundreds of thousands of people, that literally has changed how an entire country is perceived, always felt that you could have more impact through

politics rather than through business. Because I thought maybe actually you can do this through business and philanthropy and you could have an impact the way he and my mother-in-law have had. But he was the one who said, 'No, if you want to have an impact on the greater scale, the way to do it is through politics', and he was always right behind me, encouraging me, and that is why I am here today," Sunak added.

Help guidance and assistance

Sunak told his friends at the time: "I only knew James when I came back from America. I had no identity with anyone else in politics. He introduced me to Dougie and then things went on." Rishi Sunak and James Forsyth became friends when both were in college. He was best man at Forsyth's wedding to Allegra Stratton. She is now his press secretary. The Sunaks and The Forsyth-Strattons are godparents to each other's children. Forsyth gave some help to Sunak, gave suggestions, introduced his old friend to some prominent politicians, and introduced him to veteran Tory colleague Dougie Smith who used to write speeches for David Cameron. Stratton introduced Sunak to Cass Horowitz, a young social media guru, who is credited with building "brand Rishi". Horowitz is now Sunak's special adviser. It is said that Sunak had Johnson and the rest of the cabinet worried because he was more popular on Social Media than any of the Conservatives.

When an in/out EU referendum seemed unlikely, and he was called to meet with the then Prime Minister and Chancellor of the Exchequer, David Cameron, and George Osborne, hoping to persuade him to join his campaign. George Osborne tells Tim Shipman in 'All Out War' how Sunak was completely polite, but ultimately, it was clear he was not going to go through with his offer.

Indians have been woven into the fabric of British society for over 100 years. They have settled there. They have been doctors, nurses, teachers, shopkeepers, restaurant owners, friends and neighbors for the people there. The Englishmen rarely remember and bother now that they are surrounded by Indian community. People of Indian origin are now a part of life there. Sunak may have been an outsider once, but he didn't remain an outsider for long. He carved a niche for himself. In May 2014, just five months before he was elected to the safe Conservative seat of Richmond in rural Yorkshire, he argued in a BBC interview that politicians should no longer treat all Britons as "BAME" – "Black and Minority Ethnic" should not be seen together. Each specific community should accept them separately with their conditions. At the time, the Conservatives were failing to attract non-white voters whose attitudes and circumstances made them natural Tories. Sunak said at the time that he was in no way in favor of mass immigration. He makes a distinction between immigration that happened 50 or 60 years ago and the situation now. There was a time when their grandparents or parents came to this country, integrated, worked hard, unlike what they are seeing now - which in their perception is not the same as of old. His analysis of this era was right and accurate: there are fewer 'Whites' in the Conservative Party today than ever before, while still being largely opposed to immigration. None of the four most important positions in Truss's first cabinet was held by a white man. The 'breakout star' of the last election was Kemi Badenoch, who lived in Nigeria until the age of 16.[2]

A portrait of modern Britain

The Conservative Party has governed Britain since 2010. Sunak started working for the Conservative Party in 2010. In order to make a place for himself and to attract attention to his specialties, he adopted the best and simplest experiential way. He volunteered to conduct research on UK minority communities for Policy Exchange. During this period he also joined Policy Exchange, a leading Conservative think tank, for which he became head of the Black and Minority Ethnic (BME) research unit in 2014. That year Policy Exchange published a pamphlet 'A Portrait of Modern Britain'. It was written by Sunak along with Saratha Rajeswaran, deputy head of the BME unit.

'A Portrait of Modern Britain' could help politicians understand ethnic minorities and the differences between them. Importantly, there are no European groups among the ethnic minorities it discusses, so from the outset we know it is about race. He felt that for too long, the media had focused on BAME groups. It is treated as a single entity when over 100 different languages were spoken in London playgrounds alone. His report attracted attention. Here is an excerpt from the introduction to this report 'A Portrait of Modern Britain' -

> The face of Britain has changed. A Somali immigrant and a mixed-race girl from Yorkshire were among the heroes of Britain's 2012 Olympic triumph. Mo Farah and Jessica Ennis captured the spirit of the nation and came to represent the incredible diversity of Britain. Black and minority ethnic (BME) people now form a significant and rapidly growing part of the population. However, understanding these communities has not kept pace with their growing importance. From a political point of view, there have been few attempts to properly understand Britain's minority communities and there is a tendency in the media to assume that all BME communities can be treated as a single political entity – as if all ethnic minorities held similar views and lived similar lives.

but clearly there is no single 'BME Almighty'. More than 100 different languages are spoken in London playgrounds alone.[3]

Further in this report -

This report begins by answering the question: 'Who are Britain's BME communities?' It is based on a comprehensive set of survey, census, and academic and polling data. Create a broad picture of the five largest minority communities in the UK. The report outlines the demographics, geography, life experiences, attitudes and socioeconomic status of each of these major ethnic groups. These research findings are brought to life through 'pen portraits' of contributors spanning the worlds of politics, medicine, media, social action and religion.

The conclusions of the report are clear. BME communities will continue to be an ever more important part of Britain. There are clear differences between communities. These differences should be understood by policy makers and politicians. A Portrait of Modern Britain serves as a rich, authoritative and accessible reference guide to further that understanding.[4]

Richmond, Yorkshire

Suddenly, people started talking about him and he started attracting the attention of politicians. When former Tory leader William Hague announced he would not stand for re-election in May 2015 for the rural constituency of Richmond, Yorkshire, one of the safest Tory seats in the country, it was shown to many aspiring leaders. Rishi opted for it. Hague left the seat because he got the feedback from the constituency activists that they had already made up their mind to choose another Yorkshire man to fight the seat. They wanted a farmer but when they found Sunak amidst them they were confused.

Hague recalls now, "Nobody had heard of him but his effect on the association was dramatic. They had in their minds the sort of person they wanted and then this totally different person walked in. To their credit, they did a total U-turn. The key thing is he was obviously very intelligent without any trace of arrogance. That's a very unusual combination in politics. He's an extreme case of that." To those who said, "We miss William Hague, we like William," Rishi replied, "I'm the next William Hague; I just got a better complexion!"

Angus Thompson, president of the Richmond Conservative Association, recalls, "When Sunak became a candidate for Richmond, he needed a solid base in the constituency. There he decided to purchase a stately manor house in the village of Kirby Sigston in Hambleton, about four miles east of Northallerton. This Grade II listed building was set in several acres of parkland and features a beautiful lake. He made a deal with the landlord to rent the place, promising to buy it if he became the local MP." The voters were amused to find Sunak, who doesn't eat beef, learning to milk cows and buying a big house to live there. In his maiden speech, he used a joke he has often told in order to describe how he had fitted in there: "Wandering through an auction market, I was introduced to a farmer as 'the new William Hague'. He looked at me, quizzically, then said, 'Ah yes, Haguey! Good bloke. I like him. Bit pale, though. This one's got a better tan.' [Laughter.]"

Sunak thought that what if a minority wins from a minority seat. There were only two minorities in Sunak's constituency – he and his wife. Sunak joked to his friends about him and his wife being the only immigrant population in the constituency. "To be honest," said Sunak, "I think it's patronizing to assume minorities should only run in minority seats." During those days, Ben Judah ventured to meet Sunak in "the England of hill farmers, poltergeist inns, and the safest Conservative seat in the country" where he sought election from a borough that was home to only 122 desis (and quickly sprouted a sizeable UKIP backlash). Ben Judah, British Journalist and author of *This is London* and *fragile Empire* writes, "Sunak's Billionaire father-in-law, Narayana Murthy, however, was so enthusiastic that he had flown in, and had even been leafleting on his behalf, wearing a Rishi sweatshirt."

The result of the election was announced on May 7, 2015. In the general election he won over 51 percent of the vote with a majority of 19,550. He defeated council group leader Robert Light, former chairman of the local party Wendy Morton and ex-soldier Chris Brannigan.

He organizes a grand feast every year for the people of his constituency. The villagers fondly call him 'The Maharaja of the Dales'. On political ideology, Sunak once jokingly said that his family represents the entire ethnic diversity in his constituency. (His father-in-law used to distribute pamphlets to strangers wearing a T-shirt during the election campaign. Those poor people may not have realized that this old man is not a simple enthusiastic worker, but a prominent rich and respected person of India. We are Indians. Many times the people of India just think of proposing Mr Narayana Murthy's name for the post of the President of India, instead of him Britain has elected his son-in-law.)

His landslide victory in 2015 when David Cameron secured a majority Conservative government was in power was not so remarkable because nobody knew about Sunak and could foretell about his political life. People thought that he was a highly educated rich man who wanted to help the ordinary folk by fixing the things for them. He wanted to give back to the society. He was more like a social activist than a scheming politician. During his early election days, another politician who had his roots in Pakistan met him and found in Sunak the same kind of zeal as he had. Sajid Javid has this to say about him, "He's someone who takes a natural interest in business issues. I felt we were very uch on the same page: on business, the economy, free enterprise, lower taxation, less regulation." Yes, he sees everything with an economic angle and not necessarily with a political one. His tag-line is, " What's the profit?"

Soon after becoming an MP in 2015, Sunak wrote a report for the right-wing think tank, the Center for Policy Studies (CPS), calling for the creation of 'freeports' around the UK. It was co-founded by Margaret Thatcher. The policy idea was that tax-free, non-regulated space would revitalize industrial coastal cities. It was tried in the 1980s by former prime ministers after proving unsuccessful, before being abandoned again by Prime Minister David Cameron in 2012. Sunak also worked for Policy Exchange, another right-wing think tank. Unlike the think tank CPS, it does not declare its donors. Before becoming an MP, and after becoming Chancellor, he lectured at the Institute of Economic Affairs.

In Sunak's brief political career, there were two important turns and twists that changed his life. The first was definitely Brexit in which he joined the Leave group. The second one was favoring Boris Johnson when he was a candidate for the Tory leadership.

Brexit

The EU is the proverbial Waste Land. T.S. Eliot wrote, "Lilacs out of the dead land…what are the roots that cluch, what branches grow out of this stony rubbish? Son of man, you cannot say, or guess, for you know only a heap of broken images, where the sun beats, and the dead tree gives no shelter, the cricket no relief, and the dry stone no sound of water."

'Brexit' is the name given to the departure of the United Kingdom from the European Union. It is a portmanteau of 'Britain' and 'Exit'. A referendum was held to obtain a majority vote to leave the European Union. David Cameron called for a referendum in 2016 on whether Britain should remain in the European Union (EU). The electorate were offered two choices: Remain (in the EU), or Leave. There was no explanation about what 'leaving' meant, or indeed how any future relationship with Britain's largest trading partner might be managed.

Sunak had to decide which side he would back in the EU referendum. He told Nick Robinson he came to the question "with an open mind", was not ideological about it but "went through it analytically…" "I looked through the numbers". He decided to back Leave, in part because "having the flexibility and the nimbleness to adapt" to a rapidly changing world "would be of enormous value to us".

It is said that Sunak's decision to support Leave was not liked by Cameron. He tried to persuade the newly elected MP but Sunak didn't change his stance. As a new MP Sunak took a big risk defying David Cameron to back leave in the referendum. David Cameron says his "greatest regret" is that those who advocated to stay in the EU lost the vote — which ultimately divided the country, paralyzed the government and left Britain increasingly at risk of leaving the European Union without any deal. He writes about it in the new book "*For the Record*"."The greatest regret is that we lost the referendum that I didn't prevail, that we could've fought perhaps a better campaign, we could have conducted perhaps a better negotiation — perhaps the timing wasn't right — and that I didn't take the country with me on what I thought was a really important issue," Cameron said.

According to Imogen Howse, "Sunak was a public supporter of the Leave campaign ahead of the referendum, formerly selling Brexit as a "once in a generation opportunity to take back control". He also said the vote would result in a "freer, fairer and more prosperous" Britain. His voting record on TheyWorkForYou reinforces this stance, with votes against greater integration with the EU revealing an enduring belief in separating the UK from the union. He was also amongst the Tories supporting a no-deal exit back in 2019."[5]

On 23 June 2016, Britain held a referendum on EU membership. The question before voters was: 'Should the United Kingdom remain a member of the European Union or leave the European Union?' 51.89% of voters voted to leave the EU. The UK left the EU on 31 January 2020. A majority vote and a transition period were in place to leave until 31 December 2020. During that time nothing changed and the UK continued to comply with all EU laws and regulations. During this, talks were also held on the new relationship between the UK and the EU. On 24 December 2020, the negotiators of the EU and the UK reached an agreement on the new relationship between the two sides. The EU and the UK set out the terms of the deal in three agreements: Trade and Cooperation Agreement, Information Security Agreement, Nuclear Cooperation Agreement. On January 1, 2021, the rules set in these agreements came into force.

Brexit was seen as a "once-in-a-generation opportunity for Britain to take back control of its own destiny". The 2016 referendum on Britain leaving the European Union Months before, when Boris Johnson came out in support of Brexit in a dramatic turn, Sunak, despite being a lesser-known politician, declared his support. Sunak, a 36-year-old backbencher and newly elected to the House of Commons, did not play a major role in the EU referendum. But by becoming an early supporter of Brexit, Sunak went on to rise unusually quickly in British politics. According to Tony Travers, professor of politics at the London School of Economics, his early support of Brexit "put him on that right side of history within the Conservative Party". No one could say Sunak had escaped that and he could have undermined Brexit. He was a supporter of Brexit, but with a kind of moderate, common-sense Brexit rather than an ideological one."

I read his article on "Why I will vote for Britain to leave the EU" (Friday, 26 February, 2016). It is given here for your perusal.

> IT has been by the far the toughest decision I have had to make since becoming an MP, but on June 23 I will vote to leave the European Union. It pains me that I have reached a different conclusion to people I greatly respect; notably the Prime Minister and my illustrious predecessor, Lord Hague. For me, this is a once in a generation opportunity for our country to take back control of its destiny. Of course, leaving will bring some uncertainty, but on balance I believe that our nation will be freer, fairer and more prosperous outside the EU. Outside the EU, we can decide our own immigration policy, ensure our own laws and courts are sovereign, and enhance our position as a dynamic, outward-looking trading economy.
>
> I have spent my business career working around the world, investing in countries like the US, India and Brazil. I have also helped British companies expand internationally. My own experience convinced me that not only can our businesses thrive in these exciting markets, but that they must. Since we joined the Common Market, Europe's

share of the world economy has halved and is still falling. Whilst China's GDP has doubled since the recession, Europe is the only continent in the world (alongside Antartica, that is) that has failed to grow at all.Canada, South Korea and South Africa all trade freely with Europe without surrendering their independence. As one of Europe's largest customers, I see no sensible reason why we could not achieve a similar agreement. Six million jobs in the EU are linked to UK trade and we buy £60 billion more from Europe than Europe buys from us.

Nationally, only five per cent of businesses export to the EU, yet all businesses are stifled by excessive EU red tape that does everything from mandating the width of our hedgerows to prohibiting our Government from favoring British produce. It is our small, local businesses that would benefit the most as we remove the burden of Brussels bureaucracy.

I believe that appropriate immigration can benefit our country. But we must have control of our borders and we can only do that outside of the EU. As an EU member, every one of Europe's 500 million citizens has a legal right to move here and there is nothing the UK government can do to limit those numbers. It can't be right that unelected officials in Brussels have more say over who can come into our country than you.

Regular readers will know I care a great deal about supporting our local farmers. Many of them are concerned about their future outside of Europe and without the financial support of CAP.

If we leave the EU, we will immediately save £20 billion. UK farmers currently receive £2.5 billion from

CAP so the UK will certainly have the resources to put in place a British Agricultural Policy. Not only could we financially support our farmers but we could also free them from the most costly European regulations.

This is a complex and difficult decision for all of us. In the end, this is not about my vote or that of any other politician. Our future European relationship will be decided by all of you, the British people. I look forward to discussing it with you all over the coming months.[6]

"Post-truth may have delivered Brexit, but it is now the key obstacle in the working of the British government. Johnson has been dubbed as the first post-truth British prime minister and he may well be the last too" comments a historian Shruti Kapila. Of the four post-referendum Tory prime ministers, two, Theresa May and Liz Truss, voted to stay in the European Union. In January 2018, Theresa May made Sunak a junior minister in the Department of Housing, Communities and Local Government, where Sajid Javid was Secretary of State. A year and a half later, Sunak had to decide who to support in the Tory leadership race, and together with two other junior ministers, Oliver Dowden and Robert Jenrick, he supported Johnson. After Johnson had won, he made Sunak Chief Secretary to the Treasury.

Alexander Boris de Pfeffel Johnson voted to leave but he probably did so out of personal ambition. On the other hand, one must remember that Sunak had been a diehard Brexiteer since his schooldays. Writing for his school magazine, *The Wykehamist*, after Tony Blair's New Labour won the 1997 general election, he opined that the new prime minister "has plans for the possible break-up of the United Kingdom and membership of an eventual European Superstate." He voted for' Brexit out of an ideological, economic reality-defying conviction that it was in the country's best interests.'

Britain's story over the years has been one of sad disaster. 'Brexit' was a major blow to the country's ongoing policy and it goes without saying that the country is yet to recover from the cost of exiting the European Union. Brexit saw the UK withdraw from the European single market and customs union, while free movement between member states and the jurisdiction of European courts ended. The UK left the EU in full in January 2021, after years of political wrangling since the divisive referendum in 2016 to split from the bloc.

Alexander Boris de Pfeffel Johnson

During the last general election in 2019, the Tories with the intention of getting 'Brexit' (keeping Britain out of the European Union) made the then Prime Minister Boris Johnson victorious. In other words, Boris Johnson secured his historic win in the 2019 election with a promise to "get Brexit done". He had to pay more attention to those parts of the country that had been left behind as a result of globalization, especially in the industrial north of England.

In his recent book "The Age of the Strongman", foreign affairs editor of the Financial Times Gideon Rachman identified a new global political pattern. Many of the present day leaders fashioned themselves as authentic and wildly popular embodiments of 'the people'. From Jair Bolsonaro in Brazil to Vladimir Putin in Russia to even Xi Jinping in China, Narendra Modi in India, Donald Trump in America and Boris Johnson in the UK, these leaders ' have led their countries towards a more personalized type of leadership that embraces nationalism, a rhetoric of strength and a fierce hostility to liberalism." Boris Johnson too flirted with this style of politics-in his attitudes to law, diplomacy and dissent within his own party.[7]

Across the media, Johnson was praised by many. Tim Shipman of The Sunday Times wrote, "Boris Johnson now squats like a giant toad across British politics." But within a year he was gone. "His fall is the most remarkable political defenestration in modern British political history because so few believed it would ever actually happen." Sebastian Payne wrote in his book on him.

Boris Johnson's tenure was marred by several scandals and he was forced to resign. The three P's in his life –Paterson, Partygate, and Pincher- all of these crises suggested that he was away from the real grip. Whoever meets Sunak will be convinced of his stability, calm nature and seriousness. Indians will not have any problem with his height. He is the polar opposite of the pompous, ostentatious, snooty Boris Johnson. The Greek philosopher Heraclitus said, "Character is destiny." Johnson as prime minister and Sunak as chancellor did not work well together because their views did not match. Johnson's theory was "Cakeism". You can have your cake and eat it too. In policy terms, this meant the magical view that Britain could have a European-style safety net and pay American-style taxes. This is what we Indians call riding two boats together. This irresponsible approach endeared Johnson to the Tory public for a time, but worried Sunak. This was not the thinking of Rishi Sunak. "The Fall of Boris Johnson: The Full Story" has this to say about the role of Rishi Sunak in his fall.

> Sunak became Britain's new prime minister by promising to unite the party. Then he did not say much about Brexit, but it has troubled the country for the last six years and remains the biggest challenge of the government. Addressing this will make it easier to fix the budgetary mess. "One of the great opportunities of Brexit is our ability to do more trade with countries around the world."

Saying this Sunak expresses his opinion. He added: "Let me be unequivocal about this: Under my leadership, the United Kingdom will not pursue any relationship with Europe that relies on alignment with EU laws."[8]

Becoming an MP was the first step in his uninterrupted political career. Many politicians spend their whole lives trying to become chancellor, but Sunak got there in five years. He voted in the 2016 referendum, quickly aligning himself with Johnson, and his only misstep is said to be joining Michael Gove's leadership camp after David Cameron resigned. In 2016 he voted to leave the European Union in the Brexit referendum, arguing that leaving the EU would make Britain "freer, fairer and more prosperous". He called it his "toughest decision since becoming MP" but said it was a "once in a generation opportunity for our country to take back control of its destiny". He rectified this two years later, when Theresa May ousted him in disgrace, and he dutifully returned to Johnson's side. He was rewarded with a cabinet post as Chief Treasury Secretary under the then Chancellor Sajid Javid. He served under Javid, at one point calling him a "mentor" and "good friend" – they watched Star Wars: The Rise of Skywalker together. ("Great night with the boss - Jedi Master @SajidJavid," Sunak now wrote enthusiastically in a tweet.)

Johnson's loyalists believed Sunak's arrival in the Treasury was critical in his downfall. One close ally painted a scenario in which he survived: If SaJ (Javid) had stayed as chancellor and people who had genuine affection and loyalty to the PM had been in Number 10, he could have been alright. The cardinal sin was the loss of the treasury; that created Sunak as a problem. It created economic policy as a problem that could never be managed. 'From the partygate scandal onwards, the chancellor decouped from the Prime minister and began to pursue his own agenda, seen through the series of wobbles that culminated in his resignation and leadership bid. There was paranoia among Team Johnson about his maneuvers, which was not entirely misplaced.[9]

Sunak insisted he wouldn't "demonize" his former boss. "Did I disagree with him? Is he flawed? Yes and so are the rest of us. Is it no longer working? Yes and that is why I resigned," he said in his speech. "But I will have no part in a history that seeks to demonize Boris."Rishi Sunak's conduct highlights, says Peter Osborne, one of the unhappy consequences of having a liar as prime minister. Sunak, a young politician on the rise, was obliged to substantiate Boris Johnson's lies ...to contradict the official line would mean leaving the government.

'No one could deny that those backing Boris Johnson in the leadership contest (which he did not actually take part in) knew exactly who – and what – they were voting for. The same cannot necessarily be said for Rishi Sunak, a man whose career to date has been riddled with contradictions. His supporters say he is a man of the people, while detractors characterize him as "Davos Man" (a reference to his background as an investment banker and hedge fund manager).' The commentary continued: 'If the former Chancellor is to win the ultimate prize (which he has since), he will need to shake off the "slippery Sunak" tag and convince Tory MPs of what he truly stands for.' Today we are in a position to do a comparative study of both Boris Johnson and Rishi Sunak. And we can see that if one is the past, then the other is the rising sun. Boris Johnson was married to Anglo-Indian Marina Wheeler. This marriage lasted for 27 years. He spent the winter holidays in Delhi chatting with his Indian relatives, who were thrilled to have a blond, dashing son-in-law. Some fit the two into Max Weber's equation, saying that Sunak is made of an 'ethics of responsibility', while Johnson seems to be made of his own 'ethics of irresponsibility'. In "The Fall of Boris Johnson: The Full Story" Sebastian Payne concludes, " Johnson was well known as a celebrity politician before he became prime minister, he was chosen by the Conservative party precisely because he did not fit the norms and would break convention to deliver Brexit. It was no surprise that he did not govern in a conventional sense, but few anticipated just how chaotic it would be. Through three Downing Street operations, he failed to make the job fit with his personality... he was always living on his wits, close to the edge, taking risks, bragging his way through, and relying on personality rather than preparation. It is a recipe for the wheels falling off."[10]

The Coronavirous Chancellor

> I know Rishi and I know he's more than up to the role. He's smart, engaging and unfazed by the big responsibilities he faces. He also knows what all chancellors know: spending the money is the easiest bit of the job; raising it is the hardest. George Osborne

Boris Johnson appointed Sunak chancellor on 13 February 2020 after Sajid Javid quit. He had not run a government department before that. Sunak had been chief secretary to the Treasury for the previous seven months. Two months before his promotion the first covid cases had been reported and confirmed in the UK. Sunak was one of the decision makers during the pandemic. He promised to do 'whatever it takes' to support people and businesses through the emergency. Just 39 days after Sunak's promotion Johnson announced the first lockdown. Sunak has always maintained "I will always protect the most vulnerable ...we did it in covid and we will do that again. His message on March 20 was liked by the media and public both. Even his political opponents praised him when he said, "When this is over, and it will be over, we want to look back at this moment and remember the many small acts of kindness done by us and to us. We want to look back on this time & remember how we thought first of others & acted with decency."

Sunak endeared himself to the national consciousness by making appearances at the daily government briefing on the coronavirus. Then when the general public found Boris Johnson evasive and insincere, Sunak appeared to them as a firm and decisive figure who was helping them in their hour of crisis. He provided a massive £30 billion in aid with the promise that no one would be left behind. Previous Tory chancellors had not been so generous. Sunak helped generously. And his confidence freed people from the blood-sucking fly-sucking austerity of the Sajid Javid-era. Sunak was found to be "not in the least swanky or ostentatious" but who can "inspire the country and revitalize the party".

As prime minister in the 1930s, Stanley Baldwin characterized the Conservative Party as an alliance of throne, church, and empire. In the past 10 years, Britain has seen five prime ministers, seven chancellors, six home secretaries and 10 education secretaries. The government had become a joke. In the process, the reservoir of ministerial experience and knowledge seems to have been exhausted. Rishi Sunak has emerged as the most popular chancellor of the 1970s since the Labor Party's Dennis Healy, according to a new poll. Labor voters are also pleased with his performance. According to Ipsos MORI, 64 percent of the British public was satisfied with Sunak's handling of the economy as Chancellor of the Exchequer. Roughly one in five people were dissatisfied, but four were also satisfied. Mori said he was the best leader since Healy in April 1978, with 67 percent of the public supporting him. According to Burton-Cartledge, "Rishi bears a striking resemblance to former

Prime Minister Cameron: economically Thatcherite, but socially liberal. I can't see him cringing back at harsh rhetoric about migrants."

Let me put it this way. There was a collective realization among the people and politicians that here was a man of the moment. They found him smart, energetic and full of empathy. He was just forty years of age but he behaved like a responsible elder to them.

Extract from Chancellor of the Exchequer Rishi Sunak's keynote speech at conservative Party Conference October 2020 in which He reminded his audience that back in 2016, as a newly-minted MP, he was told that his career would be over if he did not back Remain in the EU referendum. Instead, he reminded the Tory activists; he stuck to his principles and backed Leave.

> Being appointed Chancellor in February this year was an immense honor. Even though my first conference speech as Chancellor isn't quite how I expected it to be, it remains a privilege to talk to you today. And I am here today because of so many different people. My family, whose love sustains me. My colleagues in government and in Parliament, whose backing has never wavered. My association in Richmond, North Yorkshire, who placed their trust in me, and my party, whose members, councilors and activities worked tirelessly to deliver a Conservative government in December last year. Politics is a team sport, and there is always a multitude of hardworking people behind any effort.[60]

Sunak becoming prime minister marks his rapid rise to political power. He was first elected as an MP in 2015 and spent two years on the back benches before becoming a junior minister in Theresa May's government. From 2015 to 2017 he was a member of the Environment, Food and Rural Affairs Select Committee and Parliamentary Private Secretary at the Department for Business, Energy and Industrial Strategy. In January 2018 he was appointed to his first ministerial post as Under-Secretary of State at the Ministry of Housing, Communities and Local Government. Sunak became a vocal supporter of Boris Johnson's party, and, when Johnson became leader and prime minister, he too rewarded Sunak with a promotion. Johnson gave Sunak his first major government role, appointing him as Chief Secretary to the Treasury in July 2019 and then promoted him as Chancellor in 2020. He became the Finance Minister of the UK. After a long time a leader like Sunak came forward as one of the more intelligent, civilized and calm personalities to lead the British Government. He inherited a crumbling public sector that was flawed in almost every way.

During Sunak's tenure as second-in-command at the Treasury Ministry, tensions were rising between his boss, Chancellor of the Exchequer Sajid Javid, and Johnson. When Javid resigned in February 2020, Johnson replaced Sunak, who at age 39 became the fourth youngest person to hold that position. Almost immediately Sunak was faced with manifold challenges due to the arrival of the COVID-19 pandemic in the UK.

Sunak has experience fighting economic crises, handling the UK during the COVID-19 pandemic, and has presented himself as a 'sound finance' candidate. During the pandemic, Sunak introduced £400 billion ($452 billion) of measures aimed at boosting the economy, including a generous furlough scheme, business loans and restaurant dining discounts. But that stimulus came at a huge cost and the government has been scrambling to find ways to save. As the British economy was shut down by the government-enforced lock down, Sunak employed the powers of his office to try to economize and offset this. The wage subsidy for employees was aimed at job retention and to ease the burden of the lockdown for individuals.

Sunak's "Eat Out to Help Out" scheme, which aimed to support restaurants and pubs with government-subsidized food and drink, was seen by some observers as an encouraging success, but some critics saw it as a way to increase Covid-19 indicated as playing an important role in Nevertheless, Sunak's image as a super slick, social-media savvy, impeccably dressed, handsome, but down-to-earth politician went on during the pandemic. You would be surprised to know that when the whole world was crying foul in 2020, the English media was busy calling Rishi Sunak "Dishie Rishi" and "Britain's Sexiest MP".

Revelations

But this euphoria after some time turned into an outcry. There were some revelations that had to be given. In April 2022, there were some revelations about Sunak. Perhaps most alarming was the revelation that his wife, who is an Indian citizen and non-domicile had unaccounted wealth. Murty was a non-dom: she paid British taxes on any earnings in the UK but not on any income overseas and elsewhere which was a perfectly legal choice. She retains her Indian citizenship just as Nick Clegg's wife, Miriam, had retained her Spanish citizenship when he was in government. The act is believed to have saved £20 million ($24 million) in UK taxes over a period of around seven and a half years. Her act was not illegal but it adversely affected Sunak's credibility and growing reputation. As a protective husband, Sunak found it "very upsetting" when his wife was targeted. Her money was her money, and the stake she held in the multibillion-pound family business Infosys was strictly her business and he was not to be blamed. He even compared himself to the actor Will Smith, who lashed out at the comedian Chris Rock after the latter joked about his wife's hair.

The result was that Akshata Murty quickly revised her tax status, stating that she did not intend evading taxes, and that it was the right course of action according to her. Sunak's patriotism was also questioned. It was learned that he had decided to stay in the U.S. until the end of October 2021. Green card was taken. Due to this, there was a possibility of sending the message to the people that if they failed, they would leave the country and settle in America.

Partygate

Partygate was a political scandal in the United Kingdom in 2020 and 2021 regarding parties and other gatherings of prominent leaders and staff of the government and Conservative Party held during the COVID-19 pandemic, when public health restrictions prohibited most gatherings. While the country was under several lockdowns, they ate, drank and danced. The unruly aides not only broke the rules when they went to the garden of Prime Minister's official residence number 10, they also broke the swing of the Prime Minister's newborn baby while that same morning, the Queen, following England's COVID-19 rules at the time, attended the funeral of the Duke of Edinburgh. But Rishi Sunak, one of the most prominent ministers in the government, gave indirect support to the Prime Minister.

Staying away from the glare of the media, he said, "The Prime Minister was right to apologize, and I support his request for patience." Reports of the incidents attracted the attention of the media, police and general public. Public reaction and political controversy ensued. At the end of January 2022, twelve such parties were investigated by the Metropolitan Police, with at least three attended by then Prime Minister Boris Johnson.

Police issued 126 fixed penalty notices (FPNs) to 83 individuals who police found had committed offenses under COVID-19 regulations, including Johnson, his wife Carrie Johnson and Chancellor of the Exchequer Rishi Sunak, who all apologized and paid the fine.

In April 2022, Sunak was fined by the police for violating the government's rules against social gatherings at that stage of the pandemic by being among the guests at Johnson's office birthday party in 2020. He claimed that his attendance at the party was unintentional and was the result of showing up early for a meeting with the Prime Minister. Sunak said he had been working all day and "meeting with MPs". He thought that the number 10 ceremony and drinking was a "work event". He clearly did not want to make any direct statements supporting Johnson that would harm him, especially when he's eyeing the top job himself.

A poll of party members by the 'Conservative Home' website on the same day found Sunak easily top of cabinet satisfaction ratings, with Johnson placed at the bottom of the list. This was in contrast to a poll in December 2020, in which Conservative Party members were asked who should take the post after Johnson stepped down, with only five out of 1,191 naming Sunak. Describing Johnson and Sunak as 'Tory Thelma and Louise' and 'the loan shark chancellor and his innocent cronies', Labor pulled their guns fully on Sunak as they began to believe that Sunak would be the future Prime Minister and the next Tory would be the leader. Whatever happened, there was a lot of grit. As many words as many words!

The consequences of this incident did not prove to be so serious for Sunak, but the Prime Minister had to accept it. This 'Partygate' scandal has put Johnson on fire. A series of scandals involving Johnson unfolded one after the other. Allegations of sexual misconduct by the prime minister against former Conservative deputy chief whip Chris Pincher began to be discussed. Sunak and Javid both resigned from the cabinet on 5 July 2022.

In the book "The Fall of Boris Johnson: The Full Story" by Sebastian Payne, the narrative starts with this scandal.

> What Johnson should have done at this stage was to tell MPS that his team would look in to what had happened and he would report back. Instead, the prime minister and his allies became 'like rabbits in the headlights', according to one official. "They just got caught and went further and further with the denials. The issue was that too many in the prime minister's core team were directly implicated in partygate. Within the Cabinet, it dawned that a real scandal was brewing. One member said, "It's the classic Watergate lesson, the cover-up is worse than the event."

Political events can be classified as turning points or talking points. Though partygate was not a political event, yet it was a turning point and the talking point both.

On 5 July 2022, Sunak and Health Secretary Javid resigned almost simultaneously amid a scandal surrounding the sexual harassment allegations against Chris Pincher, which arose after it was revealed that Johnson had promoted Pincher to the position despite knowing of the allegations beforehand. Sunak was the second of 61 Conservative MPs to resign during the government crisis. Sunak resigned as he could no longer tolerate Johnson's lies, laziness and deadly lack of seriousness. In fact, he resigned in protest. In his resignation letter Sunak said: "The public rightly expects the government to be conducted properly, competently, and seriously," Sunak scolded him in his resignation letter. "I recognise this may be my last ministerial job, but I believe these standards are worth fighting for." In his resignation letter, he also wrote "Our people know that if something is too good to be true then it's not true."

He resigned in protest at what he saw as a culture of dishonesty and unforgivable ducking of hard questions. His resignation caused uproar within the Conservative Party. There was a lot of criticism. There were disputes. Johnson was forced to resign as party leader. Although some Tories also criticized Sunak's behavior, they did not spare Johnson. They announced their intention to replace him as leader. Johnson was forced to step down. Johnson remained as a caretaker prime minister, and the party began to select his replacement.

Boris Johnson can be compared with Shakespeare's 'King Lear'. The play's betrayal speaks directly to the endless in-fighting in the Tory party. Lear repents having ignored his people:

> Poor naked wretches, wheresoe'er you are,
>
> That bide the pelting of this miserable storm,
>
> How shall your houseless heads and unfed sides,
>
> Your looped and windowed raggedness defend you
>
> From seasons such as these? Oh, I have ta'en
>
> Too little care of this!

On 8 July 2022, Sunak stood in the Conservative party leadership election to replace Johnson. Sunak launched his campaign in a video posted to social media, writing that he would "restore trust, rebuild the economy and reunite the country." He said his values were "patriotism, fairness, hard work". Sunak pledged to "crack down on gender neutral language". Sunak's pledges during the campaign included tax cuts only when inflation was under control, scrapping of the 5% VAT rate.

The Parliamentary Party of Conservative MPs narrowed the field of candidates for the leadership from eight to two by their votes. At the end of that process, Sunak and Foreign Secretary Liz Truss remained the two candidates as the final pair. The names of these two were put to vote by the entire membership of the party.

Sunak was the first candidate or candidate of his kind. He was the first Hindu to lead Britain. He had to put in some extra labor to win. Some doubts had to be cleared. To achieve this goal, he had to dispel the perception among some conservatives that he would not be able to understand the needs of the average British citizen in a time of catastrophic inflation because they are so wealthy. The British hoped that the country would benefit from his ability. Lord Salisbury said many years ago that the British electorate would never agree to be represented by a 'black man'. But that was a thing of the past.

Liz Truss and those Wretched Weeks

Mary Elizabeth Truss is from the Conservative Party. She was 47 years old, and had been an MP for 12 years and a cabinet minister for eight years, having been in cabinet with three prime ministers. She was born in Oxford, and grew up in Scotland and then Leeds in the north of England. She also briefly lived in Canada before taking the tried and tested route to Westminster. She also took a degree in philosophy, politics and economics from the University of Oxford. Truss is married to accountant Hugh O'Leary, with whom she has two daughters. She shares the values of the Christian faith and the Church of England, but is not a regular practicing religious person.

Truss looked to easily defeat his rival Rishi Sunak by wooing the Conservative Party grassroots with the promise of reducing taxes from day one. The just-published book 'Out of the Blue' by Harry Cooley and James Healey tracks Liz Truss' transformation from geeky teen Lib Dem to Tory PM, revealing the events of her office and the month-by-month scenario — that's what Liz Truss says, only to plunge her administration into chaos and announce her resignation after a record-breaking 44 days. Target achieved.

She was a high-profile, self-proclaimed loyalist leader during her three turbulent years in office under her predecessor, Boris Johnson. Many Tories assumed that Johnson had been brought down primarily by his Chancellor of the Exchequer, Rishi Sunak, or by a malicious media conspiracy led by the BBC, but Liz Truss, Johnson's foreign secretary, was freed from the stigma of betrayal. In the leadership contest that followed Johnson's forced resignation; many considered Sunak his rightful successor.

Truss insisted that she was not a Margaret Thatcher clone or duplicate (although Truss has been seen emulating the late Conservative Prime Minister Margaret Thatcher's best dress and mannerisms). Ms Truss was a Remainer, but even before the race began, she posed herself as a follower of Margaret Thatcher, In August 2022, Truss enticed party members by promising a new and revitalized British economy following Margaret Thatcher's path. To do this she promised sweeping tax cuts along with new spending. Truss claimed she would promote economic growth without hurting public finances. Sunak called her plans "fairy-tale economics". He told the BBC at the time, "Liz's plans are promising too much for everyone. I don't think you can eat your cake and have it at the same time." He warned that her plan could increase inflation and cause a reaction in financial markets.

Chris Blackhurst, a former editor of The Independent, commented that in the UK PM race, "dishy" Rishi Sunak rose like a soufflé and fell flat. "Truss was nice but no superstar, and definitely not a future leader. For seven weeks, while the contest has been meandering along ("raged" is putting it far too strongly), Mr Sunak has been fighting a losing battle." As a former editor Blackhurst has really pinpointed one of the reasons for his defeat, "It did not assist Mr Sunak's cause that the right-wing press were against him. The Telegraph, Sun and Mail all backed Ms Truss, often attacking Mr Sunak with venom. Their favourite "Dishy Rishi" was long gone. Only The Times was in his corner."

Liz Truss ran her leadership campaign largely promising of cutting taxes and curbing trade union power, while also pledging to be tough on crime. Rishi Sunak, initially opted to take a more cautious approach, prioritizing 'responsible' public finances and ruling out personal tax cuts until inflation is "under control". Later he announced he will cut the basic rate of income tax from 20% to 16% by the end of the next parliament if he becomes prime minister. Meanwhile, writing in The Daily Telegraph, Sunak proclaimed: "I am a Thatcherite, I am running as a Thatcherite and I will govern as a Thatcherite." Mr Sunak, could not make the proper connection with the MPs. It is said that He was seen by those who were voting, as too brainy,to intelligent, too sharp, too quick and smart. They saw Sunak's behaviour differently, categorising him as a traitor, a Brutus that knifed their fair-haired Caesar.

When the election results were announced on 5 September, Sunak received 42.6 percent of the vote, compared to 57.4 percent for Truss. She was declared leader and became the prime minister. Sunak sat down in defeat. Perhaps he lost because he was seen as Brutus, he behaved too much like a masculine man, and Truss's only mantra signaled the retreat to conservative ideology. In an article for The Times today, Sathnam Sanghera argues that Mr Sunak's leadership campaign is "a clear illustration of how white privilege works", because despite being "by far the most qualified candidate … he has still had to prove himself repeatedly against utterly woeful white candidates." Another Indian scholar Shruti Kapila, professor of Indian history and global political thought at the University of Cambridge, said that there are many reasons why Rishi Sunak lost UK PM chair. But race isn't the main one. Her forecast was: Sunak will likely join the global elite of billionaire clubs that he truly belongs to and do what they do—make money while spending luxuriously. As the man who nearly became the first Indian-origin prime minister of the UK, Sunak will above all be remembered for his wealth, at a time when Britain became much poorer and far more unequal… Sunak's career marks the point of divergence between the once twinned politics of imperial Britain and the Indian nation.[11]

Truss lasted only six weeks. The personality-driven populism that marked Boris Johnson's premiership was already over. Truss brought nothing but confusion. A love for former PM Margaret Thatcher and her mantra of "low tax, high growth" brought by Truss could install her as leader—even if for all of 45 days— but could not sustain her. Thatcher, ghosts and all, was truly over. Unlike Margaret Thatcher, who used her magic as Leader of the Opposition to prepare the British public for radical change, Truce foisted them on an unhappy public without warning.

Truss is known for her economically liberal views and her support for free trade. She supports the neoliberal philosophy of supply-side economics, often referred to derogatorily as "trickle-down economics." She founded the Free Enterprise Group of Conservative MPs, a pro-free market collection of parliamentarians arguing for a more entrepreneurial economy and fewer employment laws. Truss's chancellor Kwasi Kwarteng presented a mini-budget, which pushed Britain into economic catastrophe overnight. First, she sacrificed her chancellor, who was clearly on a suicide mission and was being nicknamed by public as 'Kamikaze Kwarteng'. Secondly, the Indian-origin Suella (dubbed Cruella) Braverman's prejudiced and hateful views on race stalled the Free Trade Agreement with India. Braverman's blistering resignation letter warned Truss for not sticking to her right-wing guns. She was extremely critical of Liz Truss, "I have concerns about the direction of this government."

Not only did people drown, the ministers themselves also drowned. Inflation soared and markets already spooked by dismal performance from the Bank of England rebelled. When Margaret Thatcher was made to resign against her wishes as prime minister, she had famously lamented: "I never lost a general election; I never lost a confidence vote in the House of Commons; I never lost majority support within the Conservative Party; and yet I am out of office." Liz Truss could express a similar sentiment. In fact one day she firmly declared "I am a fighter, not a quitter", and the very next day she was out of office through some mysterious process.

The shelf-life of Truss as Prime Minister was shorter than that of cabbage bought from the farmyard. (There were some questions about whether it was actually a head of lettuce and not cabbage.) I don't say this, the whole world said and ridiculed her. Like the Solomon Grundy of the nursery rhyme, who was born on a Monday and buried on a Sunday ("That was the end of Solomon Grundy"), Britain's one of the youngest prime ministers boasted of her 45 days in office after one The humiliating ending slammed "I'm a fighter and I'm not going to quit."

Capitalizing on the prime minister's loosening grip of power, 'The Daily Star' started broadcasting a live feed of a head of lettuce purchased at a Tesco for 60 pence next to a picture of Truss, and asked the question, "Will Liz Truss still be Prime Minister within the 10-day shelf-life of a lettuce?" This proved to be the shortest tenure in British history so far. Her effort to impose £45 billion ($50 billion) in tax cuts while capping energy prices for two years ran a huge budget deficit and promised to open up fractured financial markets. Sunak was a severe critic of Truss' economic plan, as his plan was panned by investors, the International Monetary Fund and credit rating agencies. The U.S. President, Joe Biden, called Liz Truss's original economic policies "a mistake" and said the economic turmoil that followed the government's mini-budget had been "predictable". While Sunak also advocated for lower taxes, he said tax cuts could only be made after inflation was brought under control, which could take several years. His warning over the summer that the truce's unfunded tax cuts could panic financial markets came true. When Truss and his Chancellor Kwesi Kwarteng revealed their plan, the British pound fell to a record low against the US dollar. UK government bond prices rose at the fastest pace ever, causing the cost of borrowing to skyrocket. Although Conservative Party rules protected Truss from a vote on his leadership for a year, discontent among Conservative MPs grew rapidly, and calls for his resignation grew. Truss announced his resignation on 20 October. The world's oldest election winning machine, the party of Disraeli, Churchill and Thatcher - the party of Boris Johnson - had turned itself into a global laughing stock. Even the head of the UK supermarket chain Tesco has come out in the open and said it had no concrete plans for growth. The US President, Joe Biden, called Liz Truss's economic policies "a mistake" and said the economic turmoil that would follow the government's mini-budget was "predictable".

It is quite clear that Truss was no Thatcher, even if the Tory party had chosen her as its leader. Truss, Maria Zakharova comments, would be best remembered for her 'catastrophic illiteracy'. Mr. Johnson didn't haunt Liz Truss, like Banquo's ghost tormented Shakespeare's Macbeth because Ms. Truss served a mere 50 days. Again there was a need to search for a prime minister. Sunak's main political rivals, Boris Johnson and Liz Truss, were defeated and were unlikely to return. Senior leaders of the party rallied behind Sunak. The share market and the market slowly started breathing a sigh of relief.

Between 1989 and 1999, India had five general elections and seven different prime ministers. Liz Truss may have lost her mind before 45 days, but her term was three times longer than Atal Bihari Vajpayee's 1996 term. That's why we should not make fun of anyone. Let us also not forget that over the past 25 years UK governments have elected MPs to push through a range of constitutional changes. The result of some important steps taken was that parliamentary sovereignty continued to weaken within., devolution of power to elected assemblies in Scotland and Wales; House of Lords reform, the creation of the Supreme Court, party leaders being elected by party members rather than MPs, holding a referendum on electoral reform, Scottish independence, and Brexit are just some of the steps that have had far-reaching consequences.

This time, 100 nominations from 357 Conservative MPs were required for the candidate to be eligible. This meant that only three candidates could advance for consideration. Three months earlier, Jeremy Hunt had finished eighth out of eight candidates in the race to become prime minister. Some now felt that they would now be able to undertake the rescue of Britain from Ms Truss' failed financial experiment. Hunt wrote in the Daily Telegraph, "To restore stability and confidence, we need a leader who can be trusted to make difficult choices. We also need someone who can make those choices public members who are concerned about jobs, mortgages and public service. We have a leader who can do that, in Rishi Sunak." Rishi Sunak supporters have started pitching him as the British equivalent of a technocratic Mario Draghi: the only man who can calm the gilts. He presented himself as the candidate brave enough to confront audiences with tough trade-offs. "In this leadership election, I haven't taken the easy road," he said.

The Second Coming

Again the two finalists were to be voted on by the party membership. Rishi Sunak was not as reckless as Ms. Truss, but he lacked Mr. Johnson's brash personality and charisma, leaving many MPs at a loss. Sunak, who still had widespread support among MPs, became their initial choice.

Following Truss's resignation on 20 October 2022, Penny Mordaunt (Penelope Mary Mordaunt) of the House of Commons was the first candidate to announce her candidacy. Mordaunt made a second bid to become Conservative leader and Prime Minister. She pulled out of the election after being unable to gain the necessary endorsement of 100 MPs, allowing Rishi Sunak to become leader unopposed. Sunak later retained Mordaunt in his cabinet, continuing as leader of the House of Commons.

Defense Secretary Ben Wallace has been a popular choice, but he always chose not to, and first he gave Johnson his conditional endorsement. Following the July 2022 United Kingdom government crisis, Wallace was seen as a contender to become the next leader of the Conservative Party and thus Prime Minister, but he ruled himself out from entering the contest. on 10 July. In a statement on Twitter, he said his focus was on his current job and "keeping this great country safe". He later endorsed Liz Truss in the election. Following the election of Truss as Prime Minister, Wallace was reappointed to his post on 6 September. He went on to retain his post when Rishi Sunak became prime minister on 25 October.

Boris Johnson had resigned only a few months earlier, yet he wanted to come back. He was on vacation in the Dominican Republic, he ran back on foot. Voters said that Boris has an uncanny ability to bamboozle people; they (the voters) were perplexed. They (Johnson and Sunak) were once close allies — two Tory Brexiteers working at the very top of government to steer Britain through the pandemic. They then became the deadliest of enemies, when the apprentice knifed his master in the back and embarked on a fruitless campaign to pinch his job. Now the poisonous rivalry between Boris Johnson and Rishi Sunak has reached its dramatic third act — an extraordinary struggle to take back control of the Conservative Party following the disaster of Liz Truss' brief tenure." Commented Politico.[12]

But cutting short his Caribbean holiday to try to resolve a cost of living crisis was not good politics. Though he garnered public support from some of the Brexiteer like Jacob Rees-Mogg and in the pro-Boris media, it was not enough. First, Johnson tried to strike a "deal" with Rishi Sunak but didn't succeed. He bowed out insisting he had the required 100 nominations to make the ballot, but realized he would not be able to form a stable government. On October 23, the day before the nomination, Johnson withdrew from the candidacy. Perhaps he had noticed that by then more than half the MPs had already committed to nominating Sunak. He realized and came to understand that no ousted prime minister has returned to No. 10 in nearly 40 years, since Labour's Harold Wilson in 1974. Nobody since Bonar Law in the 1920s has led the Conservative Party twice. His chances were zero.

The third contender, Penny Mordaunt was falling short of the 100 MPs' votes needed to send the leadership contest to a vote of the grassroots party members. Penny Mordaunt was unlikely to win because of her lack of experience. Her failure to garner enough nominations to run in the leadership election left the way clear for Sunak. When Mordaunt dropped out shortly before the deadline, the way was cleared for Sunak. She wrote on Twitter: "We have chosen our next Prime Minister. This decision is a historic one and shows, once again, the diversity and talent of our party." She added that Sunak has her "full support". He was the only remaining candidate to be confirmed as leader of the party, setting the stage for him to become prime minister. "The UK has had enough entertainment for a generation," remarked Robert Shrimsley in the Financial Times, speaking on behalf of the exasperated British capitalist class, "and now desperately needs a period of undramatic stable government." Former health secretary Matt Hancock had said then . "His style of leadership is diligent and thoughtful, which makes it easy to support him, not only when he's making decisions you agree with but even when he's making decisions you don't." "I back Rishi Sunak to be our next PM. He has the plan and credibility to: restore financial stability, help get inflation down and deliver sustainable tax cuts over time; and unite the Conservatives by bringing the best talent into government to deliver for the British people," tweeted former Cabinet minister Dominic Raab, among the first of nearly 50 MPs to openly declare support for Sunak.

What a strange charisma of politics, democracy and destiny that in December 2019, Boris Johnson was elected Prime Minister by a vote of about 14 million people, in September 2022 Liz Truss was elected by 140,000 Tory members and two months before that Sunak became prime minister just by saying 'yes' to more than two hundred Tory MPs. British democracy is so old that it has become more flexible now. He won the approval of 202 Tory MPs to replace Liz Truss as prime minister. Newsnight's political editor Nick Watt said then that "his colleagues find him "very personable", but also someone who is very clear and certain in what he thinks."

Journalist Anita Pratap in her opinion- piece reminded her readers of a parable as follows: The early bird catches the worm, but the second mouse gets the cheese. Rishi Sunak lost to early bird Liz Truss in the September Tory race to become party leader and British prime minister. But in the second race to the top to replace her, Sunak became the clever mouse that got the cheese—the tempting, to-die-for trophy that British politicians covet. He became the 57th prime minister of the United Kingdom, with much broader party and public support than his predecessor.

The rationale for choosing Mr. Sunak was that as former Chancellor of the Exchequer, Sunak was trusted and respected by the market and could stabilize the exchange rate and the market for government bonds .The regulation was set by motion and as a result everything went topsy-turvy. Sunak had proved his worth on both the economic and business fronts. His handling of the British economy as Chancellor of the Exchequer during the pandemic had been widely praised and had consistently spoken of the need for more foreign investment and trade. After Liz Truss' brief tenure ended in failure due to inadequate economic policy, it had become increasingly important for Sunak to live up to his reputation and resolve.

Liz Truss had done her successor a huge favor by showing her how markets respond to negligence. The Labor Party condemned her for this, and several Conservative MPs also lashed out. Hence no party and parliamentarian could expect any credibility if they advocated re-use of 'magic money tree'. The Bank of England was now expected to raise interest rates to six per cent by the end of the year, raising household bills for millions of mortgage-holders and hitting business investors hard but good for the economy.

At the time of Rishi Sunak becoming Prime Minister, something similar happened during the time of India's Dr. Manmohan Singh (his former secretary even wrote a book by the same name on this feat). Partly it's the roundabout way they got to 10 Downing Street, but it's almost like a silver medalist winning a gold medal after the pre-declared winner fails a drug test. Perhaps how a leading commentator Minhaz Merchant puts it in a more befitting manner than I could when he signs off in his two part write-up "Race and Rishi": Rishi Sunak is the first non-white British prime minister among 57 past British prime ministers. Despite the compulsion—and compulsion it is—of multiculturism, a general election in Britain would not have resulted in him being prime minister. It took the toxic prime ministerships of Boris Johnson and Liz Truss and the economic crisis caused by the Russia- Ukraine war to convince Conservative Party MPs that Sunak was the most sensible choice to serve as interim prime minister.[13]

The Address: I am not daunted

Rishi Sunak made his first official speech as Prime Minister of the United Kingdom on 25 October 2022. Shortly after meeting with King Charles III at Buckingham Palace, the new Prime Minister addressed onlookers, fellow MPs, and most importantly, the public, to set the tone for his new administration and outline some key priorities. While his acceptance speech on 24 October was remarkably brief, this speech was to the point. Sunak's tone was somber and sober and contained no sense of celebration and merry-making. He thanked his predecessor's Prime Minister for his "noble objective" of reforming and bringing changes in development, but did not hesitate to say - "but some mistakes were made. Not maliciously, or not bad under stress - quite the opposite in fact - but mistakes nonetheless. And I have been elected as the leader of my party and your prime minister, in part, to try to fix them."

Solving problems was at the heart of this entire address. Sunak said, "economic stability and confidence" would be at the center of his agenda and that "difficult decisions would have to be made." It was a signal for the cuts that he and his chancellor, possibly Jeremy Hunt, will pursue to rein in public spending in the coming weeks. Besides, he promised to fulfill the promises made in the 2019 manifesto. He included promises of a 'stronger NHS, better schools, safer roads, control of our borders, protecting our environment, supporting our armed forces, raising standards and building an economy that embraces opportunity'. It also pledged that they would prioritize Brexit as well. He also added that: 'I also understand that I have to work to restore trust after what has happened'. He tried to tell all that he understands his dharma well. "I understand that I have work to do to restore trust after all that has happened," he said. "Trust is earned and I will earn yours." It will be a difficult task, that's for certain but he has determination to conquer and defeat all difficulties.

Let me remind you that Sunak was Chief Secretary to the Treasury from 2019 to 2020 and Chancellor of the Exchequer from 2020 to 2022. Then as Prime Minister he now says that we are in deep economic trouble. Anyone would be surprised to hear this.

Sunak Ministry

Rishi Sunak was invited by King Charles III to replace Liz Truss as Prime Minister of the United Kingdom on 25 October 2022, following Truss's resignation and the subsequent Conservative leadership election. The Sunak ministry was formed from the 58th Parliament of the United Kingdom, as a Conservative majority government. Sunak began appointing his cabinet on 25 October 2022.

On his first day as Prime Minister, he assembled a Cabinet that included some safe bets, a few familiar faces - and one highly controversial choice.

Jeremy Hunt remained as chancellor, a role he was given during the Truss ministry after Kwasi Kwarteng was dismissed on 14 October. Dominic Raab was also re-appointed Deputy Prime Minister and Justice Secretary, a role he was given during the premiership of Boris Johnson. James Cleverly remained as Foreign Secretary with Suella Braverman returning as Secretary of State for the Home Department, a role from which she had previously resigned during the Truss ministry. Ben Wallace remained as Secretary of State for Defence, a role from which he had previously during the Johnson and Truss ministries. Michael Gove returned as Levelling Up Secretary, a role he was sacked from by Johnson, and Grant Shapps was demoted from Home Secretary to Secretary of State for Business, Energy and Industrial Strategy. Penny Mordaunt remained as Leader of the House of Commons and Lord President of the Council, roles from which she had during the Truss ministry. Other key appointments include Simon Hart as Parliamentary Secretary to the Treasury and Chief Whip of the House of Commons, Nadhim Zahawi as Party Chairman, Oliver Dowden as Chancellor of the Duchy of Lancaster, Thérèse Coffey as Environment Secretary, Mel Stride as Work and Pensions Secretary and Mark Harper as Transport Secretary.

Sunak was criticized because he appointed Gavin Williamson and Dominic Raab to the cabinet. Both were accused of bullying, a charge they both denied. Williamson resigned after allegations that he used improper language to former Chief Whip Wendy Morton and had bullied several staffers during his time as a Cabinet minister under Theresa May. Raab faces an independent investigation into complaints arising from his prior tenures as Lord Chancellor and Foreign Secretary under Boris Johnson. Sunak was also criticized for returning Braverman to the cabinet, despite her being previously sacked by Truss for breaking the Ministerial Code; Braverman left Truss's government due to an alleged security breach when Braverman shared secure information with a colleague. Sunak said that his appointments to the government were in an attempt to reflect a "unified party".

Thatcherism

Mrgaret Hilda Thatcher, Baroness Thatcher, LG, OM, DStJ, PC, FRS, HonFRSC (13 October 1925 – 8 April 2013), was Prime Minister of the United Kingdom from 1979 to 1990 and Leader of the Conservative Party from 1975 to 1990. She was the first female British prime minister and the longest-serving British prime minister of the 20th century. Margaret Thatcher attempted to stir Britain from its economic decline with policies encouraging hard work and entrepreneurship during her 11 years as British PM. She practiced what she preached. She got by on only four hours of sleep daily, nodding off after a regular glass of whisky. As prime minister, she implemented economic policies that became known as Thatcherism.

There are people who say that Sunak is a zealous Thatcherite who have provided tax cuts for the rich with a multi-millionaire infamous for providing tax cuts for himself and his family. Sunak believes that Margaret Thatcher was the best leader of the Conservative Party during the first Tory election in Yorkshire because of her many electoral victories and the many changes she made to improve the countryIn Rishi's own words, his family values were shaped by the best principles of Thatcherism—hard work and success. And in his early life, Thatcher's grocery store was replaced by Sunak's pharmacy counter. (We may even get a glimpse of the Thatcherite ethos in the rise of her father-in-law, Narayan Murthy, a story of which his well-behaved son-in-law and prime minister is so proud of.) In short, Margaret Thatcher is the ideological core of Sunak. As a Conservative, he is often urged to follow Thatcher and Lawson's legacy.. He has always been a "people must look after themselves first" Thatcherite. He is a believer in common sense, not theory. He is a "modern non-ideological conservative". If Sunak, from his bundle of experience, can bring forth the ever-cautious old Thatcherian fortitude and ideological clarity for his proven credentials as an administrator, it will be great. As a newly elected MP in 2015 he argued that "public spending should not exceed 37 percent of GDP in normal times", an arbitrary figure that only revealed Sunak's ideological leanings. Today, in a new era of permanent crisis, such a figure can only be achieved through turbo-austerity and a sharp break with European norms. In 2016, Sunak wrote a report for the Center for Policy Studies. The Institute is a think tank co-founded by Thatcher., In this report, you have championed free ports, created economic zones free from standard taxes and regulations, etc. For Sunak, who supported Leave in the 2016 EU referendum, the appeal of Brexit was to tilt the UK in an even more pro-market direction. Their aim has been to fulfill the unfulfilled dream of Margaret Thatcher. In many ways, Sunak is Britain's most Thatcher-like prime minister after Thatcher herself. She is today portrayed as a centrist, declaring in July 2022 that "I am running as a Thatcher and I will govern as a Thatcher".

I am tempted to add that both Rishi and Margaret Thatcher are not that tall in height, she is five feet five inches and he is only five feet six inches, but both of them have commendable political stature. The British media respects him as a Dishi Rishi, and his charismatic personality is no less feared in the anti-Labour Party. It should be expected that like Thatcher, Rishi will also take strict steps to bring economic reforms back on track through strictness.

"Rishi Sunak isn't a centrist technocrat – he's a proud Thatcherite. The new prime minister represents the same free-market world-view favoured by Liz Truss. His ascension represents a triumph for the conservatives' Thatcherite wing. Tory members were offered two varieties of neo-liberalism: Reagnite tax cuts from Truss or Thatcherite fiscal discipline from Sunak. The implosion of the former has created the ideal pretext for the latter." George Eaton, senior editor of the New Statesman further says, "In his technocratic aloofness, Sunak resembles an IMF official poised to impose a "structural adjustment programme" on a stricken developing world economy. After Liz Truss's kamikaze economics, the UK once again has a "grown-up" at the wheel. The narrative has been set: Sunak is an unbiased, competent leader who will administer harsh but necessary medicine."[14]

Rwanda plan

"It is lawful for the government to make arrangements to relocate asylum seekers to Rwanda and for their asylum claims to be determined there." Lord justice Lewis announcing the High Court's decision on Rwanda deportations.

The Rwanda asylum plan (officially the UK and Rwanda Migration and Economic Development Partnership, also known as the Rwanda asylum scheme, Rwanda plan and Rwanda deal) is an immigration policy first proposed by the British government, whereby people identified by the United Kingdom as being illegal immigrants or asylum seekers will be relocated to Rwanda for processing, asylum and resettlement. Those successful in claiming asylum will remain in Rwanda and not be permitted to return to the United Kingdom. The first flight under this plan received legal clearance from the High Court and was scheduled for 14 June 2022. A last-minute interim measure by the European Court of Human Rights led to the flight being canceled.

Sunak's policy preferences make it clear that he is against outsiders. This was also one of his issues when he was contesting against TRS for the post of Prime Minister. Sunak has been a strong supporter of the "Rwanda Plan", pledging over the summer to cap the number of refugees Britain would take each year and promising to do "whatever it takes" to make the asylum plan succeed - such as tightening up the definition of who was eligible to claim asylum. Once he told BBC Radio 4: "This country has a proud history of welcoming people but it's also vital that we're in control of who's coming here."

He also proposes to move immigrants who enter the UK illegally to Rwanda. The controversial policy would involve an initial payment of £120 million to Rwanda in return for sending any refugees of the UK's choice (a pilot program is proposed to start with 1,000 people). The lump sum amount will be replenished if more expatriates are accepted in that country. "Law-abiding citizens are disheartened when they see boat after boat full of illegal immigrants coming their way and our sailors and coast guard seem powerless to stop them," he said on Twitter. "Every year thousands and thousands of people come into the UK illegally," Sunak warns, "often we don't know who they are, where they are from and why they are here. These are not bad people, but it is making a mockery of the system and it must stop. This current state of lawlessness and openness to all is not an elegant path for a serious country like ours." His 10-point immigration plan, which he released around that time, proposes to withhold aid to poor countries that do not comply with their immigration policy and do not cooperate with programs to take such people back. The Conservatives have so far been unable to implement this policy only because the European Court of Human Rights has intervened. The threat of Rwanda has failed to curtail the flow of migrants coming to the UK. The government is spending about £4.7m a day housing asylum seekers in hotels.

Friendly communication

Brexit has left both the UK and the EU a little vulnerable both economically and politically, which is why the likes of Putin, Xi and Trump were so excited about it. No one has yet fully implemented Brexit and it is still eating into Britain's economy and politics, thanks to Rishi, not because he maintains that Brexit was a good idea, but because they are constantly trying to manage and limit its damage.

All the frustration of the country is now focused on this one person who sits at the helm of their democratic system. They expect him to end poverty and hunger, make them rich, protect them from infectious diseases, and stop climate change. In the meantime, he must avoid any political-misrepresentation – as well as manage statements from several hundred MPs. They expect him to be on top of the daily crises and proxy crises posed by the demands of round-the-clock news – as well as beaming their ideas across the horizon and solving long-standing issues. Ross Clarke has summed up the challenges and problems facing Rishi, saying that our expectations of the PM have been going up while our own tolerance of stress has been going down. The general population asserts ever greater entitlement to shorter hours, more holiday and time off if the pressure becomes too great. Yet we expect the PM to be omnipresent, with their performance under constant surveillance. The space in office once enjoyed by prime ministers has been entirely eroded.[15]

Rishi Ready?

Every winter if it snows

We hear their sneering, and it goes:

"I thought the world was heating up!

Where's your global warming now?"

To hear their wisdom we desire

Now half the country is on fire

But all those jeering voices have

Gone very very quiet somehow...[16]

The first major task of the government is the better management of 'energy' in the coming season. He retained Jeremy Hunt as Chancellor of the Exchequer, who was appointed by Ms Truss when she fired her Treasury chief. Former Goldman Sachs financier Sunak and Chancellor Jeremy Hunt can reassure markets whether there is a credible plan to control debt. This would require both tax increases and spending cuts, and would be an unpleasant act that would be criticized by journalists in newspapers. There are two big challenges before Sunak, the first is government spending. He has always considered himself a low-tax Tory, but he has also been an MP who believes that spending needs to be controlled first. And this control cannot be done quickly.

With no money to spend, the Tories must return to public service reform. This is an agenda that has been neglected for the last six years. The second challenge is how to get the economy going. Truss and Quarteng were absolutely right in their argument that development is an imperative. His problem was that a long-term tax plan had never been properly thought through before. Sunak and Hunt will need a new path. Sunak is all too well acquainted with the problems of public welfare. Now that unemployment is at a historically low level, there is a large number of economically inactive people, of whom about five million are out of work and still enjoy government benefits. Some of Sunak's problems are political as well. Normally, a new prime minister has some honeymoon period with the electorate, but the public is sick of Tory psychodrama. The Conservative Party has a net favorability rating of minus 47. So Sunak will have to deal with a public fed up with Keir Starmer's demands for a general election.[17]

The presence of three former Prime Ministers as MPs in the Parliament in which Rishi Sunak is the Prime Minister will always keep him alert. The presence of so many former leaders in Parliament offers a glimpse into the internal turmoil of the Conservative Party and the upheaval it has caused in Britain's system of governance. It also creates a peculiar working environment for Mr. Sunak as he himself becomes the latest member to take charge of the party. Mr. Sunak served in Prime Minister Boris Johnson's cabinet before stepping down as Britain's top finance minister, Chancellor of the Exchequer. There he took a step which gave rise to the rebellion and which ultimately led to the resignation of Mr. Johnson. Now both Boris Johnson and Liz Truss as Members of Parliament will be watching Sunak's every move.

As the fifth leader of the Conservatives in the last six years, Sunak also has to face the uphill task of uniting his increasingly fragmented party. Although Sunak has been able to claim the support of a majority of Conservative MPs, he remains a divisive personality due to his role in ousting Johnson when he resigned from his government in July.

Sunak will undoubtedly bring a more serious tone to Downing Street. He neither tolerates one of Johnson's clownish antics, nor does Truss's moderate enthusiasm make any sense, and as Helen Lewis of 'The Atlantic' rightly notes, he is a fiery and passionate personality like Frasier's Niles reminds her of a crane.

Rishi Sunak's road has not been easy, but the extra enthusiasm of many migrants like him has made his road difficult. The contributions of those leaders who are both outspoken in this matter and also strict to the extent behind not allowing their stance on immigration to be very liberal make his task strenuous and uneasy. It will be no easy task to manage the decisions and attitudes of former Home Secretary Priti Patel and her Tamil-Goan successor, Suella Braverman. It will not be easy to cross the 'living bridge' as envisaged by Narendra Modi in his tweet. Foreign secretary James Cleverly says it is 'lovely to see' how much India has welcomed the Sunak premiership – but experts feel it would be wrong of New Delhi to expect too much too fast. After Boris Johnson and Liz Truss, Mr. Sunak just paid lip service to the importance of the UK's relationship with India but failed to oversee the completion of a much sought-after free trade agreement (FTA) between the two countries by the deadline of Diwali. The highly ambitious FTA with India is naturally the first and biggest challenge he faces when it comes to better ties with India.

In an effort to rebuild party unity, Sunak has re-nominated several cabinet members who served in senior positions in Mr. Johnson's government, including Suella Braverman, who is popular in the party's moderate wing and has been appointed home secretary. She has been advocating for stricter immigration restrictions. Sunak had to make some strong comments on his first day as PM over his reinstatement of Suella to the same post and his strong support of the controversial Rwanda immigration policy. Many Indian political thinkers feel that some of the major

The Rise of Rishi Sunak

points of the free trade agreement between India and Britain are now certain to change. The objective of this agreement is to double the trade between the two countries by 2030. But this will be possible only when both the countries adopt some flexible approach. The other important pact is Migration and Mobility Partnership Agreement (MMPA) which was signed between India and the UK in May 2021. It has to be implemented now. This landmark agreement will allow young British and Indian nationals to work and live in each other's countries and accelerate the removal of illegal migrants.

Keshav Guha, well-known for literary and political journalism and author of the book 'Accidental Magic', in an opinion piece written for 'NDTV' (Nov 1,2022) explains how Rishi Sunak is going to be the Prime Minister. Sunak's appointment has reassured the markets. Whoever the PM, a Conservative defeat in the next election is now all but certain; of the available options, Sunak is probably best placed to limit the scale of the losses. For all that, his resurrection of Braverman suggests that he represents continuity - with the projects of austerity and Brexit that have defined the past 12 years of Conservative rule.[18]

Sunak's intelligent personality may make him less likely to be blamed for everything, while not being praised for the positive results he produces. But he seems unconcerned about fame or accolades, he wants to get on with everyone like the Karmayogi of the Gita. Sunak took his parliamentary oath with his hand on 'Bhagavad Gita' but his political working style is more materialistic. People say 'his mind works in Excel'. The fear is that the stress of this high-octane lifestyle may break his petite edgy frame somewhere. Will he have to remind us to have our meals on time? We all should hope that he will continue to see his ideals, his household life in the same way as he will see the country. Do not overdo anything. Avoid the extremism of politics.

There used to be a famous statement called the divine right of kings to be in power. The Tories continue to believe that no one is ever going to win an election to a Labor government because they haven't elected them for so long. It would be better if Rishi Sunak doesn't have any such illusion. Listen to your detractors and critics too. Regardless of whether Coventry South's Labor MP, Zarah Sultana, comments via Twitter: "A heartwarming story of a young boy born to wealthy parents, sent to an elite private school, then to Oxford Sent, who got a job in investment banking, before becoming the wealthiest MP in Parliament and voting for policies that plunged millions of working class people into poverty.

You have to be a politician, not just a techno whiz kid. Being a British politician is a much trickier task than people imagine. Our own Meghnad Jagdishchandra Desai, Baron Desai Professor Emeritus of the London School of Economics, has this piece of advice for you, Rishi Sunak: First Job- Steady the Ship!

> I have seen how someone can be a great cabinet minister, but fail as a politician. You will have to develop a political persona. Everyone will give you a lot of space since the country is in dire straits. I do not recall in the nearly 60 years I have been here of the country being at a lower ebb in its national confidence and international reputation. So, you will have to demonstrate that you are in charge. Jeremy Hunt, who stepped in as chancellor for Liz Truss after she sacked Kwarteng calmed nerves, but then the manner of Liz Truss's last day in the commons once again sank the ship. You can leave the finances to Jeremy Hunt and turn your attention to addressing the people who are bemused and worried as to who, if anyone, is in charge.[19]

So good luck, Rishi Sunak! If you continue to be the Prime Minister till the next election, it will be the fruit of your hard work. "Past performance is no guarantee of future returns.

No need to tell this to an economist like you. Leave the matter beyond this for tomorrow.

Readers! Before you turn the page to read the next chapter of this book, I want to give you a treat. I am going to give you a tiny-tale. Read it and in your free time –contemplate- Is Rishi Sunak like the fisherman of this parable?

> A fisherman sees a body floating down stream, and jumps in to rescue it. The same happens a few minutes later, and then again, and again. Finally, the fisherman ignores the tenth body and starts running upstream. "Why aren't you rescuing that poor man?' shouts an observer. The fisherman replies that he's going to find out how to stop these poor people getting pushed into the water in the first place.

Sunak faces a daunting task. In the words of Shakespeare's Henry IV, "uneasy lies the head that wears the crown".

***

Referneces

1 https://www.telegraphindia.com/opinion/anywhere-man-in-rishi-sunak-britain-has-the-markets-person/cid/1894449

2 https://www.theatlantic.com/ideas/archive/2022/10/rishi-sunak-wealth-britain-prime-minister/671846/

3 https://policyexchange.org.uk/wp-content/uploads/2016/09/a-portrait-of-modern-britain.pdf

4 https://policyexchange.org.uk/wp-content/uploads/2016/09/a-portrait-of-modern-britain.pdf

5 https://www.nationalworld.com/news/politics/rishi-sunak-views-policies-brexit-tax-immigration-net-zero-3891344

6   https://www.rishisunak.com/news/why-i-will-vote-britain-leave-eu-0

7   https://www.amazon.in/Age-Strongman-Leader-Threatens-Democracy-ebook/dp/B09HJZNQ5R

8   https://books.google.co.in/books?id=x4uAEAAA QBAJ&pg=PT216&dq

9   Sunak, Rishi (2020) 'keynote Speech (5 October) Conservative party Conference 2020, https://www. conservatives-com/news/rishi-sunak-read-the -chancellors-keynote-speech-in full (Accessed December 2022)

10 https://www.amazon.in/Sebastian-Payne-ebook/dp/ B0B96HJ9HP

11 https://theprint.in/opinion/there-are-many-reasons-why-rishi-sunak-lost-uk-pm-chair-but-race-isnt-the-main-one/1117952/

12 https://www.politico.eu/article/boris-johnson-vs-rishi-sunak-the-mother-of-all-leadership-battles/

13 https://openthemagazine.com/columns/race-and-rishi/

14 https://www.newstatesman.com/quickfire/2022/10/rishi-sunak-thatcherite-prime-minister-since-thatcher

15 https://www.spectator.co.uk/article/rishi-sunak-faces-an-impossible-job/

16 https://www.theneweuropean.co.uk/liz-and-rishi-two-jokes-that-arent-funny-anymore

17 https://www.spectator.co.uk/article/is-rishi-ready-sunaks-first-test-will-be-getting-through-winter/

18 https://www.ndtv.com/opinion/what-sort-of-pm-will-rishi-sunak-be-we-have-big-clues-3479138

19 https://indianexpress.com/article/opinion/columns/ prime-minister-rishi-sunaks-first-job-develop-a-political-persona-steady-the-ship-8229273/

❐

8

SPEECH LESS AGENDA

"Rishi Sunak's political potential is huge. He ranks as highly as anyone I've seen coming into politics."

–William Hague

Today, when ethnic nationalist and extreme right-wing majoritarian parties are getting stronger in many democratic countries around the world, at such a time, in white population and Christian-dominated Britain, the command of the post of Prime Minister is being handed over to Sunak, who believes in Hinduism and is not white. This has a great symbolic significance. Adding our own voice to what our Prime Minister said, we can say that the UK and India share a lot. We are all excited about what our two great democracies can accomplish as we strengthen our security, defense and economic ties. We the people of India are only celebrating his incumbency for our own reasons, but there are a lot of challenges in front of him. He also needs our blessings and it is also his need that he now turns to fulfill the resolution that he had placed before his countrymen in his address.

His speech lasted five minutes and 56 seconds. In 2019, Boris Johnson gave his speech for 11 minutes and 13 seconds.

On 25 October 2022, Rishi Sunak said in his first speech outside 10 Downing Street that he had to correct the mistakes of his predecessor PM Liz Truss. In words and deeds Sunak has shown seriousness about repairing the damage caused by Boris Johnson's conduct and Liz Truss's mismanagement. Ali Mitib says that in an attempt to break with Liz Truss's tumultuous reign, Rishi Sunak abandoned her higgledy-piggledy lecturn for his first speech as prime minister, instead opting for a simple design. He justified why he was there and then reassured the public that he will be compassionate as he implements spending cuts. During this, referring to the Ukraine-Russia war, he said that Britain is facing a serious economic crisis after Vladimir Putin's brutal war, which will now have to make difficult decisions in the coming times and promised that future generations. For this, they will not leave the loan and will pay it themselves. Presenting himself as unifying and reconciling, Sunak promised to "bring his party and country together". As a realist, he didn't shy away from telling the unpleasant truth about tax cuts and inflation, saying -

> I have just been to Buckingham Palace and accepted His Majesty the King's invitation to form a government in his name. It is only right to explain why I am standing here as your new Prime Minister.

> Right now, our country is facing a profound economic crisis. The aftermath of COVID still lingers. [Vladimir] Putin's war in Ukraine has destabilized energy markets and supply chains the world over.

> I want to pay tribute to my predecessor, Liz truss. She was not wrong, to want to improve growth in this country. It is a noble aim. And I admired her restlessness to create change.

But some mistakes were made. Not born of ill will, or bad intentions. Quite the opposite, in fact, but mistakes nonetheless. And I have been elected as a leader of my party and your Prime Minister, in part, to fix them. And that work begins immediately.

I will place economic stability and competence at the heart of this government's agenda. This will mean difficult decisions to come. But you saw me during COVID doing everything I could to protect people and businesses with schemes like furlough. There are always limits, more so now than ever. But I promise you this, I will bring that same compassion to the challenges we face today.

The government I lead will not leave the next generation, your children and grandchildren with a debt to settle that we were too weak to pay ourselves. I will unite our country not with words, but with action. I will work day in and day out to deliver for you.

This government will have integrity, professionalism, and accountability at every level. Trust is earned and I will earn yours. I will always be grateful to Boris Johnson for his incredible achievements as Prime Minister. And I treasure his warmth and generosity of spirit. And I know he would agree that the mandate my party earned in 2019 is not the sole property of any one individual. It is a mandate that belongs to and unites all of us. And the heart of that mandate is our manifesto. I will deliver on its promise.

A stronger NHS [National Health Service], better schools, safer streets, control of our borders, protecting our environment, supporting our armed forces levelling up and building an economy that embraces the opportunities of Brexit, where businesses invest, innovate, and create jobs. I understand how difficult this moment is.

After the billions of pounds it cost us to combat COVID, after all the dislocation that it caused, the terrible Ukraine war must be seen successfully to its conclusions. I fully appreciate how hard things are. And I understand that I have work to do to restore trust.

After all that has happened, all I can say is that I am not daunted. I know the high office I have accepted, and I hope to live up to its demands. But when the opportunity to serve comes along, you cannot question the moment, only your willingness. So, I stand here before you ready to lead our country into the future, to put your needs above politics, to reach out and build a government that represents the very best traditions of my party.

Together, we can achieve incredible things. We will create a future worthy of the sacrifices so many have made and fill tomorrow and every day thereafter with hope.

Thank You ![1]

Like so many others Raj Mohan Gandhi also tried to read his well crafted speech to make others understand his vision. He called Rishi Sunak's speech a Perfectly-Crafted First Speech. On the other hand, Imogen Howse wrote. "In contrast with many of his predecessors, Sunak's tone was somber and contained no sense of celebration at having been chosen as Conservative Party leader, and, consequently, Prime Minister. He spoke of the "profound economic crisis" the country has been facing and warned once again of the "difficult decisions" he's facing."[2]

In his brief speech, he praised the contribution of both his predecessors without talking much about their predecessors and promised to do the work left by them., Used short but emphatic words to calm potential enemies. Some critics of this victory speech said that there is nothing special in it. It seems that a pre-recorded announcement has been made at a railway station. Sunak said: "I will be forever grateful to Boris Johnson for his incredible achievements as prime minister, and I cherish his warmth and generosity of spirit." It was kind of Sunak to express his gratitude to the person who had left no stone unturned to oppose him. He did not speak any harsh words towards Liz Truss, but learned from her mistakes and talked about completing her unfinished work. Being an Indian, we should not forget that the biggest reason for Sunak's defeat from the truce was his not being an Englishman. Keeping this in mind, he vowed that the government he is leading will not leave any debt to the next generation and he will make it happen., We should not be ashamed to say that they probably get the trust of the post because of their Indian or foreign origin and they will work to get it.

This statement had two main objectives. The first objective was to consolidate and unify the fragmented and rudderless Tory party. The second was to assure the country that he had a credible plan to repair Britain's battered economy as millions of people were facing hardship. In his speech, Sunak dismissed Ms Truss's destructive agenda of tax cuts without it, making it clear it would be his job to "fix" the problems she brought up.

The speech also underlined that he is an inspiration to many. One who mocks him only proves that he is the enemy of aspiration. They forget that aspiration is the most valuable treasure of their life. He set the tone of his performance as a future lawmaker and gave an insight into the qualities of the head and the heart. He didn't make another 'Gettysburg- like' or Churchill's ' Blood, sweat and tears' kind of speech but in his maiden speech, he made a point. He could tell and explain why he was there.

Ten Point Agenda

Sunak will aim to restore a momentum of credibility and stability after a period of turmoil in British politics for most of this year. A message has to be given to the distressed public that his vision is focused like Arjuna and he will first look at his country then he will move outside.

No British leader since World War II entered No. 10 Downing Street facing such a difficult time as the challenges Sunak faces as the country faces rising energy bills, hospital waiting lists, borrowing costs and inflation. The challenge has been exacerbated by the brief crash-and-burn premiership of Liz Truss. As a result of his now-infamous mini-budget, which was scrapped almost entirely after causing chaos in the financial markets, conservative opinion polls have the opposition Labor Party trailing him by more than 30 percentage points. His job now will be to reassure people that the government will support them during another tough economic period – only this time they are in a much tougher position. The popularity he enjoyed during the pandemic has waned, and he takes office after a major government crisis - the third Tory prime minister to take office within three months. Some concrete steps have to be taken at the earliest to get the support of the people. But how they will remove the chaos spread by the first leaders is a big question and in response to which Sunak has a 10-point program or plan. The public is distressed, it is in a hurry. That's why every step has to be taken care of.

Sunak bills himself as a "transformative" and age-changing leader. He wants to rebuild the economy to restore confidence in the minds of his countrymen. Want to reunite the country. Sunak faces a mountain of challenges and many issues to contend with. There are also many pressing matters. They have programs and skills to get rid of all these. Sunak's ten point program as per 'Ready for Rishi' released on August 9, 2022 is very straightforward, truthful and practical in itself.

Our glorious country stands at a crossroads. And the decisions we make in the next few weeks will determine our future. I want to tame the cost of living so we can grow the economy and cut taxes. Keep Brexit safe and deliver on the opportunities Brexit offers us. Win the next general election so we can defeat Keir Starmer and avoid a disastrous Labour-led coalition supported by the SNP, which will literally tear our country apart.

1. Restructuring the Economy - A long-term plan to beat inflation, encourage investment to spur growth, and cut the basic rate of income tax by 20%.

2. Abolishing VAT on Energy Bills - Temporarily eliminating VAT on energy bills to support every household during the winter.

3. Removing the NHS backlog - fixing waiting lists and fines for missed appointments to stop the abuse of our NHS.

4. Delivering Brexit - ending all EU laws holding back the economy before the next election.

5. Tackling illegal immigration - tightening rules on refugees, limiting the number of refugees and implementing the Rwandan Partnership.

6. Curbing crime - Automatic custodial sentences for career criminals and setting up an emergency task force to track down grooming gangs.

7. Changes in education - teaching maths and English till the age of 18, promoting technical education like apprenticeships and cracking down on poor quality degrees.

8. Strengthening the Union - Fixing the Northern Ireland Protocol, leveling investment in Scotland, Wales and Northern Ireland and standing up to Nicola Sturgeon.

9. Protecting our Green Belt - building homes on brownfield sites, allowing rapid development of residential housing within planning permission, and preventing any inappropriate development on our Green Belt.

10. WIN THE NEXT GENERAL ELECTION - Fully funding campaign managers on each 80:20 target seat and giving more power to members.

Rebuilding the economy - In his first official speech as UK Prime Minister, Sunak acknowledged that the country is "facing a serious economic crisis" and that "difficult decisions" need to be made to deal with it. To this end, he pledged to place economic stability and trust at the center of his government's agenda. The most pressing economic priority for his government is keeping inflation under control. For this, Sunak will take some decisions which may be unpleasant. Sunak has retained recently appointed Jeremy Hunt as chancellor while reshuffles the former cabinet. He was brought in by Liz Truss shortly before his departure. Hunt now makes quick changes to Truss and Quasi Quarteng's disastrous mini-budget, calling it a new move.

"I will cut taxes in this Parliament session itself, but I am going to do it responsibly. I don't cut taxes to win elections, I win elections to cut taxes." "I want to cut taxes and I will cut taxes, But we will do it correctly and appropriately. And really the only way to do this in a sustainable way over time is to ensure that the Conservatives win the next general election. And I believe I am the best person to defeat Labor Party leader Keir Starmer and ensure that election victory," Sunak told a general meeting.

Women-Rights - In his previous leadership bid, Sunak claimed he would make women's rights a priority in his manifesto. He tweeted then: "If I become Prime Minister I will protect women's rights and ensure women and girls enjoy the same freedom most males take for granted in feeling safe from assault and abuse." Sunak also said that sexual violence against women and girls should be treated as a "national emergency". In the last leadership contest in summer, Sunak said police will be instructed to take tougher action to tackle "grooming gangs" and officers must be focussed on "fighting actual crime" instead of "policing bad jokes on Twitter". "As a father of two girls, I want them to be able to go for a walk in the evening or to a shop at night without any fear of threat," he said.

Tackling illegal immigration - On 13 October 2022 at the inauguration of the European Diplomatic Academy., the foreign policy chief of the European Union Josep Borrell addressed the audience which can tell us about the mentality of Europe: "Europe is a garden. The rest of the world is a jungle... And the jungle would invade the garden. Gardeners should take care of it. But they will not protect the garden by building walls around it... because the jungle has a strong growth capacity... the walls will never be high enough to protect the garden... The gardeners have to go to the jungle... otherwise; the rest of the world will invade us...." Mr Borrell went further, concluding by telling his young "gardeners" that "your duty will not be to take care of the garden itself but of the jungle outside".[3]

If Britain thought that leaving the EU would solve its concerns about migration, it was wrong. A sharp rise in people trying to cross the English Channel in small boats has fueled a new sense of crisis in the government's mind – with Tory MPs increasingly talking about it. Suella Braverman is the latest in a long line of UK home secretaries. And till now they too have failed to deal with this problem like others. Priti Patel, the previous UK home secretary, appointed in 2019, vowed to make migration crossings an "exclusive event". Having failed to hit their target, they resolved to make the Channel an "impossible" passage through a controversial plan to actively push back small boats for UK border officials. Later he was forced to give up his proposal considering it impractical. Over 100,000 asylum seekers are currently waiting for a Home Office decision, and while they wait in limbo they must be financially supported by the taxpayer as they are prohibited from working under UK law. Thus they are an unnecessary burden on the country. In April 2022, the UK signed a £120 million deal with Rwanda for asylum seekers in the East African country. Seven months have passed since a flurry of challenges in the courts against this, no such flight has left the runway, which could have driven such people out of British soil.

Another move by Sunak is to support the controversial Rwandan deportation policy. In addition to supporting this, he also strongly supports stricter rules within the UK refugee system. The appointment of Suella Braverman as the new Home Secretary has made it clear that she has no intention of showing any flexibility. Sunak believes that the European Convention on Human Rights (ECHR) "cannot and should not be allowed to inhibit our ability to properly control our borders," and wants the UK to "acknowledge every year." be allowed to control the number of refugees to be admitted." It appears that Sunak will do "whatever it takes" to implement the "Rwanda Policy" and further cement the basis for equal partnership.

Sunak and Borrell, both, are not so different from each other after all, despite very different cultural and ancestral backgrounds. He previously told *BBC Radio 4*: "This country has a proud history of welcoming people but it's also vital that we're in control of who's coming here." Sunak was proud to come from a family of immigrants, but believed the UK must control its borders.

Rishi Sunak's government is as anti-immigrant as any in Britain's recent history as he has to listen to the average voters' plea. There are voters who feel that they give "a hundred million pounds to India to tarmac their roads while where they live has so many potholes." There are voters who see that those who work hard are struggling while others cross the Channel illegally to claim "freebies" and "act like they're in forgetfulness". These voters are not voiceless now. They have social media and Sunak has to listen to their voice. Sunak has to give highest priority to these domestic voices.

"On immigration, his stance is likelier to be governed by his anxiety about not being perceived as too liberal. While subtler in articulation, he is on the same page as other Indian-origin Tories like former home secretary Priti Patel and her voluble Tamil-Goan origin successor, Suella Braverman, the kind who get in and bolt the door behind them. Indeed, Sunak courted some heated comments on his first day as PM by reinstating Suella and emphatically backing the controversial Rwanda Immigration Policy, under which illegal immigrants from anywhere are packed off to that African country. This is one of the major sticking points in the promising Free Trade Agreement with India that aims to double the trade between the two countries by 2030."[4]

Clearing the NHS backlog - Sunak sees the current NHS backlog as "the biggest public service emergency ever". He has pledged to make this his "first public service priority" and intends to create a "Backlog Task Force" to help "treat patients" in a faster, more efficient way. Sunak is against privatization, and says he will really go to great lengths to prevent misuse of funds due to wait times and backlogs. If privatization is coming through the back door in the field of medicine, then that too has to be dealt with. Writing in 'The Sunday Telegraph', Sunak has proposed a temporary £10 fine for NHS patients who skip doctor appointments. Sunak proposes, "If people aren't showing up on time or are forgetting or not showing up to appointments, then they're taking those slots away from people who need them, then that's not fair." I am committed to a fair health care system that is free to use, but not free to abuse." He wants to "eliminate the one-year wait" for patients to have the complex operation by September 2024, six months ahead of the government's current target. They also want to ensure that "everyone who has been waiting more than 18 weeks for a process is contacted by their trust within 100 days."

Climate Change - Sunak is committed to upholding the government's goal of reaching net zero by 2050, and was the only candidate in the first leadership race to do so. And until then they want to keep a ban on building new onshore wind farms. They intend to launch a "massive expansion" into offshore wind, so that the UK can be self-sufficient in its energy production by 2045. Sunak is committed to increasing North Sea gas production and that as long as "local communities" support it, till then support fracking too will go on. Despite his promises on renewable energy, Sunak was criticized for not placing "the clean economy and climate action at the heart of his mission" when he was chancellor.

Britain has failed to pay more than $300 million promised to two major climate funds, exposing it to further international embarrassment in the final days of its tenure as the world's official climate action leader. There is talk that Mr. Sunak is paying lip service to environmental issues while promoting greenwash policies. Such politics paves the way for, in the words of UN Secretary-General Antonio Guterres, 'climate hell'.

Industrial action - Sunak has pledged during its leadership campaign to ban strikes by workers involved in essential public services such as railway workers, NHS workers and teachers. The pledge was part of the Conservative Party's 2019 manifesto, which Sunak has now made very clear that he will vigorously pursue as prime minister.

Like the abortion-truce - in 2021, Sunak voted in favour of regulations enabling the Northern Ireland secretary to commission abortion services in Northern Ireland. More recently, he abstained on the amendment to introduce 'buffer zones' around reproductive healthcare clinics in the UK, as well as the amendment to make the pills by post scheme a permanent option. Sunak has also not been very vocal about his stance on abortion. Since becoming an MP in 2015, he has abstained from voting on abortion rights almost every time. However, she cast her vote in support of abortion in April 2021, when she voted in favor of giving the Secretary of State for Northern Ireland the right to open abortion services in the country. But, like Truss, Sunak stalled a parliamentary vote on establishing a buffer zone around abortion clinics.

On Women and their Safety - Sunak has also been in news for his comments on women. He specifically talks about the upliftment of women entrepreneurs and workers. In this regard he considers his 'emotional factor' that is his wife and two daughters. He said in the past he and "many of us men" had taken safety "for granted". So tackling that and making it safer for people is something that's just personally quite important to me. "I want to make sure that my kids and everyone else can walk around safely. That's what any parent wants for their children."

LGBTQ matters – Sunak has expressed his views about transgender issues several times. Speaking to grassroots Conservative supporters on July 29, 2022, Sunak described the 2010 Equality Act as a "Trojan horse", which has allowed all kinds of nonsense into public life that has killed the English language rewritten so that we can't even use words like 'man', 'woman' or 'mother' without also implying that we are offending someone." In April 2022, Sunak said that "biology is critically important because we think about some of those very practical questions. Respect should be given to the views of women who are concerned that some of the things they've worked really hard for and the rights that are important to them will be eroded." stated that prejudice against trans people is wrong and that they would strive to "promote a space in which people feel safe, able to explore complex issues and find a way out."

He claims the Conservative Party is an "open, welcoming family to everybody across society." He was prepared to combat and launch a "manifesto for women's rights", but confidently responded "no" when asked if trans women were in fact women.

Business relations with India – The sense of prideful entitlement that is in the mind of every other person across India regarding Rishi Sunak will not work for the smooth flow of the foreign policy and trade policy. It is also natural to be worried because it will not be surprising if he starts taking some tough decisions while keeping himself unconnected with India. By re-appointing Suella Barvarman as Home Minister, he has already given a signal and message that the free trade agreement he wanted to bring with India around Diwali will now be re-examined and brought forward. They think that the people of India will now try more to enter their country unauthorizedly on this pretext. If our mutual trade doubles by 2030, both will be benefited. If India is asking for some relaxation in the visa rules, then those who take the visa will also contribute to strengthen the UK economy. They want to sell their whiskey to India. But India has food-products, jewelry and rags to sell. You can also guess who needs whom more. Next let us see on which side the camel sits. Sunak himself believed in this, so he said many encouraging things in bilateral talks with Indian Finance Minister Nirmala Sitharaman in September 2021, now is the time to do them.

The relationship between two counties, like two persons, is always 'two-way' or reciprocal. It can't be one-sided. Sunak has repeatedly said he wanted to change the UK-India relationship to make it a more "two-way exchange" that opens up easy access to UK students and companies in India. He said.

> We are all very aware of the opportunity for the UK to sell things and do things in India, but actually we need to look at that relationship differently because there is an enormous amount that we here in the UK can learn from India."I want to make sure that it's easy for our students to also travel to India and learn, that it's also easy for our companies and Indian companies to work together, because it's not just a one-way relationship, it's a two-way relationship, and that's the type of change I want to bring to that relationship.[5]

Raphael Behr, columnist for The Guardian, suggests to Rishi that he may be more popular than his party (just as Atal Bihari Vajpayee was, and now Narendra Modi is) but he must be a force to be reckoned with and looking to be in control, which means having an agenda that follows the rules. He should do something better than cleaning up someone else's mess. Otherwise he is in the position of caretaker and moderator in a reckless party that is another Tory accident waiting to happen. Above all, cheerleaders within India should be under no illusion that Sunak, or for that matter, Kamala Harris (if an opportunity to make a more important and independent decision comes to her) will help India in any way. They will act as citizens who have reposed trust in them, and not as persons of Indian origin or as Hindus. That identity of theirs is confined to a purely personal realm, unlike in India, where religious identity is the basis of politics.[6]

After an exhaustive discussion of the first Hindu Prime Minister, the first Asian, the first British Indian, the first non-white Rishi Sunak, it is time for the conclusion. Let's get back to work - 'Keep work and carry on'. Sunak has come to the office of UK Prime Minister as one of the more intelligent, gentle and calm figures to lead the British government in a long time. They've got a wrecked economy. To fix this, a well-organized plan and its successful implementation will be required. Careful leadership will be required in each of Whitehall's departments. But the talent pool for that leadership has been ravaged by the Tory party's infighting over the past decade, and by defending itself and the party. Margaret Thatcher used to say that every prime minister needed a "Willie". His allusion was to the famous mentor Willie Whitelaw. Good leaders need friends who speak truth to power, that's the policy. Willie was lacking in Britain's last three prime ministers. One could say that he was mentored but couldn't find a suitable friend. Every sensible prime minister has an "honest friend". Winston Churchill had Norman Brooke, who at least claimed to have prevented his worst decisions. Harold Macmillan had John Wyndham, Harold Wilson had Lady Falkender, Tony Blair had Alastair Campbell and Peter Mandelson. Boris Johnson had Dominic Cummings, who had a lot of enthusiasm for change. Simon Jenkins, therefore, believes that late Saber Rishi too had a 'Willie' or Will need a mentoring partner. Last 10 years In 2010, Britain has seen five prime ministers, seven chancellors, six home secretaries and 10 education secretaries. The government has become a joke. In the process, the essence of ministerial experience and knowledge has been lost. Mr. Hancock's plea and Sir Gavin's humiliation are symptoms of that decay. Much resentment has accumulated in the Parliamentary Tory party over the avoidance of talk by saying 'what's gone is gone'. Voters can feel the slow pace of the administration even as it claims to be under new management. Yet there are capable men and women sitting at the back of Parliament whose only crime was Brexit and their disbelief in Boris Johnson. It is hard to believe that Sunak could not collect a handful of these and take advantage of their advice. They desperately need Willie for themselves.[7]

Rishi Sunak is fed up with Boris Johnson's dishonesty and the "guest image" of the truce as the younger generation spends this year of Britain using negative words such as "chaotic", "disorganised", "failed", "indecent" and "uncertain". Sunak has vowed to win back the public's trust by delivering a government of "integrity, professionalism and accountability". Saying that "trust is earned and I will win your trust", he became a favorite of many.

Somebody has rightly said that even being the PM of Britain is not a trophy but a job. When war is wreaking havoc on the world economy, Sunak, who has voted thrice for Brexit, has There is a lot of work to be done. He must unite his parliamentary party; to form a cabinet that is orderly and pleasing to its MPs; It has to be kept in check while improving the economy; ensuring UK support for Ukraine does not waver; political and trade uncertainties in Northern Ireland must be addressed; And cross-channel illegal immigration must be dealt with firmly. It should also be kept in mind that his rival party should not make an edge in the upcoming elections and Rishi Raj may be in danger. Only heartless parliamentarians and those indulging in the politics of jealousy would attack a young man who could leapfrog sky high in politics and personal life just to serve their own interests. On the strength of ability and dedication, he has reached where he is today by elevating himself. Nevertheless, there is no doubt that his another big challenge will be to convince the common voters that they are not oblivious to the growing concern for their livelihood, but are aware that their decisions will not only benefit them, but also their children will affect positively.

Sunak has brought credibility and stability to British politics after several wasted years of turmoil. Britain had seen and appreciated his chancellor form during the Corona epidemic and he realized his priorities too much. But, now that he is on the world stage as a politician, Britons and we Indians are waiting to see what his instincts and priorities are as Prime Minister. The people of India are also watching his foreign policy with great interest.

According to Euronews, Sunak "is often seen as belonging to the pragmatist and centre-stage of the Conservative Party." Liz Truss opposed the fiscal policies of her predecessor,and although he is described as a Thatcherite, he is seen as less economically moderate than Truss. He supports Ukraine against Russian aggression and is a strong supporter of economic sanctions against Russia, but does not appear to favor British military intervention in Ukraine. Sunak supported the recognition of Jerusalem as the capital of Israel.

On China

In 2015, then Chancellor George Osborne echoed the Chinese ambassador's claims that China and the UK were in a "golden era" of bilateral relations, but by 2020 relations had somewhat soured under Boris Johnson's government. Sunak's position on China has not always been so blunt and to the point.

Speaking as chancellor, he called for a "mature and balanced relationship" with China in order to "pursue with confidence an economic relationship in a safe, mutually beneficial way". Global Times described his approach as "clear and pragmatic" then. But in the first leadership election he hinted that he was willing to close all Confucius Institutes in the country. In his first major foreign policy speech as premier in 2022 he drew a clear line under the much-vaunted "golden era" of UK-China relations pursued by former Prime Minister David Cameron. "Let's be clear, the so-called 'golden era' is over, along with the naïve idea that trade would lead to social and political reform" he said, "We recognize China poses a systemic challenge to our values and interests, a challenge that grows more acute as it moves towards even greater authoritarianism" he added. However, he did acknowledge that the UK "cannot simply ignore China's significance in world affairs" and therefore his approach would be one of "robust pragmatism" taking a "longer-term view". The US, Canada, Australia, Japan and many others understand this too together they can "manage this sharpening competition, including with diplomacy and engagement". He is of the view that the UK is a country "that stands up for our values, that defends democracy by actions not just words" but as the world evolves "so does our application of those values". Under his leadership the status quo will be changed as he does things differently.

He called China the "biggest long-term threat" to Britain, saying that "they torture, detain, harass their own people, including in Xinjiang and Hong Kong, in violation of human rights, and they have made a constant dent in the global economy rigged." He accused China of supporting Russian President Vladimir Putin and also said that China is "stealing our technology and infiltrating our universities". China is a country with fundamentally different values to Britain; an authoritarian intends to reshape the international order through leadership. "I'm very clear that China poses a systemic challenge to both our values and our interests and it represents the single biggest state threat to our economic security and that's why it's right that we take the steps that are necessary to protect ourselves," he told Sky News on the sidelines of the G20.

Theresa Villiers, wrote in *Jewish News* that Mr Sunak wants to capitalize on Britain's relationships with Gulf states to widen the Abraham Accords. Sunak described Saudi Arabia as a "partner" and "ally", but said the British government could not ignore human rights violations in Saudi Arabia. He "regards Iran as a major threat to regional stability and beyond because its ballistic missile programme is in breach of the UN resolutions and continues apace." He favours a hard line on Iran and welcomes the Abraham Accords between the UAE, Israel and Bahrain.

According to him it is absolutely right that the British Government joins with its allies and partners around the world as they consider how to ensure energy security for this country. As British chancellor, he opposed US President Joe Biden's plan to introduce a minimum 21 percent global trade tax. In August 2022, he proposed a broader containment strategy by broadening the definition of "extremism".

On crime, Sunak proposed an automatic one-year extension to prison sentences for prolific offenders, as well as reducing the minimum sentence from twelve months to six months for deportation of a foreign offender. He proposed life imprisonment for leaders of gangs involved in juvenile delinquency and for police to record the ethnicity of those involved in such gangs.

Rishi Sunak wants to chart a new path for Britain post-Brexit, with his eyes firmly set on a region close to his heart – the Indo-Pacific. His foreign trip as prime minister to the G20 summit in Bali was successful because of this. Britain's strategy will include fostering closer ties with emerging economies in Asia, including this year's G20 host Indonesia, which is aligned with neither the West nor Russia or China. The goal is for the UK to have the widest presence of any country in the region. After Sunak's first big change on the global stage, it is clear that Asia is a region of immense potential and opportunity for this UK prime minister.

Narendra Modi has already spoken to Sunak and he has been of the view that recognizing the "importance of early conclusion of a comprehensive and balanced FTA", it should be concluded soon. Sunak has already understood its importance and has made up his mind to take it towards perfection consciously but soon. It goes without saying that his dealings with India will be watched here and there with great curiosity and expectation. The truth lies in the name of Rishi Sunak that it would be inevitable to see him as a 'Sage' and 'savior'.

The UK finalized a reciprocal migration agreement with India ahead of Rishi Sunak's first one-on-one meeting with Narendra Modi. Under an agreement reached during the G20 summit in Indonesia, degree-educated young Indian nationals will be able to travel to the UK Up to 3,000 visas will be given to work in the UK for up to two years. The same number of visas will be offered by India to Britons and will be available to people aged 18 to 30. The scheme, which was first announced last year, will begin early next year. In Sunak's words, "I know all too well the incredible value of our deep cultural and historical links with India. I am delighted that more of India's brightest young people will now have the opportunity to experience life in the UK – and with It will also be a golden opportunity to enrich our economies and societies." Speaking to reporters attending the G20 summit, Sunak said a trade deal with India "is a great opportunity for the U.K. It was a great opportunity". But he added: "I will not sacrifice quality for speed. And that goes for all trade deals. It is important that we get them right rather than rushing them and so that is the approach I will take. With India Secondly, remember the trade deal is just one part of our broader relationship which is incredibly strong and really strategic and happens on many different aspects of policy. You know, trade is an important part of it, but This is not the only part and we will make progress in all of them."

To Sunakism

There was a day when there was British rule in India and the intellectual class of the country could not even say anything directly to the British rule. It was not possible to say bluntly about the injustice of the English ruler located across the seven seas. Poets used to say – *Andhadhundh* machyo sab desa. Today, many writers, litterateurs and intellectuals of the world including India fearlessly say this. Even at the time of 1857, the people of India could not shake their heads due to fear – the fear of which the people of India could not shake their heads. But now people openly describe the tyranny of British rule in their country. Yes, now he definitely has a deep affinity towards him and wishes for his welfare. All this is due to Rishi Sunak. It has to be clarified by giving an example or quote.

Economically, Britain is devastated. It will undoubtedly be the most fragile economy in the developed world, with no green shoots to be seen. It is one thing to raise taxes and cut government expenditure but it is equally important to address domestic consumption and inflation and attract investors to England, neither of which seems likely.

Rishi Sunak had to ask one of his ministers to resign, while the Deputy Prime Minister faced criticism. Labor Party leader Keith Starmer is also proving ineffective and a situation is being reached where his predecessor, Jeremy Corbyn, is prepared to stand as an independent candidate for the mayoral election of London, if the seat is not held by his own party. Is given. Britain's place in the global community of nations Margaret Thatcher's famous phrase was "The ladies not for turning". It was adapted and ridiculed in connection with Liz Truss's endless series of U-turns. But now it would seem that there is also a 'man is for turning'. That means even sages go back on their words. The harshest criticism of Sunak lies in his cabinet selection, primarily his decision to reappoint Suella Braverman as Home Secretary. It is felt that Sunak brought Braverman in because he declared support for her during the weeks-long campaign. Considering how close Penny Mordaunt was to securing the desired number of MPs for the PM nomination, she deserved a more senior position in cabinet.

Rishinomics

In this age of internet search engine optimization, there is a game to be played. Whenever someone new comes on the scene –in politics, sports, or culture –thousands of articles pop up entitled, "who is …?" "It is meant to be one of the best ways for sites to pick up internet traffic. But age, height and net worth only tell you so much about Rishi Sunak. Thus begins an article by James Forsyth. He is talking about Rishinomics.

Similarly, Rishi Sunak writes on 20 July 2022 in "The Telegraph" before he became the PM, "If I become PM, I will deliver the radical set of reforms need to unleash growth. I will be the heir to Margaret Thatcher." Sunak offers his life-long competence and prudence in this idea. As a principled pragmatism his financial prudence through Rishinomics is an offer no one can refuse to accept. Though it may bring hardship to the people of the sixth largest economy as a corporation tax rise and national insurance may come to stay because of this act. Adam Marshall, the former director general of the British Chambers of Commerce (BCC), who liaised with Sunak when he was chancellor during the height of the pandemic in 2020, says: "I found him to be across the detail and genuinely curious about getting feedback from the business community."

Trussonomics failed miserably as Liz Truss was "the radical tax-cutter". On the other hand, Rishi is "the cautious fighter against inflation". Sunak does not like to make promises of unfunded tax cuts at a time of soaring inflation. He wants to bring down taxes once he has "gripped" inflation. The real difference between them is "timing and tone".

Challenges and pitfalls

Rishi Sunak's reputation for public economic competence was forged during lockdown and proved in the summer leadership debate. Now he must be both book-keeper to a nation in a new crisis, and peace-keeper to the deeply divided Conservative party. Forming his Cabinet and policy are the first steps in a long journey. Dr Matt Cole, University of Birmingham

'Whenever you think of Rishi, think of wealth.' is a slogan Sunak would not like to be repeated and propagated. His upper-class background and immense wealth has been a pitfall in his political career. He is advised to avoid a clumsy show-off of his wealth when the entire country is reeling under economic pressure. He should not think that people don't notice what he and his family wear and eat. He shouldn't try to hide his wealth behind an ordinary-guy façade. They do notice and get annoyed. He should never give the impression that he is too rich to be the PM. His ideal for this can be his father in law. He should understand the anxiety many in Britain feel as the economy staggers under the combined weight of Covid-19, Brexit, and the Ukraine war.

He is doing his bit in this regard. "As a Conservative, I believe in hard work and aspiration and ...that's my story," he told the BBC earlier this year. I don't judge people by their bank accounts; I judge them by their character. And I think people can judge me by my actions over the past couple of years."

Only time will tell how well Rishi Sunak does, and how much confidence he can instill in his party and indeed the British public. One hopes they do well, and will be able to fix this mess. Otherwise, there are fears the Conservative Party will have no future. Given the disastrous economic climate, the grandiose Johnsonian vision will no longer find followers in Britain. At a time when the opposition Labor Party looks set to win the next general election, Sunak Will have to try his best to win from his side. For this he will have to endear himself to the Conservative Party elite. His economic policy is not going to be liked by the common people as well as the special people, so he will have to take a tough stand on issues like immigration. In Rishi Raj, there may not be prosperity like Ramrajya, but whatever the economic future of Britain The map is with him, he will definitely not let disaster pass him by.

Sunak needs a foreign policy if he wants to reset the UK's relationships internationally. Johnson and Truss were both foreign secretaries before entering No. 10 Downing Street. Sunak rose to power after a seven-year parliamentary career as chancellor who was very successful in overseeing the economic response to coronavirus. It is expected that his foreign policy will be based on a strong economic footing. But the economy is weak. "Whether it's the Indo-Pacific tilt [to strengthen economic ties in the region], making Britain into a science and technology superpower, or funding defense, aid and diplomacy — whatever it is you want to do in terms of global ambitions, you need to be able to pay for it. And it's a lot harder if you've got a weak economy."[7] This is the question raised by critics and commentators.

Certain Cassandra -like soothsayers proclaim, "whoever he ends up being as Prime Minister; Sunak will probably not be able to divert the torrent that is coming. The Conservative Party is tired of being in government and the public is tired of it. It's Time for it to depart and conduct the argument about whether it wants to go for culture wars with Kemi Badenoch, a civil war with Johnson, something of the night with Dominic Raab or all-out war with Braverman. The obvious best move would be to beg Sunak to stay but this has become a self-destructive party."[8]

The challenges and ptifalls are there and will remain for a while. But the greatest one is their ongoing post-Brexit "identity crisis." His government's long-term goal should be to clearly articulate its vision for Britain's place in the world and invest in the country's "soft power."

References

1 https://www.ndtv.com/world-news/rishi-sunaks-first-speech-as-uk-pm-full-text-3461114

2 https://www.nationalworld.com/news/politics/analysis-rishi-sunak-first-speech-prime-minister-3893049

3 https://www.thenationalnews.com/opinion/comment/2022/10/18/the-eu-must-act-against-josep-borrell-for-his-jungle-remarks/

4 https://www.indiatoday.in/magazine/editor-s-note/story/
20221107-from-the-editor-in-chief-2290662-2022-10-28

5 https://www.indiatoday.in/world/story/rishi-sunak-as-uk-
pm-where-do-india-uk-relations-stand-2289493-
2022-10-26

6 https://www.theguardian.com/commentisfree/2022/
nov/07/rishi-sunak-margaret-thatcher-wise-advice-
backbenches

7 https://www.politico.eu/article/wanted-foreign-policy-
britain-uk-rishi-sunak-g20/

8 https://www.newstatesman.com/comment/2022/10/how-
long-will-rishi-sunak-last

9

THE ARGUMENTATIVE STANCE

"I didn't get into politics to say what sounds good. That means sometimes taking the difficult road, landing the less popular message, telling the truth."

—Rishi Sunak

On 30 March 2022, an article By Ben Walker was published in a magazine. The title of the piece was 'Has Rishi Sunak's bubble burst?' It turns out when he's not doling out the cash, Dishy Rishi isn't so popular after all. "What a journey. He started off with better ratings than any politician since the heydays of Tony Blair. He was talked up as a flexible operator suited to playing to the gallery. When Boris Johnson's premature obituaries were written in December in the midst of partygate, he was cast as the obvious successor to guarantee a Conservative victory in the next election. But with the Spring Statement behind him, and an increasingly disquieted public disappointed with its meager offerings, Rishi Sunak's net approval rating is falling as fast as Johnson's was a few months ago."[1]

Perhaps the answer to this question was given by political research manager Chris Curtis in subsequent months. "Ever since announcing the furlough scheme in March with a declaration that he was willing to do "whatever it takes" to protect the economy, Rishi Sunak has been the most popular serving politician in the country. Polling conducted by YouGov after Wednesday's statement shows the latest rafts of announcements have helped to solidify this status. Six in ten (59%) now think he is doing a good job as Chancellor of the Exchequer (up 10% since June) with just 11% thinking he is doing a bad job (unchanged since June). This makes him the most popular man to hold the office in 15 years, since Gordon Brown still held his reputation as the "Iron Chancellor" in the run up to the 2005 election."[2]

Following his appointment as chancellor, Sunak arrived in public discourse from relative obscurity. In the early stages of the COVID-19 pandemic, he was popular by the standards of British politics, described by one analyst as having "better ratings than any politician since the heydays of Tony Blair". Various polls showed Sunak remained overwhelmingly popular among Conservative supporters and many other Britons throughout 2020. Public attitudes towards Sunak remained broadly positive in 2021, though his popularity declined steadily over time. By early 2022, with the cost of living becoming a growing focus of public concern, Sunak's response as chancellor was perceived as inadequate and he received some of his lowest approval ratings, which continued as the Sunak family's financial affairs came under scrutiny. By the time he resigned as chancellor in July 2022, Sunak's approval ratings slightly recovered. In an Ipsos MORI poll in September 2020, Sunak had the highest satisfaction score of any British Chancellor since Labour's Denis Healey in April 1978, and was widely seen as the favorite to become the next Prime Minister and leader of

Conservative Party after Boris Johnson. Sunak developed a cult media following, with jokes and gossip about his attractiveness widespread on social media and in magazines, gaining the nickname "Dishi Rishi." 'Big spender Rishi Sunak is the most popular chancellor since Labour's Denis Healey in the 1970s, according to a new poll, which showed even Labour voters are pleased with his performance.'[3]

His future Tory leadership hopes were boosted when the poll suggested voters rated him above Boris Johnson for being "good in a crisis" and having sound judgment.

***

"I am of the view that India is by far the world's most significant source of undiscovered and undervalued talent. It is akin to Germany and central Europe in the late 19th and early 20th centuries, and someday will be seen as such. It is possible to believe this and still have mixed or uncertain views about India's future as a nation, just as central Europe in that time faced plenty of turmoil."[4] Tyler Cowen

Now that the British-Indian politician Rishi Sunak has become the Prime Minister of the United Kingdom, some show indifference but some left liberals can't digest it. Left-leaning politicians and intellectuals are increasingly fretting over Sunak and his wife's movable and immovable assets and status, and are criticizing them for the same. Rishi Sunak witnessed both bricks and bouquets from the world media as he scripted history by becoming the first person of color to become the Prime Minister of Britain, which in the past had colonized most of the world.

Rishi Sunak, 42, is the youngest prime minister in over 200 years of UK politics. Also remember that the average age of his cabinet is a decade older than his, at 52. Team Sunak has

The Rise of Rishi Sunak

Dominic Raab(48), Jeremy Hunt(55), Suella Braverman(42), James Cleverly(53), Ben Wallace(52), and Michael Gove(55). It was 49 during Truss and 48 under Boris. It is important to have people around you with great and long experience who can benefit from constant mentorship and listening. In his young image, political thinking, fast-paced speed, calm nature with sea-like seriousness, self-confident personality amazes with its complete aura. His own demure style has earned him the title of 'Dishi Rishi' by the British media. Prior to Sunak, William Pitt 'the Younger' became Britain's youngest Prime Minister.

The youngest prime minister in the entire history of Britain was known as William Pitt the Younger. At only 24 years old in 1783, he was not only the youngest prime minister of Great Britain, but the first to hold that exact title. He was also the last person. He left office that year, but served again from 1804 to 1806, when he died at the age of 46. Sunak has gone from MP to Prime Minister in only seven years – faster than any other Prime Minister in the modern era. David Cameron achieved the same in nine years, but Pitt the Younger holds the overall record with only two years. Extremely rich, young and the first person of color (Gaurang not being) to become Prime Minister of Britain, Rishi Sunak is also making history as the first practicing Hindu to lead the country. Sunak's success is a triumph of diversity: he is the first British of Indian origin to become prime minister, and as a Hindu, the first non-Christian. But this is also a victory for the establishment. At one time in India also it happened that the President of India Abdul Kalam was a Muslim, Prime Minister Manmohan Singh was a Sikh and UPA chairperson Sonia Gandhi was a Christian.

It is also noteworthy that Rishi Sunak will be the 5th Prime Minister of Britain in the last six years. His appointment as Prime Minister comes after Liz Truss announced her resignation as the

56th Prime Minister of Britain on 20 October 2022. Truss now has the undeserved record of sitting in the PM's chair for just 44 days. The record for the shortest tenure as PM was previously held by George Canning, who held the post for 119 days until his death on August 8, 1827.

Criticism

His background of Indian origin and extreme wealth makes his every move intensely scrutinized by his critics. The simple fact of a man of Indian origin occupying the highest office of the British Government is like a strange kind of modern drama.- a drama that has clear traces of the age-old tales of a vassal-turned-prince. Now what does it mean that they represent British Indians only in a nominal and symbolic way. His parliamentary constituency of Richmond, York, is a predominantly white rural area with only about 1 per cent Asian. Rishi Sunak must now find himself juxtaposed between fairytale and brutal reality. Mitali Saran feels sorry for poor Rishi Sunak. He may have become Britain's youngest and first non-white Prime Minister by walkover, in the shitstorm that is current British politics, but he's also India's first British-Indian Hindu-Elite Prime Minister of another country. Not only is every Indian who knows someone who knows someone who knows Narayana Murthy's dog walker's cousin going to want a piece of Sunak, for a possible invite/contract/visa/citizenship, but his public life will also be dogged by a chorus of embarrassing triumphalism from India."[5]

Lord Ashcroft KCMG PC is an international businessman, philanthropist, author and pollster. He is Rishi Sunak's biographer also. As a biographer he says that he is the first to acknowledge that Sunak has his critics. Some accuse him of having torpedoed Boris Johnson's premiership this summer. He has also been labelled too slick for his own good. And the fact that he grew prosperous as a financier, and then married the daughter of a highly successful Indian businessman, is held against him, too. India today's editor –in chief Aroom Purie has the last word, "if he fails, he may go down in history as a colorful night-watchman that the Tories sent to a crumbling pitch in failing light."

First about his color...

"Rishi Sunak: Young, ultra-rich and UK's first PM of color" This is how France24 describes him. For some, it is a 'watershed moment', for others, "it's time to revisit claims about racism in the Anglosphere, including the widespread assertions of systemic/institutional racism that now inform and in many cases guide public policy, corporate hiring and university staffing and admissions ...The rise of Rishi Sunak to the highest political office in the United Kingdom is a good thing for several reasons, but not least for demonstrating the success of individual Britons irrespective of color and creed."[6] Opines Samir Shah "as well as being a Hindu, he is a 'person of color', the description beloved of certain sections of the commentariat. Already the race lobby has written columns about how his elevation to PM is not a sign of Britain's success in race relations. I find the phrase 'people of color' offensive. Describing people as not white (parenthetical thought: isn't white a color?) is deeply negative. It implies that 'white' is the default setting and every other skin color is a deviation. The phrase serves only to place us in a subordinate position, and that plays to the victim narrative equally beloved of the same sections of the commentariat."[7]

Even in India, how were they saddened to see - People's President Droupadi Murmu and former President Ram Nath Kovind being in office? Their pen doesn't work anymore, but the tongue definitely works like scissors.

Next his Heritage

"I am now a citizen of Britain. But my religion is Hindu. My religious and cultural heritage is Indian. I proudly say that I am a Hindu and my identity is also a Hindu," Sunak said in 2017, when former Prime Minister Theresa May made him a minister in her cabinet. In August 2022, when Sunak was considered a likely candidate to succeed Boris Johnson as prime minister, he was spotted performing a "gau pooja" (cow worship) in London. A large section of Hindus in India consider the cow sacred and revered. But Sunak is an advocate of saving and growing meat from all kinds of cattle. However, as a British leader, he has and should have many such commitments. Rishi Sunak is the UK's first prime minister of color and the first Hindu prime minister. He has made his commitment to his faith clear by performing puja, and by taking the oath as an MP on the Bhagavad Gita. As prime minister, Sunak will likely enjoy the backing of the Indian diaspora, one of the largest ethnic minorities in the UK, numbering close to 1.5 million people.

Wealth and Richness

Super Rich?

In fact, Rishi is not super rich, but his wife is just like American Kerry. TV comedians used to make fun of him by calling him Cash and Carey. But this fact is easily forgotten by the leftists. This is a detailed analysis of the same leftist media coverage, reading which one can think that he who is rich in pots is Rishi Sunak, while the truth is something-somewhere else. Some people may reject Rishi Sunak out of envy, but they may also admire him and those who manage like him to get on in the world. The current and recent senior Cabinet Ministers from ethnic minorities — with some exceptions like Sajid Javid, the former Chancellor and Health Secretary, and Kemi Badenoch, the Trade Secretary and Equalities Minister — most share a privileged background. Kwasi Kwarteng is the son of wealthy Ghanaian parents and educated at Eton. Nadeem Zahawi's grandfather was a government minister in Iraq, his father a businessman, director of Balshore Investments, and he went to a private school.

Rishi Sunak too is educated privately and rich- very rich. Infosys Chairman Emeritus N.R. Akshata Murthy, daughter of Narayana Murthy and wife of Rishi, has a personal net worth of around $4.5 billion. With Akshata, who receives $715 million through her 0.93 per cent stake in Infi, the couple's wealth becomes immense. Sunak's racial identity is less important to most Britons than this fact about him. People feel sorry for him and his wife being rich. He has earned this money. His wife has found it. Sunak does not hide his wealth, he shows it. People become the center of attraction and comments. : The tailored suit, a Peloton exercise bike, that absurdly expensive self-heating cup. To those sensitive to the noble vibrations of the British class system, it seems to make them "new money" because unlike Sunak, Boris Johnson went to Eton and won a scholarship. Sanuks are uncommon among these modest people. Some also maintained that Sunak had held onto a green card until October 2021, allowing him permanent residency in the United States. His critics have at times made allegations about how determined he was to live out the rest of his life in Britain. Forbes estimates Sunak and his wife Akshata Murthy's net worth to be around $810 million. In contrast, it is more than a quarter of a billion dollars, compared to King Charles III's personal wealth of $500 million.

Sunak, a father of two daughters, has his own personal real estate portfolio. The couple owns four luxurious homes in the UK and California, which are estimated to be worth $18.3 million. The largest asset he owns is the Manor House, a heritage-listed two-storey countryside mansion dating back to the 19th century in the village of Kirby Sigston in North Yorkshire, which he bought in July 2015 for $2.3 million. The Sunaks are reportedly spending $450,000 to set up a leisure center with a 40-foot swimming pool, a gym and an outdoor tennis court. In London, his main residence is at 16 Hesper Mews in upscale Kensington, a four-bedroom terraced house which he acquired in 2010 for $7.1 million. Sunak also has an apartment on Old Brompton Road in South Kensington, which he bought in September 2001 for around $300,000. In California—where Sunak and Murthy met as students at Stanford's Graduate School of Business—they have a beachfront penthouse that costs $7.5 million. It's unclear how much Sunak earns so far, but his new position as prime minister comes with a sizable salary. He will now earn more than $185,000 a year, nearly double his $95,000 salary as a lawmaker. Although he is certainly not as wealthy as his billionaire wife, Sunak worked in the field of economic management for more than a decade before entering politics in May 2015. He was then elected to Parliament in the constituency of Richmond, Yorkshire. His official financial disclosure details are unclear: for his financial assets it is only stated that he holds a "blind trust/blind management agreement".

In Hinduism, amassing wealth is not a sin but a virtue. There is a passage in "Manava-Dharma-shastra" – which encourages its adherents to be money–oriented and materialistic. There is even a goddess of wealth, Lakshmi. She is one who is widely worshiped. Sunak's economic policies are geared to wealth creation. In Christianity, the Gospels of Matthew and Luke suggest you cannot serve both God and mammon. In Hinduism you can. Let me tell you that in the USA the Vice President's name Kamala is the name of the goddess of wealth. In a thought provoking article in The Spectator, our dear friend Samir Shah comments, "Hinduism is wise to the pitfalls of accumulating wealth. The religion recognizes that wealth is needed to perform many of the duties required to be a good Hindu. And dharma is the lifelong duty to behave virtuously. Spending money for the welfare of others is a virtuous action. Compassion for those who do not have wealth is also considered a duty. It might have been politically expedient for Sunak, as chancellor, to implement the furlough scheme and 'eat out to help out'. But anyone expecting the new PM, for all his millions, to be a ruthless capitalist is in for a shock. His adherence to dharma will rein in the excesses of artha." Nothing more is required to add and say. This is the dharma. In the Bhagavad Gita, Lord Krishna sets out four principles of life. These are: Dharma, Arth, Kaam, and Moksha. The second one being *"artha"*, which is one of the meanings of which is "wealth". You may argue dear reader that it could mean "meaning" also. In some texts, *"artha"* means instruments of satisfaction too. The Bhakti cults even say *"artha"* is the instrument by which you love God. The flexibility of Hindu Dharma is such that one can interpret the meaning in more ways than one. Our Rishi Sunak, who studied Economics and not theology, took the first meaning of 'artha'. What else you can expect from a hedge-fund-manager?[8]

Beyond Symbolism

A part of the media is not in favor of discussing and indicating Rishi Sunak's elevation as symbolic. CNN (Opinion) can be cited here. Kehinde Andrews, professor of Black studies at Birmingham City University and the author of the book "The New Age of Empire: How Racism and Colonialism Still Rule the World" says that we should not fall for the symbolism of

Rishi Sunak's premiership. He argues that Sunak was not elected — the other Conservative candidate for the top job conceded after failing to meet the threshold of nominations — so this tells us little about voter attitudes in the wider electorate to racialized minority candidates. The fact that his skin is brown and his parents are immigrants does not mean he automatically has any affinity to the millions of Black and brown citizens who are victims of his party and its policies. All his ascension in the Conservative Party ranks proves is that race doesn't matter if you wholeheartedly embrace the party line. It may be tempting to fall for the symbolism, but Sunak does not represent racialized minorities in Britain. Migrant histories are far too diverse for any one person to do so."[9]

On the other hand, the symbolism of this tale of Rishi Sunak is tremendous. Certainly for those who share his color and cultural lineage. Yet, A British Indian in 10 Downing Street has a meaning beyond racial resonance. This is more than desi pride. Without diminishing the importance of a foreign surname - somewhat like Obama's - in the history of power in Western democracies, it could be argued that this Sunak story reveals the evolutionary paradoxes of conservatism in Britain. At Diwali two years ago it became clear to the world that Sunak was a practicing Hindu.

Begani Shaadi mein!

The political arena of India started challenging the Bharatiya Janata Party after Rishi Sunak became the Prime Minister as if Narendra Modi had a hand in making Rishi the Prime Minister. Chidambaram said in a tweet, "First Kamala Harris and now Rishi Sunak. The people of America and Britain have embraced non-majority citizens of their countries and elected them to high positions in government. "He also said," I think India and the parties that follow majoritarianism should learn a lesson. MP Mahua Moitra said, "I am proud of Britain, which is my second favorite country, for electing a British Asian to the top position. He said, "India should be more tolerant and more accepting of all religions, all backgrounds. Congress MP Shashi Tharoor said Britain has outgrown its racism, shown a tremendous willingness to assimilate and accept people of other religious faiths and above all has seen the merit of the individual. We must be prepared to look beyond certain considerations of caste, religion and class and language and region. The reward the country should give is merit. It is also a matter of pride for Britain and Britons that he enabled a man seen by some as an "outsider" to reach his country's highest political office. Politicians like Shashi Tharoor comment that Indians should learn something from this example; magnanimity is a quality that is our heritage even today.

As soon as Sunak became the Prime Minister, a new debate started in India: when will the minority community in India or should we say that the Muslim community becomes the Prime Minister? There was so much debate on social media that #MuslimPM became the top trend. Mehbooba Mufti, who was the CM of Jammu and Kashmir, while trying to surround the Government of India on the pretext of Sunak, said that Britain has accepted an ethnic minority as its PM. While we are busy following divisive laws like CAA and NRC. In the race to go ahead of all these, A.I.M.I.M. Its head Asaduddin Owaisi said, "I have already said that one day a girl wearing a hijab will become the Prime Minister of India." India will follow the tradition of electing one of the minorities to the top post, this is their intention, but they do not remember that this has been happening here. Just now the election of Her Excellency the President Mrs. Droupadi Murmu has taken place. They are the original residents. Tunku Varadarajan writes for The Wall Street

Journal, "But Mr. Sunak's rise presents an important truth to Indians: that their erstwhile masters are much more tolerant than they are. Indians should look to Britain for guidance on how a merit-based society works, and how minorities are treated as equals. Seventy-five years after its independence, India still has so much to learn from Britain, so much to emulate."[10]

By the way, some self-proclaimed journalists and writers of Indian origin are venting their anger by writing and speaking in Indian and foreign media. Like Nidhi Razdan and Pankaj Mishra, there are many others who have suffered. But quoting his writings with context will have to give them undue importance. The UK getting a Hindu Prime Minister is not a historic moment for them. They believe that this is being shown. Pankaj Mishra, referring to 'Hindu Supremacists' (a term used by Leftists/ Islamists for Nationalists and BJP supporters), said that for them Rishi Sunak is 'Deshi Bro'.

Sunak represents just 2.3 per cent of Britain's electorate. Muslims are almost 15 per cent of India's voters. Does India need to learn from British politics? In fact, British democracy offers valuable lessons to the whole world on how to accommodate religious and racial diversity. Mr Sunak becoming prime minister could accelerate a process already underway in the UK of the long-standing appeal of left-wing parties among ethnic minority voters. India should also be very proud in this regard. For example, in 2004, Hindu-majority India elected a Sikh (Manmohan Singh) as prime minister from a party led by an Italian-born Catholic (Sonia Gandhi). President APJ Abdul Kalam, who administered the oath to Mr. Singh, was a Muslim who was given the opportunity by the so-called Hindutva Bharatiya Janata Party.

Some people are still perplexed as to why Rishi Sunak's Hinduness should matter. It matters because of the imperial context, tweeted Satnam Sanghera, author of *"EmpireLand: How Imperialism has Shaped Modern Britain"* (2021). "Rishi Sunak, son of GP and pharmacist, becoming Chancellor but then nevertheless being portrayed as a doctor on front page of Daily Mail is the most Asian thing that has ever happened." His tweet after a while was, "Rishi Sunak's campaign is classic illustration of white privilege: he's plainly the most qualified, but keeps having to compete with woeful white candidates."

Rishi Sunak is not an Indian, this is the unalterable truth. He is British by birth. Even the talk of his 'Indian origin' is an exaggeration - an exaggeration as his parents are East African Asian. He migrated to East Africa in 1935 from Gujranwala in pre-independent India. In Pakistan, the birth of Rishi Sunak's ancestors is another unfinished agenda of Partition. In Gujranwala, the city of wrestlers, a group of residents, including some wrestlers, came out on the streets to greet the British PM. Naila Inayat, a freelance Pakistani journalist writes "Wait until they find out that Joe Biden has already called up Sunak, and there is even a video of it. The same video confirms that anyone dipping a biscuit in Chai is a certified desi. Now the US president calling UK PM 'Rasheed Sunook' is no coincidence, had his family stayed in Pakistan Rasheed would have been his name today. Food for more conspiracies…"[11]

Abuses

In the BBC "word cloud" program people were asked to describe Rishi in one word. Yes, there were other far more positive adjectives like "clever", "smart", "capable", but what stayed were the abuses. Among the popular phrases to describe the PM were "rich", "okay", "capable" and "liar". Other descriptions included "boring", "posh" and "arrogant". But some viewers were surprised when they saw the words "twat" and "c***" spread across their TV screens. Unfortunately -- or perhaps deliberately -- certain nasty, vulgar expletives appeared on air. They were shocking to the viewers. But they were there. To call Sunak a "t**t and a c**t" blatantly exposed what many Britons think of him.

In the words of Ganesh R –It should be clear to anyone that Rishi Sunak suffers from double or even triple jeopardy – he is not just a rightwing conservative but also a dark skinned Hindu that is not ashamed of his legacy and faith. That makes him 'wajib-al-qatl' as per the Stalinist fringe left-Islamist jihadi fanatics' continuum, as well as assorted Lutyens coolies of fascist looter dynasts that passes for liberals in today's world."

Response and Rebuttal

Still, Rishi feels like one of our own because in 2009 he was married to Narayana Murthy's daughter Akshata. Let us not forget that Akshata still holds her Indian passport, and Rishi has always been a British citizen, a British passport holder by birth. Though irreverent, provocative, opinionated Shobhaa De is not off the mark when she tweets, "Rishi Sunak is Rishi Sunak. He has not been appointed to such an important post for being someone's son-in-law. Okay???

The common man does not understand that Rishi is British by birth. We Hindus have the pride and satisfaction that one of us has got himself established at this place. Sunak has repeatedly underlined his faith in Hinduism. "British Indian is the category that I tick at the census; we have a category for that. I am completely British, this is my home and my country, but my religious and cultural heritage is Indian, my wife is Indian, I am open and forthright about being a Hindu," Sunak said in an interview to Business Standard in 2015. He was seen wearing the sacred red Hindu 'Kalava' thread during his maiden speech at 10 Downing Street.Mauli or Kalava is a cotton red thread, which is considered very sacred and is used for all religious purposes by Hindus. The thread is also used to offer clothes to the deity. Molly thread is an integral part of any puja. By worshiping and attending Hindu religious lessons, he says he is a Hindu in body and mind. Sunak made history when he lit Diwali candles and lamps outside 11 Downing Street, the official residence of the UK Chancellor. Describing the experience, Sunak told The Times, "It was in a sense Gosh, this is great, but also that's just Britain". He added, "Hopefully it's a source of collective pride".

As an MP, he took the oath of his office by laying his hands on the Bhagavad Gita. There are a range of options, from the choice of the holy book to the language in which the oath is to be taken. And so each time some members choose the Bible and some the Gita or the Quran (Alok Sharma also chose the Gita) similarly some choose to take the oath in Welsh or Urdu apart from English.

***

Symbol of hope and faith

Rishi will improve relations between India and Britain. He would certainly try to change UK-India relations by becoming the first Indian-origin Prime Minister. Sunak's vision for India-UK bilateral relations appears to go beyond the opportunity for the UK to sell goods in India; he believes that the UK must also 'learn from' India. They are not the citizens of our country but we have good relations with them. There is a relation between bread and daughter. It is our sense of belongingness because of which we Indians usually see the achievements of overseas Indians living abroad as our own. And take pride in them - be it the Indians leading Google and Microsoft or Kamala Harris, whom I had written a book in English on seeing becoming the Vice President of America. But there is a difference between Kamala Harris and Rishi Sunak. The difference is that Sunak's ties with India are distant; his own relatives are no longer in India. His grandparents originated from British India and his birthplace is located in the Punjab province of Gujranwala (now in Pakistan). Rishi Sunak's parents – retired doctor Yashveer and pharmacist Usha Sunak – are of Indian origin and moved to the UK from Kenya in the 1960s. His parents followed a thoroughly postcolonial route from India through East Africa to Britain in the 1960s. His parents followed a thoroughly postcolonial route from India through East Africa to Britain in the 1960s. After settling in Southampton, an unnamed port city in southern England, his mother worked as a pharmacist and his father as a general doctor. The couple gave their boy the best (or at least the most expensive) education they could afford. As well as his ethnic background, everything about his later career is top-notch: boarding school, Oxford, Goldman Sachs, Stanford business school, a hedge fund, then a think tank, then a political career. They are a reflection of Britain's continuing desire to combine modernity with tradition.

***

Britain's symbol of political maturity

When a person of Indian origin was selected for the post of Prime Minister by a right-wing party in Britain, it was not said by any MP that he is a person of foreign origin. That's why I will shave my head or shave my head if he becomes the Prime Minister. In terms of the place of identity in politics, comparisons are bound to be made and were made with India as well. Sonia Gandhi's foreign origin came in her way and perhaps formal power was out of reach for her in 2004 and she automatically stepped down from the seat of the prime minister and her supporters declared it as her exemplary sacrifice. In the twenty-first century, when a woman's foreign origin is made an issue by the opposition party in India, there is strong opposition. In the same century, Muhammad Sadiq of Pakistani origin was elected as the Mayor of London and Rishi Sunak of Indian origin was elected as the Prime Minister of Britain.

This is called liberalism, this is called pluralism. This is called unity. Britain has shown how liberal its society and political parties are, how mature they are. It is not the first time that the Prime Minister of Britain has been made by someone who is not a Christian. Earlier in 1868, Benjamin Disraeli became the Prime Minister of Britain whose father was Jewish. But his father had a dispute with his Synagogue in 1813 and left Judaism. After that he converted to Christianity and raised his children according to Christian religion. Remember that till 1858 people of Jewish religion were banned from entering the British Parliament. The political scenario in Britain today is something like this... The Prime Minister is a Hindu, the Mayor of London is a Muslim and the King of the country is a Christian.

One interesting thing that seems to have been overlooked in the way he took office was that he was "crowned" by an uncrowned king. For then until that day the king had yet to be crowned in a ceremony where the Archbishop of Canterbury would bestow on him the aura that the crown is a symbol of. A Hindu Prime Minister was sworn in by the Bhagavad Gita in a Christian majority country. And he would advise the king in choosing an archbishop for the Church of England! Interestingly, in Britain, the state is constitutionally Christian. But all citizens, including minorities, are equal before the law and guaranteed full democratic and civil rights.

For Britons, Sunak's Indian origins come as no surprise, nor is it particularly worthy of comment. Of the 11 MPs initially fielded, four were women, and there were only three who could be called White British Men. Two were of Pakistani origin, one Nigerian and one Kurdish, and two of Indian origin. Rishi Sunak's Indian or Hindu origins were coincidental for he was seen there as part of a wider kaleidoscope of diversity in British politics.

The rise of Rishi Sunak shows what is possible when the process is open and welcoming, observes Jammi N Rao. By focusing on the individual, and particularly on the Indian origin and Hinduism of the individual, India's media commentators have failed to note the role of British society and the open nature of the political process that recognizes merit and fosters deserving talent. Personal identity attributes such as religious affiliation and racial origin have become irrelevant. The real lesson to learn from recent events in Britain is *not* the rise of a talented and successful Indian-origin politician. The real lesson India needs to learn is about the open, democratic, and welcoming structures and systems in place in Britain that allow women, minorities, and foreign-born citizens to rise on the strength of their merit in academia, the professions, and in public life; to win electoral office; and even to stand for selection as the next prime minister of the country. [12]

Pakistan Connection

The matter does not end here. Just as the media of India is trying to link Rishi with India, the wrestlers of Pakistan are asserting their claim, the people of Tanzania and Kenya are mixing their voices, so are the Americans saying the same.

We also have some right on Rishi. He became intelligent by studying in America. He got wisdom in America and wisdom became Akshata Murthy. One newspaper writes, "Britain and America's relations in the 19th century were mostly commercial, perhaps best symbolized by Andrew Carnegie, the Scottish-born American steel baron who served as the U.S. And was famous for his philanthropy in the British Empire. Our military alliance with Britain was paramount in the 20th century. We had a relationship with Winston Churchill who was very dear to Americans, and to a degree reciprocated as a symbol of that bond we still have today. And now in the 21st century, here comes Rishi Sunak who associated himself with Wall Street and did MBA in our country. America brought up the sage of Britain, even if it was only for a short time, but this contribution is of no use.

London-based expatriate Hindi litterateur Tejendra Sharma concludes an editorial in 'Purwai' (*Rishi Ek, Sanak Hajar*) "News channels and newspapers began to find out about the ancestors of Rishi Sunak. He was said to be a descendant of Sunak, the sage of the Vedic period. We do not even know whether Rishi can speak Hindi or not... Yes, he comes from a Khatri family of Punjabi origin, so he must have spoken Punjabi." I may add here that the mother tongue of his wife is Kannada, he must also know Kannada. His friends are from Pakistan so he must know Urdu too. In one of his tweets, he wrote, "United by friendship. Ek majbuut dosti". I have watched a handful of videos in which he is speaking a few sentences in Hindi. We Indians guess from *Sthali Pulak Nyay*. Rishi does not know Hindi, is out of the question. We can guess the contents of the letter by looking at the envelope.

Dr. Mayank Chaturvedi writes in detail in 'Panchjanya' (Refreshing memories of Indian wisdom tradition on the pretext of Rishi Sunak), Britain's Prime Minister is a Sanatani from the

Rishi Sunak gotra, so the belief must be strong that he will neither run away fearing Britain's bad economy nor sit silent fearing criticism from his opponents. His Indian genes will automatically motivate him to face all the challenges and ultimately achieve success for himself. (briten ke pradhaanamantree rshi sunak gotr se sanaatanee hai, isalie yah vishavashhee shakhai ki ve na to briten kee bigadee arthavtha se ghabaraakar palaayan karenge aur na hee apane virodhiyon kee aalochanaon se ghabaraakar chup baithenge. unaka bhaarateey jeen unako s: skarata rahega ki sabhee chunautiyon ka saamana kar ant mein saphalata ka svayan varan Karen.[13]

It is not such a small thing. This victory is historic. The name Rishi, or the word Rishi, means a person who is enlightened and who has great wisdom. To address a person by the name of Rishi means to underline the knowledge of that person. We all either know or want to know the importance of our name. We want to be like our name and qualities. Rishi Sunak is also similar to his name and the quality associated with his name . No doubt about it.

For clarity and correctness, it should be remembered that by nationality, Mr Sunak is a Brit. His duty is to protect and promote British interests. As has been underlined by those who know him well, Mr Sunak's awareness of unspoken race-connected reservations about him will make him even more protective of British interests in UK-Indian negotiations. Rajmohan Gandhi[14]

There is no need to tell you what is the importance of Satyanarayan and his story in the Hindu mind and Hindu faith. It comes first in the story of Satyanarayan - *Ekda Naimisharanya Rishay: Shaunkaday: || Paprachchurmanayaḥ sarve suṭṭa purāṇikaṁ khalu |1||* (Once upon a time, eighty-eight thousand sages asked Shri Sutji about Shaunikadi in Naimisharanya

Tirtha) Shaunaka is a noun used for teachers and a branch of the Atharvaveda. Specifically it is the name of a famous Sanskrit grammarian who was the author of the Rigveda-Pratishakhya. He is said to have united the Bashkal and Shakal branches of the Rigveda. The Rigveda-Pratishakhya is attributed to Shaunaka, who taught it to others at a Satra-yajna (a 12-day mass sacrifice) held at Naimisharanya. According to Puranas, Rishi Shaunak was a Vedic teacher, who was the son of Bhriguvanshi Shunak Rishi. His full name was Indrotdaiwaya Shaunak. If we look at his lineage tradition, first of all the story named "Pramdwara ko snakebite" is found in the eighth chapter of Mahabharata in Paulom festival under Adiparva. In which the clan-gotra of Rishi Shunak has been explained in detail.

Chyavan, the son of Maharishi Bhrigu, gave birth to a son from his wife Sukanya's womb, whose name was Pramati. Mahatma Pramati was very bright. Then Pramati gave birth to a son named Ruru from Ghritachi Apsara and through Ruru Shunak was born from Pramadwara's womb. Shaunakji is called 'Shaunak' because of being the son of Shunak. Shunak was full of great Sattva qualities and was going to increase the joy of the entire Bhriguvansh. As soon as he was born, he got involved in intense penance. Due to this his steady fame spread everywhere.

It is said that Rishi Shaunak had achieved the unique honor of Chancellor by running a Gurukul of a total of 10,000 students. It is said that before him no other sage had received such an honour. Shaunak had a prominent role in the Mahabharata epic. The entire Mahabharata was narrated by a storyteller named Ugrasrava Sauti during an assembly of sages presided over by Shaunaka in the Aranya (forest) named Naimisha. 'Rishi Sunak', who is adorned by the name of this sage, has the same name and qualities.

Sankadi Rishi (Sanakadi = Sanak + etc.) refers to the four sons of Brahma, Sanak, Sanandan, Sanatan and Sanatkumar. His special importance is described in Puranas. They are the Ionij children of Brahma and are incarnations of Lord Vishnu who are counted among the 10 creations. These are from both natural and abnormal cantos.

In fact, it seems that 'Shaunik' of Sanskrit became 'Sunak' in Punjabi and keeping in view the historicity, sanctity etc. of this name, 42 years ago - on May 12, 1980, the parents of the British The child whose name was named 'Rishi Sunak' became the Prime Minister of that country today. It should be said that 'Sunak' is his surname, probably gotra only. Rishi is his name and the Hindus of North India do not usually have a middle name like the English Christians.

Hardly half of the dramatic life of this era man has been seen so far. Half is yet to come. But whatever has been seen is strange and surprising. On this you are going to read this first book written in Hindi, so this is also a unique thing. This book is the first and it is certain that it will not remain the first. The limitations of the first books are also there. But it is certain that through this book you will get acquainted with some known and unknown aspects of Rishi Sunak's life. And will be proud of Rishi as well.

Bharatvanshi Yatra - Tatra - Everywhere

Have you not yet wondered how a Hindu would run the government of a country which has an established religion (Christianity as recognized by the Anglican Church), and where the then Prime Minister had earlier this year visited the late Queen Elizabeth II At the funeral service, some passages from the Bible were read aloud. Will Sunak be able to do so on a similar occasion if the need arises? I think you can definitely do it. This is the identity and specialty of a Sanatani Hindu.

The election of Rishi Sunak as Prime Minister of the United Kingdom is "very surprising" and "an unprecedented milestone", according to US President Joe Biden. In the words of the US President, "Diwali, the festival of lights, is a reminder that we all have the ability to dispel darkness and bring light into the world. This is an option. And we make choices every day. This is true in our life and in the life of this country, especially in the life of a democracy, be it here in America or for many families in India which is completing 75 years of independence. Rishi Sunak is expected to be prime minister, I think, tomorrow when he visits the king. Quite surprising. An unprecedented milestone. And it matters. It matters a lot."[15]

In 2020, when Biden chose Indian-origin Kamala Harris as his running partner, he created history. As the Vice President of the United States of America, Kamala Harris is now the second most powerful figure in the country after the US-President. She is the first woman of Indian origin to hold this position. (See - Kamala D Harris - Dr. Gopal Sharma)

You would like to compare Rishi Sunak with Kamala Harris and Barack Obama. There is no harm either. Kamala Harris may leave a couple of sparklers on Deepawali, but she neither lets her Hindu past nor does Indian history confront her Africanness. Rishi Sunak is a Hindu by birth and practice, while Kamala Harris is a Hindu only by birth. Sunak becoming prime minister in 2022 is more significant and surprising than Barack Obama assuming office for the presidency in the United States in 2008 because black people dominated the American political scene for years and the number of Indians or Asians in American politics is low. They were more visible than they were. Obama considered himself an African-American and used the trait extensively. Taking this as a basis, talked about racism and often focused the attention of America and the world on racial issues. President Barack Obama's maternal lineage can be traced to his "great-grandfather" Joseph Kearney, a shoe repairman. Not only had this, as President, Obama visited an Irish village where his great-grandfather used to make shoes.

All the Indian newspapers are talking about an Indian running the UK and hoping that the Free Trade Agreement will now be an easy walkover. Britain needed its new prime minister to take care of itself. It is a matter of pride that a person with ancestral roots in India is now the Prime Minister of Britain. But Sunak will be as Indian as Barack Obama was Kenyan. Barack Obama was not just a freshman senator as he embarked on his first presidential campaign. He had the flair of a creator and the innovative thrill of a visionary. The process of Rishi becoming prime minister had his own distinct, if not identical, gritty excesses. Both made history. How much both of them kept their native country in mind, it is well known about one, it will also be known about the other - Barber, Barber, how many hair, They are coming forward, see for yourself, Host!

Sunak just presents himself as a Tory politician. It seems that Rishi Sunak neither sees nor wants to separate himself in this way. Sunak has succeeded in British politics as a Hindu, but this is apparently not possible in the United States, although the Indian Diaspora there appears to be more powerful in terms of education, jobs and social status.

The success of the talent of the youth of Indian origin is being heard all over the world at this time. Important Indian-origin CEOs include Sundar Pichai of Alphabet, Satya Nadella of Microsoft, Parag Agarwal of Twitter (probably not for much longer), Shantanu Narayen of Adobe, Arvind Krishna of IBM, Raj Subramaniam of FedEx, Sonia Singhal of Gap and Starbucks.

K Laxman Narasimhan is included. These are the names that are in America. One is in America, the greatest producer of managerial talent the world has ever seen. It is also noteworthy that many of these people were born in India.

"We are not a country. We are a proprietorship that wants to appropriate everything, including that which was never ours." Some commentators got it right. For us, the whole world is a family. As many words for relatives are there in our languages, there are not so many in English. That's why we have brought Rishi Sunak in the midst of ours.

Dadabhai and his ilk

Let us ponder over the background. It is always good to know what happened and in what circumstances. From the nineteenth century itself, Britain began to ensure that they transmitted to their native subjects the system and thought rooted in their own culture and values through English education. This was the signal in Macaulay's education system. A special section of India first understood the importance of English education and then made it the medium of their upliftment and used education as a tool of development. The story of Dadabhai Naoroji (1825–1917) is well known. Dadabhai Naoroji was a scholar, professor, political leader, freedom fighter and businessman and a strong supporter of women's education. He was the second Indian to be elected as a member of the British Parliament in 1892. The predominantly working class constituency of Central Finsbury elected Dadabhai Naoroji. From there Naoroji proceeded to fulfill his agenda of holding up a mirror to the shameful British rule in India. The coronation of Rishi Sunak in Britain must have brought a smile on the face of Indian-origin Dada Bhai Naoroji in heaven. For record's sake, let me tell you that nearly 130 years ago, a Parsi professor from Mumbai (Bombay) became the first Indian to be elected to the UK Parliament. Prior to him, in 1841, the Anglo-Indian David Ochterlony Dyce Sombre became a Member of Parliament by winning the election to represent the Sudbury constituency in July 1841. Not only this, an Indian MP was also elected in 1895 as a member of the Conservative Party. Sir Mancharjee Merwanji Bhaunagari KCIE (1851–1933) was his name. Have you ever heard this name? Historian Jonathan Scheer states that Mancharjee Bhaunagri, a conservative politician of Parsi descent, represented Indian aspirations in Britain. These early leaders were of Indian origin and remained "loyal, assimilated, obsequious" to the British state throughout their lives.

Europe is no stranger to Indian-origin prime ministers. Portugal counts two premiers of Goan ancestry, including current Prime Minister António Costa. Seven years before Sunak became Britain's Prime Minister, Antonio Costa, a man of Indian origin, took over as the Prime Minister of Portugal.

Leo Varadkar, whose father is from Mumbai, served as Ireland's prime minister from 2017 to 2020. He was born on January 18, 1979, Dublin, Ireland. He is an Irish politician who became leader of the Fine Gael party and Ireland's first openly gay taoiseach (prime minister) in June 2017. Varadkar's mother, an Irish-born nurse, and his father, an Indian-born physician, met while working together in England. Before settling in Dublin, where Varadkar, the youngest of three children, was born, the family also lived in Leicester and briefly in India. Leo Varadkar has become taoiseach (prime minister) again, as a result of a power-sharing agreement between his party, Fine Gael, and Fianna Fáil, led by Micheál Martin, who has stepped down as taoiseach to serve as tánaiste (deputy prime minister).

Following are some such prominent persons of Indian origin. You will be pleased to know that the rise of people of

Indian origin to powerful key positions in various countries is not limited to the UK. People of Indian origin have held high positions in other parts of the world.

1. Antonio Costa, Prime Minister, Portugal

2. Mohamed Irfan Ali, President, Guyana

3. Pravind Jugnauth, Prime Minister, Mauritius

4. Prithvirajsingh Roopun, President, Mauritius

5. Chandrikapersad Santokhi, President, Suriname

6. Kamala Harris, Vice President, United States

Mauritius has nine Indian-origin heads of state, including Mr. Jugnauth and Mr. Roopun, according to "Indiaspora", a US-based non-profit organization representing the Indian-origin community globally. Similarly, Suriname has seen five presidents from the community. In addition, four heads of state in Guyana and three in Singapore were of Indian origin. Apart from these countries, Trinidad and Tobago, Portugal, Malaysia, Fiji, Ireland and Seychelles have also elected an Indian-origin head of state so far. Today, with 32 million people of Indian origin all over the world, there are five Indian origin heads of government, three deputy heads of government, 56 cabinet ministers, and four additional ministers, according to the 2021 Indiaspora Government Leaders' List.

All these leaders who have been selected and elected reached there not because of their color of skin and ethnicity. They also come from an ethnic minority, though they follow a different religion followed by a majority of the citizens of their country. They too are brown. But their ethnic ancestry and color did not come in the way of their selection as the candidate for Prime Minister or Presidentship. They were chosen by them because they had tirelessly worked day and night for the welfare of their people. Similarly, Sunak belongs to an ethnic minority that follows a religion different from the majority of Britons. He is brown in a predominantly white and color-conscious country. Yet, when the Tory MPs elected him their leader, they did not look at his religion, ethnic origin or skin. They looked at his merit; they saw him as the best man who could do the job. "However, here is what we should know: despite the color of their skins, Indian-origin foreign politicians, or other high achievers, are people who left India (in this generation or in the past), and they are not Indians in any sense now. Their success depends on how they find favor with local aspirations despite their different racial features, and not on what they do for India. In fact, their own success will be jeopardized if they are seen to favor India."[16]

As Sanjaya Baru, former media adviser to Manmohan Singh when he was prime minister, wrote in a Times of India column, nearly 200 persons of Indian origin have been elected to political offices across 25 countries, and 10 have even been (or still are) heads of government. While some have been comfortable in their Indian skins and dealt normally with India, others have proved more prickly. Sunak will probably prove to be more of the latter. Needless to say that Sunak may turn out to be more loyal than the King and be tougher on India.

This day is the fruit of the hard work and faith of so many stalwarts who came before Rishi Sunak. Lord Salisbury, the 19th century Conservative prime minister, said that British voters would never agree to being represented by a "black man". Voters proved him wrong by electing Dadabhoy Naoroji as the first Asian member of the Commons. When Lionel Rothschild became the "first Jewish parliamentarian" in 1858, he did an important job of promoting minority participation in politics. He was elected five times before finally being able to

The Rise of Rishi Sunak

join the Commons without taking the traditional Christian oath. Ironically, Rothschild, who was MP for the City of London for 15 years, never had a chance to speak in Parliament. Whatever one thinks of Sunak's politics, Britain can be proud of its rise. Should be that the son of Hindu parents of Afro-Indian origin can hold the top position in British politics is a matter of pride. It is a matter of pride not only for the Indians living there but for all the ethnic minorities. Let me cite James Salins who asks to himself, "Am I proud a British Indian like me is PM?" and after narrating his episodic life concludes:

> Rishi has inherited a poisoned chalice. It is likely he will lose the next election in 2024 and either become a backbencher or pursue something else entirely.
>
> But it is important for people of Ethnic Minority backgrounds to see with their own eyes someone reaching the top of the British system. They say 'a picture paints a thousand words', so seeing Rishi Sunak PM at the door of Number 10 can never be taken from us.
>
> It is a symbol that will go down in the history books. It is the very embodiment of me saying to my boys 'You can be who you want to be'. I don't ever have to ponder whether we will have a Non-white Prime Minister in my lifetime anymore. It is done and I am glad.[17]

In one of the budget speeches Rishi Sunak sought inspiration from Tennyson's Ulysses as he attempted to sum up the UK's determination to face the future."That which we are, we are," the chancellor said as he reached the end of a statement which promised tax rises and continued emergency spending during the coronavirus pandemic. The quote was taken from the acclaimed last lines of the 19th-century poem which has been used by many to summon communal strength during times of adversity:

That which we are, we are
One equal temper of heroic hearts,
Made weak by time and fate,
But strong in will
To strive, to seek, to find, and not to yield

His greatest strength and inspiration is not Tennyson or Blake, he has always got inspired by the book of books- The Bhagavad Gita.

He draws inspiration from the Bhagavad Gita, especially to guide him through the difficult decisions that lie ahead as the country battles through an excruciating cost-of-living crisis. In a letter (dated 18 November 2022) to Visakha Dasi, President of the Bhaktivedanta Manor Hare Krishna Temple in Watford, the Prime Minister reiterated the "special resonance" Gita quotations hold for him.

yadyadācarati śreṣṭhastattadevetaro janaḥ
sa yatpramāṇaṃ kurute lokastadanuvartate

Whatever a great man does, that other men also do (imitate); whatever he sets up as the standard, that the world (people) follows.

How far Lord Krishna's word extends its influence over Rishi Sunak's premiership remains to be seen. But given that turbulent times surround us, with difficult decisions to come, we might take comfort in the teaching found in both the Gita and Blake. As Blake put it: "Man was made for joy and woe, And when this we rightly know, Through the world we safely go."[18]

References

1   https://www.newstatesman.com/politics/polling/2022/03/
    has-rishi-sunaks-bubble-burst

2 https://yougov.co.uk/topics/politics/articles-reports/2020/07/10/sunak-most-popular-chancellor-15-years

3 https://www.cityam.com/rishi-sunak-most-popular-chancellor-since-1970s/

4 https://www.bloomberg.com/opinion/articles/2022-10-28/rishi-sunak-shows-growing-influence-of-indian-talent-in-west?leadSource=uverify%20wall

5 https://www.deccanherald.com/opinion/desperately-seeking-self-esteem-1157762/.html

6 https://financialpost.com/opinion/rishi-sunak-skin-colour

7 https://www.spectator.co.uk/article/how-will-rishi-sunaks-hinduism-inform-his-premiership

8 https://www.opindia.com/2022/10/rishi-sunak-uk-prime-minister-indian-origin-hindu/

9 https://edition.cnn.com/2022/10/26/opinions/rishi-sunak-prime-minister-do-not-fall-symbolism-andrews/index.html

10 https://www.wsj.com/articles/britains-prime-minister-is-indias-pride-rishi-sunak-liz-truss-anticolonialism-language-immigrant-ethnicity-grievance-11666729362

11 https://theprint.in/opinion/letter-from-pakistan/in-pakistan-rishi-sunaks-origin-is-another-unfinished-agenda-of-partition/1187701/

12 https://www.newslaundry.com/2022/07/27/indias-media-is-taking-the-wrong-lessons-from-rishi-sunaks-rise

13 https://panchjanya.com/2022/10/28/255089/bharat/refreshing-memories-of-indian-knowledge-tradition-on-the-pretext-of-rishi-sunak/

14 https://www.ndtv.com/opinion/rishi-sunaks-perfectly-crafted-first-speech-by-rajmohan-gandhi-3463091

15 https://swarajyamag.com/world/sunak-is-losing-momentum-in-race-for-british-prime-minister-and-that-is-not-bad-news-for-india

16 https://www.rediff.com/news/special/james-salins-am-i-proud-a-british-indian-like-me-is-pm/20221104.htm

17 https://www.iglobalnews.com/icommunity/profiles/i-draw-inspiration-from-the-bhagavad-gita-rishi-sunak

18 https://www.markvernon.com/rishi-sunak-william-blake-and-the-gita

◻

10

IN A LIGHTER VEIN

"I am so excited to share my happiness because the new prime minister of Britain, Shri Rishi Sunak, is very close to me and my family; he is actually my cousin's father-in-law's real second wife's sister's husband's uncle's neighbor's former employer's daughter's husband. So, he is just like my brother."

During my journey and sojourn in cyberspace in search of primary and secondary material for the book, there were instances when I could not stop myself smiling and laughing and sometimes getting annoyed and angry. These days the internet, facebook, twitter, snapchat, insta, whatsapp including tik tok is full of Rishi Sunak's stories. Some of the funniest commentary on social-media cesspits saw cyber-sena telling Sunak to "act his age". The rise, fall and rise again of an Indian origin young man Rishi Sunak gave the world opportunities to express themselves in the ways they can, sometimes not the ways they should. There are youth who write poems, stories, anecdotes etc and eulogize him. A group of youngsters watching cricket treated Rishi Sunak's election also as a match between politicians and parties of England. Even on the reputed BBC, a Guest Comedian described Rishi Sunak as 'Prince Charles' in Brownface. These incidents trigger controversies too but should be taken with a pinch of salt. Take it lightly, man!

"The Queen is dead, the new King looks bored, Brexit is a dinner table joke and the pound is in a freefall." Deep Halder of 'India Today' Digital continues his conversation. "Jerry (a racist caller on Britain's popular radio show who identified himself as Jerry on the LBC radio show), said out loud what many others said under their breath. "Could you mention me becoming the prime minister of Pakistan or Saudi Arabia? No. Eighty five per cent of England are white English people and they want a prime minister who reflects that. I can't just go to India and be the Prime Minister there, can I?" Jerry also brought in the Al Qaeda angle which was funny because the subject of his racist rant was a proud Hindu. Following this, the show host shut him down saying, "I think you are fundamentally a racist, and it's absolutely fascinating that you and other Tory Party members think like this."[1]

The Internet is flooded with funny memes — showing chappals left by visitors outside 10 Downing Street (presumably because many Indians do not enter homes wearing shoes); a swastika (the ancient Hindu auspicious sign, not the hijacked Nazi caricature) on the door; and on the new Prime Minister's seeming likeness to Ashish Nehra, the former Indian left-arm fast bowler. Even Rishi Sunak has joked about people complimenting his "tan" in opening of the Conservative party hustings in Leeds.

> "The weather has been fantastic and we've been in so many people's gardens, the sun has been shining. So much so that someone even said to me the other day 'Wow, you've got a great tan'."

***

One of the best pieces I could lay my hands on was found on the "goodreads'. It is as follows.

"A common enough mistake, sir," he said. "Mr. Rishi Sunak, our current Prime Minister, is not Indian. He is what they term a Britisher of Indian origin."

"Does that mean he came from India?"

"Oh no, sir. It only means that Mr. Sunak's forefathers are of Indian origin."

"Ah!" I said as light dawned on me. "You mean his parents are from India."

Jeeves coughed deferentially. "Not exactly, sir. The current prime minister's father came to England from Kenya and his mother came from Tanzania."

"Those countries are in Africa, aren't they?" My head was in a whirl again. "Then why isn't the blighter called African?"

"Well, sir, Mr. Sunak's grandparents originally relocated to Africa from Gujranwala in colonial India..."

"Oho!" I was getting it now. "That is why you said his forefathers are from India!" I said, interrupting Jeeves.

Jeeves once again cleared his throat. "I would not say that that statement is one hundred percent accurate, sir."

I was lost again. "Why, Jeeves?"

"Because Gujranwala is in current-day Pakistan, sir," he said almost apologetically.[2]

***

"You are going to London?" a smirking Indian immigration officer said to me at Mumbai airport. "Our Rishi Sunak is there."

"What do you mean 'our'?" I asked.

"He's there, but he's ours," the officer replied.

"He's a British person whose grandparents are from East Africa," I added, bringing some pedantry to a humorless exchange.

"Yeah, they all say that," he concluded. "You'll be fine."

He stamped my passport and, with a slight wave, dismissed me certain that when I landed, I'd be taken care of by one of "ours".[3]

***

"Rishi Sunak's rise to power proves that regardless of your ancestral background, the colour of your skin or the social stigma, with sheer hard work, will-power and dedication, you can also be a pretentious white man," said Shadman's father.

"The day my deshi son will be qualified enough to be treated as a white man in the west, I'll finally be able to rest in peace," he continued. "As long as he graduates from a public university, of course."[4]

***

The Daily Show

The above South Asian pieces of humor are on one side and the type of satire Trevor Noah, who hosts 'The Daily Show' on American TV, presents are poles apart. Noah jokes that the racists among the UK's white population might even fear that Rishi Sunak would be tempted to sell Britain to India!

'You hear a lot of people saying: "Oh they're taking over, Indians are going to take over Great Britain and what's next?" and I've always found myself going: "So what?... What are you afraid of?"

'You see people in the UK, you see people like Tucker Carlson all the time saying: "You know what they're trying to do... they won't stop until black people and women are in positions of power"... So what?'

'Why are you so afraid? I think it's because the quiet part a lot of people don't realise they are saying is: "We don't want these people who were previously oppressed to get into power because then they may do to us what we did to them".'

***

In the UK, when people say "ASIAN" they're most often referring to people of South Asian descent, whereas in the US, "ASIAN" refers to people of East Asian descent. It's a cultural/ semantic difference. In the U.S. government eyes, Asian refers to people "having origins in any of the original peoples of the Far East, Southeast Asia, or the Indian subcontinent including, for example, Cambodia, China, India, Japan, Korea, Malaysia, Pakistan, the Philippine Islands, Thailand, and Vietnam." On the other hand, when British say Asian, they usually refer to Indian, differentiating Far Eastern.

Chieng, who was born in Malaysia, joked.

"Don't call Rishi Sunak the U.K.'s first Asian PM in front of Ronny Chieng."

"Indians are not Asians. I love how Indians try to have it both ways, like being Indian and Asian. Pick a lane, OK."

***

Storm over a Teacup

Soon after Boris Johnson announced his resignation, the press showed up at Rishi Sunak's London house. Akshata Murty served them biscuits and tea in expensive cups that prompted a Twitter user to comment caustically that the price of a single cup could have fed a British family for two days. The cups were allegedly from a brand called Emma Lacy and cost 38 pounds (approximately 3,600 rupees) each. They could also spot some biscuits and a bowl of nuts like cashews and walnuts, and dried fruits along with the tea as well. They could also notice how two cups had black tea while the rest of the three were with milk. Josh Gafson, a journalist who was present at the time, shared a close picture of the tray Murty bought.

"Can't believe Rishi Sunak spends £38 on mugs, Akshata Murty millionaire trying to copy Bo Jo for? Say what you want about walking tumbleweed on legs but at least he had real mugs," a user tweeted.

"Tone deaf !!! The price of that mug could feed a family for 2 days!! I would've dropped it," the user tweeted.

***

Kohinoor Tweet

Harish Goenka tweeted:

My friend's idea to get back Kohinoor:

1. Invite Rishi Sunak to India.
2. Kidnap him when he is stuck in Bangalore traffic to visit his in-laws.
3. Send instead Ashish Nehra as UK PM. No one will realize it.
4. Nehra will be told to pass the bill to return Kohinoor.

***

Adv. Sumit Arora tweeted :

Who? Rishi Sunak (PM candidate)

Where? London, England

What? Performing Cow worship

That's our rich cultural heritage we must be proud about. Tat twam asi

Wall-paper

Sunak's wealth also becomes a subject for jokes. Former Prime Minister Boris Johnson famously was unhappy about the Downing Street wallpaper and was determined to replace it as a very expensive alternative. And since he couldn't afford the new wallpaper, he persuaded a 'generous' Conservative backer to pay for it. Sunak, by contrast, is too rich to need donors. "Sunak becomes the richest-ever prime minister which means he ought to be able to afford his own wallpaper."

***

Sunder Pichai

Mother - "Look at that Rishi, Sunak uncle ka beta, 8 years younger to you, Britain ka Pradhan Mantri ban gaya, aur tum sirf ek 100 Billion $ company ke CEO ho US mein."

Pichai, "Mom, I can't replace Joe Biden."

Mother, "Try kar beta, you can do it, tum koshish hi nahi karoge to kaise hoga."

"I may be able to convince my parents but many PM/Presidents are at risk now....Indian parents have already decided the next career goal for their kids."

Vijay Mama

"Mama, I have somebody to say hello to you."

"Hello, Vijay mama."

"Hello, Rishi, how are you?"

"I hope you come here to see me. So, when you arrive, instruct your nephew Sanjay to take you to Downing Street."

"Take care."

***

One liner-

"Infosys acquires Britain. Not by law but in-law."

As Sunak wins and Akshata Murty, Narayan Murthy and Sudha Murty move into 10 Downing Street, then it can be renamed Teen Murthy Bhavan.

***

"Yes, there's a brown man in the ring… but [he] also just happens to be one of the richest Members of Parliament and has sustained a rather meteoric rise to power. So, different but same same?" Kusum Wijetilleke

***

"There will be no VAT on historical fiction by Hilary Mantel, manuals for textbooks like Gray's Anatomy or, indeed, works of fantasy … like John McDonnell's Economics for the Many,"

***

"Well dance your bhangras but if Sunak's term is as short-lived as was that of Truss, get ready your sayapa (dirges) too!!"

***

The only minority is the bourgeoisie. Going by that logic, Sunak is, and was, a member of a "minority".

***

Rishi is a role model now — if he can, they can too

***

Rishi Sunak ran for Britain's top job and lost. Then he got another shot — and the chance to say "I told you so."

***

Worse to Verse

Every winter if it snows

We hear their sneering, and it goes:

"I thought the world was heating up!

Where's your global warming now?"

To hear their wisdom we desire

Now half the country is on fire

But all those jeering voices have

Gone very very quiet somehow...[5]

****

When a boy, his mother used to

prop him on the ironing board

and steam out the creases.

Since he was about five

he's been the adult in the room

coming up with solutions

the gods of the Market will like.

He arrived with a birthmark

which, under a magnifying glass,

appears to read

Head Prefect.[6]   **by Kevin Higgins**

***

The Tailpiece!

World leaders have a long tradition of bringing pets into high office, with Sir Winston Churchill doting on Rufus the poodle. The Sunak's family dog, Nova, is a fox red Labrador retriever. It is said when Mr Sunak's two daughters met Boris Johnson's dog Dillyn, they immediately fell in love and begged their father for a pup of their own. Rishi gave in to his daughters' pleas and Nova was welcomed into the family. Rishi announced her arrival via a tweet that was captioned: "Meet Nova." Nova loves roast chicken and naps in Rishi's famous red Budget box. She is often featured on Mr Sunak's Instagram; with one post in October 2021 showing him slumped on a blue sofa with the then-Chancellor as he read documents on the October budget. The caption read: "Tomorrow's Budget and Spending Review will deliver a stronger economy for the British people. I hope you find it more engaging than Nova did."

Larry the Cat, whose official title is Chief Mouser to the Cabinet Office, has resided at No 10 for 11 years. Soon after his arrival at Number 10, Larry became the first cat to be given the title of Chief Mouser, and he is regularly seen chasing after mice or foxes outside the Prime Minister's home. Throughout

Larry's mouse-chasing career, David Cameron, Theresa May, Mr Johnson, Ms Truss, and now Sunak have all served as PM. He also has his own unofficial Twitter account. When Sunak won the latest Tory leadership contest, the account tweeted: "Rishi Sunak is becoming prime minister. His family is loaded so caviar and lobster on the menu for me from tomorrow."

The press is elated to find Downing Street's new dog appears to be settling nicely into life at Number 10 – and has even been given a Remembrance collar. Nova was filmed receiving the poppy-laden item as the prime minister donated it to the Royal British Legion. Larry the cat, however, was conspicuous by his absence – and it is unclear what sort of relationship the pair enjoys.

References

1   https://www.indiatoday.in/opinion-columns/story/rishi-sunak-uk-pm-indian-origin-hindu-inside-10-downing-street-2289125-2022-10-25

2   https://www.goodreads.com/book/show/55883282-going-for-broke/

3   https://www.theguardian.com/culture/2022/nov/17/our-rishi-sunak-comic-anuvab-pal-pm

4   https://www.theneweuropean.co.uk/liz-and-rishi-two-jokes-that-arent-funny-anymore/

5   https://www.culturematters.org.uk/index.php/arts/poetry/item/4113-meet-your-new-leader

6   https://www.thedailystar.net/shout/news/rishi-sunak-ruins-kids-life-dad-finds-another-person-compare-him-3158136

AFTERWORD

This book is neither an authentic biography of Indian-origin British Prime Minister Shri Rishi Sunak nor is it a eulogy. This is not an authorized biography, I repeat. I neither had got a chance to meet Rishi Sunak nor did I have access to his papers, letters or any other communications beyond those acquired through Google and media. I wrote the book because of his bewitching charm. Who would not be enamored by the natural attraction of the Indian name 'Rishi'? I too became too eager to know about this dashing personality. Neither did I know that he was not the son-in-law of Shri Narayana Murthy and Mrs. Sudha Murty, nor did I know anything about his belief in Hinduism. But as soon as I came to know about his parentage and *Dharma*, it got me devoting my entire time in writing this book.

The credit for writing the first authentic biography of Rishi Sunak in English goes to Lord Michael Ashcroft, former Treasurer and Deputy Chairman of the Conservative Party. The book 'Going for Broke: The Rise of Rishi Sunak' was written when Rishi was Finance Minister. Come to think of it, Rishi's biography was written before he even reached the age of 40 by a wealthy businessman and Tory politician almost twice his age. There is something in this, isn't there? Ashcroft said in 2020: "Rishi has emerged as a very capable politician at a time when capability is sorely lacking. His greatest strength is a combination of acumen, immense work ethic, good political judgment, ability to present himself well and great interpersonal skills." A commentator, Will Lloyd, wrote very succinctly on October 17, 2022 and I quote. "Rishi Sunak seems destined to be an assassin. The Chancellor's weapon is pointed, polished contrast. Where Boris is shambolic, Rishi is spruce. Boris looks necrotic, Rishi simply gleams. We know Boris is a rake; Rishi is fanatically uxorious. Boris is all appetites: embarrassingly lardy. But Rishi is all discipline, Peloton-ed every morning." Ashcroft now says: "Rishi Sunak's rise to the top of British politics has impressed me. Kinda surprising... we leave the tale at a point when our subject is liked as well as admired."

You and I do not know much about Rishi Sunak that is why this book was needed. People are asking different questions on the internet - Where is Rishi Sunak a native of? What is the caste of Rishi Sunak? Is Rishi Sunak from Gujarat? Who is the father-in-law of Rishi Sunak? Who is Rishi Sunak's wife? Who are Rishi Sunak's parents? What is the nationality of Rishi Sunak? What is the history of Rishi Sunak?

But whatever they ask, they know he is the Prime Minister of the UK. Why wouldn't they know him? Rishi Sunak is one of the most familiar figures in British politics. A diligent public relations campaign has ensured that newspapers continue to profile him and his photogenic family. Political pundits are writing about him and his policy. His country's economic policy is now associated with his tight suit and soft smile, just as it once was with Gordon Brown's crumpled clothes and angry growl. He's Britain's first ever Hindu PM, the first of Indian-descent, the youngest PM in the modern era, the PM with the fastest rise to power (it took him 7 years), he's the first millennial (born May 1980), he's the richest PM (his wife has an estimated fortune of US$1.2b), and the second shortest male

Prime Minister since Winston Churchill who was 1.1 cm shorter. He is also, significantly, the first to hold an MBA degree. Yet beyond Mr. Sunak's immense wealth and professional ability, not much is known about him. There are many reasons for this ambiguity. The star of his fortune rose so fast and quickly that the eyes of the onlookers dazzled.

In this book, I have gathered such information for you, which you would not have even thought of. We learn many lessons from Rishi Sunak becoming the Prime Minister of Britain. Common Indian young men and women will have to understand that the era they are in gives success to the talented irrespective of his caste, creed, race, color and upbringing. See for yourself, an Indian-origin Hindu becomes the Prime Minister in Britain. It is said in Sanskrit, "The king is worshiped in the country, the scholar is worshiped everywhere. If you are a scholar, you can also become a king in a distant country." Parents and their sons and daughters should realize the worth of quality education that opens the horizon. The open, democratic and welcoming structures and systems in place in the UK have allowed women, minorities and foreign-born nationals to advance on the strength of their abilities in education, professions and public life. It is also said in Sanskrit that 'the age of the brilliant is not seen.' Rishi is just 42 years of age. Therefore, if the largest Indian democracy has anything to learn from an old British democracy, then at least just learn this and leave the other things to retire and rest in the haze of antiquity!

The research for this book started when Rishi Sunak started giving signs and signals of his arrival on the world-stage. The rush to get to you as fast as possible didn't give me the opportunity to collect the material in great detail and also verify and cross-check properly what was available in cyberspace. I have given you everything –sometimes raw and uncooked- here in this book to the best of my knowledge and ability that you should have been given and that you are entitled to. However, I can claim that this is the first book written in India on Rishi Sunak and no matter how much someone writes about him in detail now, this 'half-a-story' will remain first and foremost.

That which will happen in the future

Only those who can see the future know

Therefore, let me recall only the events that are past

And describe them with my signature flow

On behalf of all of you - on behalf of We- the people - this bouquet of words is dedicated to the pride of India Shri Rishi Sunak!

Om Puurnnam-Adah Puurnnam-Idam Puurnnaat-Puurnnam-Udacyate |
Puurnnasya Puurnnam-Aadaaya Puurnnam-Eva-Avashissyate ||
Om Shaantih Shaantih Shaantih ||

–Gopal Sharma

Milton Keynes UK
Ingram Content Group UK Ltd.
UKHW031153251124
451529UK00001B/84

9 789356 844407